Fodor's

Short Escapes in France

Fodor's Travel Publications, Inc.
New York * Toronto * London * Sydney * Auckland

▼

SHORT ESCAPES IN FRANCE

Designer: Nancy Koch

Map Design: John Grimwade

Maps By: John Grimwade, Andy Christie, Alex Reardon

Editor: Marita Begley

Cover Design: Guido Caroti

Cover Illustration: Steven Rydberg

Art Assistant: Lauri Marks

Copyright © 1996
by Beachscape Publishing Inc.

SPECIAL SALES

Fodor's Travel Publications are available at special discounts for bulk purchases for sales promotions or premiums. Special editions, including personalized covers, excerpts of existing guides, and corporate imprints, can be created in large quantities for special needs. For more information, contact your bookseller or write to Special Markets, Fodor's Travel Publications, 201 East 50th Street, New York, NY 10022. Inquiries from Canada should be sent to Marketing Department, Random House of Canada Ltd., 1265 Aerowood Drive, Mississauga, Ontario L4W 1B9. Inquiries from the United Kingdom should be sent to Fodor's Travel Publications, 20 Vauxhall Bridge Road, London SW1V 2SA, England.

Also available:
Short Escapes Near New York City
Short Escapes in New England
Short Escapes in Britain

Please address all comments and corrections to Beachscape Publishing, Inc. 145 Palisade St., Suite 397, Dobbs Ferry, NY 10522; tel. 914-674-9283 and fax 914-674-9285.

ISBN 0-679-03071-9

Second Edition

PRINTED IN THE UNITED STATES OF AMERICA
10 9 8 7 6 5 4 3 2 1

ABOUT THE AUTHORS

Bruce Bolger, an avid traveler and experienced walker, has explored the countryside in more than a dozen countries spanning four continents. Currently head of a book-packaging and electronic-publishing business, he has extensive experience in the travel and publishing fields. He is a graduate of the University of California at Santa Barbara and attended the University of Paris in France. He speaks French fluently. He lives outside New York City with his wife, Shawn, and children, Kate, Chris, and Elizabeth.

Gary Stoller has been an editor at *Condé Nast Traveler* magazine since its start-up in 1987. Considered a pioneer of the concept of "investigative travel reporting," he wrote articles that were cited by judges when the magazine twice received National Magazine Awards. His articles have also won awards from the National Press Club and the Aviation/ Space Writers Association. He has a journalism degree from the University of Colorado and now lives outside New York City with his wife, Terry, and children, Kristin and Ben.

To my wife, Shawn Bolger, and children, Kate, Chris, and Elizabeth, whose loving support helped make this book possible. And to Tante Loulou, who opened up a new world for me.

♦♦♦

To my wife, Terry Stoller, and to our children, Kristin and Ben, for understanding why so many nights and weekends had to be spent in front of a computer.

Contents

VI INTRODUCTION
VIII WHERE TO FIND EACH EXPERIENCE
IX HOW TO USE *SHORT ESCAPES*

EXPERIENCES 1–4: OUTSIDE PARIS
1 Auvers-sur-Oise—Cradle of Impressionism

11 Chevreuse—In the Footsteps of a Poet

25 Barbizon—The Forest of Kings

35 Giverny—Hills of the Artist

EXPERIENCES 5–8: BURGUNDY
44 Pommard—Vineyards of Rome

54 Auxey-Duresses—The Ancient Outpost

61 Vézelay—Rural Exodus

71 Fontenay—An Enterprising Order of Monks

EXPERIENCES 9–12: PROVENCE
81 Gordes—A Town Built on a Rock

92 Murs—Medieval Mills

98 Forest of Cedars—Toujours Luberon

108 Mont Ste-Baume—Pilgrimage to a Holy Mountain

▼

EXPERIENCES 13–14: RIVIERA

117 St-Jean-Cap-Ferrat—Spirit of Somerset Maugham

125 Grand Canyon of Verdon— Bridge to Another Time

EXPERIENCES 15–17: GIRONDE

134 St-Symphorien—Village in the Forest

142 Villandraut—Palaces of the Pope

151 St-Macaire—*Bastides* of Bordeaux

EXPERIENCES 18–21: LOIRE VALLEY

160 Noizay—Cave Dwellers of France

171 Gué-Péan—Lonely Chateau

181 Thésée—Lifestyles of the Gallic-Romans

189 Artannes—Valley of the Lily

EXPERIENCES 22–23: NORMANDY

199 Omaha Beach—The Longest Day

211 Carolles—The Peaceful Side of Mont-St-Michel

EXPERIENCES 24–25: BRITTANY

220 Cap Fréhel—Castle in the Moors

229 Château de la Hunaudaye—Where Time Stands Still

▼

Introduction

When you come to France's great cities and towns in search of history, you can find monuments to the past everywhere along the grand avenues and back streets. But not even in the most silent corner of a city can you escape the sounds of modern life—trucks, cars, scooters, and machines—that forever encroach upon your effort to experience the past.

This guide is for everyone who would like to escape to the peace of the French countryside and soak up a more complete sense of the way life once was, and is today. It will take you away from the tourist crowds to unique places with spectacular vistas and remarkable histories. You can stroll alone through an ancient forest, walk along the towpath of a centuries-old canal, or picnic without neighbors on the grassy banks of a peaceful river. You can continue the mood at a recommended restaurant in a picturesque setting and then complete the experience at a charming country inn, a bed and breakfast, or even a rural hostel.

Short Escapes brings you to special places little known even to the French. According to your tastes, you can tramp around historic landmarks, plunge deep into farmland and forest, or just sit undisturbed for hours looking down at gentle waves lapping against a shore. Through the quiet, you will be able to feel what it might have been like when Celts and Romans ruled France, when the Cistercians founded their medieval abbeys, and when the great Impressionists set up their easels in the 19th-century countryside. Many of the book's suggested walking tours cover country roads and footpaths in use for hundreds or even thousands of years.

The 25 experiences in this guide are scattered around eight different regions—each with its own distinctive character, flavor, and points of historical, cultural, or natural interest. All are within a day's journey of France's major tourist spots, and some are accessible by train. Each experience is centered around a walking tour, which can be anything from a short stroll to a five-hour walk.

These experiences cost less than other forms of travel. Nobody charges admission to villages and the countryside, and rural hotels and restaurants match and even surpass their urban counterparts in comfort and luxury at much lower prices.

Short Escapes is more than a travel guide: It's designed to awaken the traveler's senses to the moods and flavors of a place and its people, and to help evoke a real sense of the past and present. We hope that the 25 experiences will have the same uplifting effect on you as they had on us. We have thrust ourselves into the soul of the country and have learned about the land in a way you can't by simply reading about it in a book or observing artifacts in a museum.

In fact, we feel we have stumbled upon a new form of travel—one which combines the cultural and sensual enrichment of traditional travel with the spiritual pleasures of walking. We ended each day with a great sense of accomplishment and, like a local resident, felt we had participated in the place.

The rewards of exploring the countryside are great: You return home having experienced the essence of France, knowing that you have felt its history, escaped from the hubbub of its cities and tourist attractions, and savored the beauty of the land and its people.

**WHERE TO FIND
EACH EXPERIENCE**

Omaha Beach **22**

● Rouen

Giverny **4** **1** Auvers-sur-Oise

Cap Fréhel **24** **23** Carolles

● PARIS

25 Château de la Hunaudaye

● Rennes

Chevreuse **2** **3** Barbizon

18 Noizay

Tours ●

19 Gué-Péan

8 Fontenay

● Nantes

7
Vézelay

● Dijon

Artannes **21** **20** Thésée

Auxey-Duresses **6** **5** Pommard

FRANCE

● Lyon

100 MILES

● Bordeaux

17 St-Macaire

16 Villandraut

15 St-Symphorien

Murs **10**

St-Jean
Cap-Ferrat **13**

Gordes **9**

Verdon

14

Forest of Cedars **11**

● Toulouse

Nice

12

Marseilles ●

Mont Ste-Baume

How to Use *Short Escapes*

We selected the 25 experiences in *Short Escapes* for their historic, cultural, or natural interest and for their general proximity to regions popular with travelers. At each location, walking tours permit visitors to get out of their cars or the train and experience special places up close. All include private, easily accessible spots to picnic or enjoy memorable views. When possible, itineraries provide optional walks for strollers or serious walkers.

Itineraries are organized by region and are chosen so that travelers staying in one of the selected lodgings can easily enjoy multiple experiences during their stay. We followed every itinerary mentioned in this book personally and purposely omitted others that gave us difficulty.

To bring your visit to life, each experience comes with a narrative on historical, cultural, literary, or natural points of interest, as well as suggestions on other unique places to explore nearby, so you don't have to be a walker to enjoy this book.

FINDING YOUR WAY

We designed this book to make it as easy as possible to follow the directions. For your convenience, each itinerary begins with basic information on duration, length, and level of difficulty. Walking tours marked "Easy" have few ups and downs, no areas of tricky footing, and no navigational challenges and are appropriate for anyone capable of walking. Tours labeled "Moderate" require a little more physical commitment and might have an area of tricky footing, but they require no particular navigational abilities or physical endurance. The few itiner-

▼

aries marked "Difficult" are appropriate to regular walkers who feel comfortable walking in a few tricky areas and finding their way in forests or hills. The text fully details whatever difficulties the traveler might encounter along the way. Serious walkers will probably find even "Difficult" trails relatively easy, compared with what they're accustomed to in the United States. And even the least experienced walkers can safely follow almost all "Difficult" and "Moderate" itineraries just a short way to a nice view or historic site, and then retrace their steps.

Unless otherwise indicated, all itineraries are loops; and walking time is based on a very leisurely 2 mph, except in itineraries with exceptional ups and downs. The numbered text directions enable you to complete a walking tour without using the map, but some may find it easier to simply follow the map and refer to the text when necessary. We strongly recommend that you use both the text and the maps, which provide navigational aids and show the places of interest as well as hotels and restaurants along the way. At each numbered point on the map, the same number in the text gives the information you'll need to find your way as well as additional observations about the terrain.

For the few more difficult itineraries, experienced walkers might enjoy having a compass and a more detailed topographical map, which can be purchased at various stores throughout France (*see* For Serious Walkers section, below).

Proceed carefully, and don't ever walk for long in any one direction unless you're sure of the way. Even on the few itineraries marked "Difficult," you will never be too far from assistance. By American standards, France is densely populated and is crisscrossed with paved roads, so you can almost always find help along the way. Should you ever get confused, feel free to knock on a door or flag down a car. If you cannot find assistance, simply turn back and retrace your steps. You'll still have seen far more of France than most tourists ever do.

Many of the itineraries follow footpaths marked with colored trailblazes that indicate the way for at least a portion of the route. A word of caution: Trailblazes can mysteriously disappear and footpath conditions change. While we have made every effort to select well-established itineraries and have walked every single one for the second edi-

▼

tion of this book, we cannot guarantee that the character of an itinerary has not been altered or deformed. We found several changes when we researched this edition and have changed the directions and maps accordingly. If you encounter a dramatic change, we'd like to hear from you.

THE FRENCH FOOTPATH SYSTEM

Before you head off on a blazed walking tour, familiarize yourself with the French trail system. The white-and-red long-distance trails, called *grands randonnés (GR)*, are particularly well marked and maintained, so we have made every attempt to include them in our itineraries. Many localities have created yellow-blazed short loop trails, called *petits randonnés (PR)*, which we have also attempted to include. In some places you'll also find other blaze colors, primarily blue. In the countryside you'll often find blazes on trees, fence posts, and rocks; in villages they appear on telephone poles, buildings, and walls. On some trails you'll find them every 10 or 20 feet; on others you'll find them only at trail junctions.

If the instructions tell you to follow the blazes during a certain

HERE ARE THE BLAZES COMMONLY USED IN FRANCE:

RED	YELLOW	YELLOW
WHITE	RED	YELLOW
Grand randonné (Long-distance trails)	*Petit randonné* (Regional loop trails)	*Petit randonné du pays* (Short loop trails)

Right turn*	Wrong way*	Left turn*

*These blazes bear the same colors as the trails being walked.

▼

portion of a walking tour, don't change trails unless directed to do so by the blazes. If you're not sure you're on the right trail, retrace your steps until you pick up a blaze, then turn around and resume your walking tour, keeping an eye out for the next blaze.

PRECAUTIONS

Although most of the itineraries require no special athletic abilities, all travelers should be sure to dress appropriately for the weather and wear shoes or sneakers designed for walking. Always carry the clothing you'll need for a worst-case change in the weather. A daypack generally can handle whatever clothing two people might need, plus drinks and a picnic, and these small packs, when empty, fit easily into your suitcase.

We have tried to select tree-shaded itineraries, but geography in southern France does not always cooperate. Beware of the region's potential for intense heat and sun. We've noted the few itineraries exposed to the sun; on hot days, do these walks in the morning or evening or travel with plenty of fluids.

Elsewhere, the usual countryside obstacles—such as muddy and rocky trails, fallen trees, and poorly cut footpaths—pose the greatest risks. There's no need to race through your walking tour. Take the time to enjoy the beauty, and watch your step.

Although we have never seen a viper in the wild, people walking in the countryside should know that these poisonous snakes live in most parts of France. You will have no problem if you take the same precautions you would in just about any forest at home: Watch where you sit down or place your feet and hands.

Finally, the hunting season varies throughout France and from year to year, but it generally opens in autumn and ends in spring. You may wish to inquire at the tourist offices about the exact dates for hunting in the regions you're visiting, and you should wear bright-colored clothing if you're walking through forests during hunting season. Even then, however, hunting is permitted only on a few select days each week.

WEATHER

Generally speaking, you'll find cooler, damper weather in the

▼

north and progressively hotter and drier weather as you move south. On certain days, though, it may be the other way around. In the north you run the risk of hitting protracted days of rain and clouds, especially in winter, although in summertime you'll often find the days warm and quite long. In the south you may confront the bitingly cold mistral wind or desertlike heat and azure skies.

GETTING THERE

Although those who travel by car have the greatest and most flexible access to France's hidden treasures, even train travelers can enjoy some of these short escapes. Wherever there is direct rail access, it is noted in the Getting There section. (Most itineraries near Paris have direct train access.) Intrepid train travelers can also reach some of the more remote destinations by bus from a major train station.

You can get specific information on train fares and schedules in the United States from *Rail Europe, 230 Westchester Ave., White Plains, NY 10604, tel. 800-848-7245; open Mon.-Fri. 9-5.*

If you are driving to a short escape, use the directions in the Getting There section and the small regional map alongside the walking tour map. A more detailed, commercially available road map will help.

Almost all itineraries have been selected in regions already popular with travelers.

OTHER PLACES NEARBY

For those who prefer to tour by car, we've provided suggestions on how to visit the highpoints of our experiences and have pointed out other places of interest in the region that are often overlooked by tourists. This way, you can enjoy the highlights of our itineraries and uncover other special places without walking more than a short distance. If you plan to spend some time in a region, call or fax ahead to the tourism office to get the latest information on schedules.

DINING & LODGING

For those who want to continue the mood created by the day's experience, we've selected a few restaurants and hotels in the country-

▼

side near our itineraries.

To be included in *Short Escapes,* a restaurant must either have an excellent view, be rustic or historic, or serve good food that's popular with the locals. Generally, you'll get the best and least expensive meals by ordering from the menu of the day. These meals almost always include one or two entrées, the main course, dessert, and coffee for one flat price. Restaurants fall into four categories based on the per-person cost of their daily dinner menus:

Very expensive	**Over 350 francs**
Expensive	**200-349 francs**
Moderate	**100-199 francs**
Inexpensive	**Under 100 francs**

It usually pays to have someone in your hotel call ahead to reserve a table, especially on weekends and holidays.

Many towns in France have *fermes-auberges,* or local farms open for a weekend lunch or dinner served by the owners. This is country home cooking at its best—you're in the home of a farmer and dining with locals. To inquire about such establishments, or to make reservations and get directions, contact the local tourist office; several have been included in this book.

The most inexpensive way to savor France's myriad specialties is to shop for lunch in the local food stores and enjoy the fruits of your efforts on the walking tour. You can pick up cheese, luncheon meats, and bread in specialty shops or local grocery stores—but remember to do your shopping by noon because nearly everything closes for two hours or more at lunchtime in the provinces. If you happen to be in town on market day, you can select your lunch from an ample variety of vendors who usually set up in the main square.

All country inns, bed and breakfasts, and other lodging establishments we've chosen either are rustic or historic, have an excellent view, or are a great value. Nearly all have less than 20 rooms and are located in extremely quiet areas. Almost all have direct telephone service and private bathrooms with shower and bath. We have checked

▼

each one for cleanliness and up-to-date maintenance.

Bed-and-breakfast places known as *chambres d'hôtes* are very popular. Many *chambres d'hôtes* belong to the organization Gîtes de France, which maintains a rating system of room standards and a complete up-to-date directory of members and their facilities and attributes. You can obtain an official national bed-and-breakfast guide free of charge from the *Service National d'Information, Maison des Gîtes de France, 35 rue Godot-de-Mauroy, Paris 75439, tel. 1/49-70-75-75; open Mon.-Sat. 10-6:30.* The best of these *chambres d'hôtes* offer beautiful rooms in magical rural settings, but even the best have a room or two sharing a bathroom or toilet. If you want a private bath, say so when you make your reservation. Almost all *chambres d'hôtes* include Continental breakfast at no additional charge, and many offer relatively low priced dinners with the family.

You can often get a free brochure listing each region's bed and breakfasts—with photos and multilingual information about each one's facilities and comfort level—by writing to or visiting the local tourist office. Although you can generally reserve a room in a hotel by phone or fax, the bed-and-breakfast owners often have rudimentary knowledge of English. We have noted when owners speak English; otherwise, you can write in English.

In general, you should write to request a reservation well before you go, and give the proprietor different dates if possible. Once you've received confirmation, you can hold the reservation by sending a personal check in U.S. dollars. The bed-and-breakfast proprietor holds it until your arrival. At that point, you get the check back and make all your payments in francs. You can telephone directly if you or someone you know speaks French or the owner speaks English. If you're already in France and want to book a room, you can call ahead with the assistance of a hotel or tourist office employee, who will usually make the call for you if you pick up the cost.

France also has a growing number of *auberges* or *hôtels de charme,* generally quite small and located in old homes or converted estates, and we have included them when possible.

For budget travelers and the backpacking crowd, France has an

▼

extensive network of hostels known as *gîtes d'étapes*. Usually located near a major hiking trail or area of natural beauty, the *gîtes* provide dormitory living, generally clean bathroom facilities, and even inexpensive meals prepared by the owners ($12 to $15 with wine). Most *gîtes* have kitchen facilities that you can use at no charge, and many will let you set up a tent on their grounds if you prefer. For a complete list of *gîtes d'étapes,* write to the same organization responsible for *chambres d'hôtes* or to the local tourist office. To reserve your place, follow the procedures for *chambres d'hôtes*.

Lodging prices are double-occupancy and are designated as:

Very expensive .... **Over 750 francs for two**

Expensive .... **350-749 francs**

Moderate .... **200-349 francs**

Inexpensive .... **Under 200 francs**

You'll find that some hotels and restaurants well suited for one itinerary may also be within easy access of another recommended itinerary. Some regions do not have a wide selection of restaurants and hotels in keeping with the ambience of this book. In such cases we recommend establishments that come as close as possible to our standards and warn you of the shortfalls.

Many of the hotels also have restaurants, so you can stay on a *demi-pension* basis; that is, eating two meals in the hotel's restaurant as part of a package price. Determining whether this arrangement makes sense for you requires a little judgment, because the menus offered often don't include drinks or specials of the day. You can make your decision on the day of your arrival, when you've had a chance to review the menu and its prices.

All hotels and restaurants in this book accept a major credit card unless otherwise noted; the most inexpensive restaurants and bed and breakfasts usually require cash or traveler's checks.

Fortunately for travelers, most French towns provide signposts clearly pointing the way to most of the area's hotels, restaurants, and

▼

even *chambres d'hôtes,* so keep your eyes out for signs when you're following our directions to hotels or restaurants.

TOURIST OFFICES

France has an extensive network of local tourist offices (called an Office de Tourisme or a Syndicat d'Initiative) open to travelers during the week and on weekends, especially during vacation periods. To take advantage of these offices, select the area you're interested in and write in English requesting everything they have on the history, walking trails, restaurants, and hotels of the region, specifying *chambres d'hôtes, gîtes d'étapes,* or *fermes-auberges.* Although these offices vary greatly in the depth of information offered, they often supply maps indicating the location of historical sights, hotels, bed and breakfasts, and restaurants, as well as walking-tour routes. You should also ask for their most current hours of operation, so you can stop in when you're there, and the hours of museums or attractions you wish to visit.

As you enter every town, you'll almost always notice road signs indicating the tourist office (usually marked with the letter *I* for information). Volunteers there will often direct you to the restaurants or hotels you're interested in and to places of interest. If you ask, they'll usually phone ahead and make reservations. Unfortunately, the volunteers often do not have a great command of English in the more out-of-the-way locations, and they don't always have full knowledge of the region's most attractive hideaways.

You will find the phone number and address of the tourist office for each location featured in this book in the corresponding chapter. Otherwise, contact the *French Government Tourist Office, 444 Madison Ave., 16th Fl., New York, NY 10022, tel. 900-990-0040 (95 cents a minute for information). Literature is available for free at offices in New York, Chicago, and Los Angeles.*

FOR SERIOUS WALKERS

France has a highly developed system of marked long-distance *grand randonné* hiking trails as well as a fast-growing network of *petits randonnés,* or day walks. Because walking has become a national pas-

▼

time in France, a huge selection of maps and literature exists (mostly in French) for those interested in exploring France on foot. The government publishes highly detailed topographic maps showing historic sights and, in certain revised editions, the exact position of well-known footpaths. The IGN maps (for Institut Géographique National) use multilingual symbols, so confident map readers can use them to follow the itineraries in this book or to create their own. The most detailed maps and those must useful for walkers have a scale of 1:25,000.

When you're visiting a particular area, you can generally buy the local IGN maps in a *librairie* (bookstore) or even a *bureau du tabac* (where newspapers, candies, and cigarettes are sold). For every itinerary mentioned in this book, we have provided the numbers of the corresponding IGN maps. You can order a directory of IGN maps, the maps themselves, and walk books through *Au Vieux Campeur, 48 rue des Ecoles, Service Vente à Distance (Long-Distance Service), Paris 75005, tel. 1/46-11-43-53; fax 1/60-11-49-66; open Tue.-Sat. 10-7:30; English is spoken, but a recorded message in French will greet you.*

The national long-distance trails and many local trails are maintained by the F.F.R.P., or Fédération Française de la Randonné Pedestre. It publishes dozens of guides to these trails, along with notes on history and *gîtes d'étapes,* but most of the information is in French. It also maintains a book and map shop in Paris that's open to visitors and will mail a catalogue of books and brochures anywhere in the world for those who want to order by mail and credit card: *64 rue de Gergovie, Paris 75014, tel. 1/45-45-31-02, fax 1/43-95-68-07; open Mon.-Sat. 10-6; closed Sun. and holidays.*

NEW TELEPHONE NUMBERS PLANNED

As of press time, the French government plans to introduce new regional codes in late 1996 that will be added to current phone numbers, meaning that most phone numbers will have 10 digits, instead of the current eight for most parts of France and nine for Paris. The planned codes are: 01, Paris and suburbs; 03, northeast France; 04, southeast France; 05, southwest France; and 02, northwest France.

Cradle of Impressionism

EXPERIENCE 1: AUVERS-SUR-OISE

The old thatched roofs have gone, and the urban sprawl of Paris has crept uncomfortably close. Yet much remains of what that gifted band of 19th-century painters known as the Impressionists sought in Auvers-sur-Oise: old houses lined up against the steep ridge; narrow streets and twisting footpaths; a sweeping plateau above, with fertile fields of grain stretching to the horizon. As you pass by the very same houses and landscapes made famous in the paintings of the Impressionists, the words of Vincent van Gogh still ring true: "Auvers is very beautiful. It is the real country, characteristic and picturesque."

The Highlights: A historic country village where great Impressionist painters lived and worked, well-preserved medieval houses, sweeping panoramas, Van Gogh's last home and grave site.

Other Places Nearby: The old quarter of Pontoise and its 15th-century church and Pissarro museum, L'Isle Adam with its picturesque bridges and nearby gardens.

Relics found in the area date the town to the 2nd century, but for most of its existence it remained a tiny backwater. Situated on the banks of the L'Oise river, it was invaded by the Normans in the 9th century, and it suffered its share of battles in the Hundred Years War (1337-1453) and the religious wars of the 16th century.

1

▼

On the walking tours outlined below, you'll see the town's oldest structure, the **Notre-Dame d'Auvers** church. Construction of this Romanesque-Gothic church, started in the 12th century, centered around a small chapel used by King Louis VI's widow, who lived in Auvers after her husband's death. The church's architectural design was strongly influenced by Notre-Dame cathedral in Paris, although the shape of its roof and four-sided belltower is rare in this part of France. Inside, you'll find 14th- to 17th-century statuary and a pleasing procession of ribbed vaulting, slender pillars, and decorated capitals. From the back, outside the church, art lovers will recognize the facade pictured in one of Van Gogh's best-known works, *L'Eglise d'Auvers* (the Church at Auvers).

You'll also pass the town's other oldest buildings on these itineraries. Along the second walking tour, you see against the hillside the weed-covered ruins of a 13th-century chapel, **St-Nicolas-des-Lépreux** (St. Nicholas of the Lepers), which once served a leper colony. The second walking tour also takes you by the recently restored **Château d'Auvers,** which was home in the early 16th century to an Italian banker (a local nobleman lived here later and significantly renovated the structure). The tourist office and town museum occupy another of the oldest houses, **Les Colombières,** a 14th-century manor house updated in the 17th century. Some of the oldest houses along the walking route date to the 13th century.

Charles-François Daubigny was one of the first of the Impressionists to discover the village. As early as 1854, he spent a summer here with Jean-Baptiste Corot and Honoré Daumier. In the next 30 or so years, the village was visited by Camille Pissarro (who lived in nearby Pontoise), Paul Cézanne, Paul Gauguin, and finally Vincent van Gogh. The studio of Daubigny, now open to the public, became a gathering place for artists. To help visitors recognize the landscape and village scenes painted here, the town has placed glass-encased copies on the very spots where the artists set up their easels.

Above the valley of the L'Oise, you can walk through the lush farms on the plateau. Cézanne and Pissarro, prodigious walkers them-

▼

selves, undoubtedly tramped along some of the pathways described here; a sketch of *Cézannes at Auvers-sur-Oise* shows the famous painter on foot, an easel on his back, a canvas in one hand and a walking stick in the other. Both painters captured numerous local sights on canvas, such as Cézanne's *Dr. Gachet's House* and *The Hanged Man's House* and Pissarro's *In the Garden* and *Cows on the Road to Pontoise*.

Auvers-sur-Oise probably is best known as the final home to Vincent van Gogh, who passed an emotionally turbulent but highly productive 70 days here before taking his life in July 1890. Early that year, Van Gogh left the hospital at St-Rémy-de-Provence and, on the advice of his brother, went to Auvers, where he met Dr. Paul Gachet, an art patron who had helped many of the Impressionists. Van Gogh took up residence in a small room beneath the roof of the former Café Ravoux, just across the street from the town hall. While there, he produced many famous paintings, including: *Portraits of Dr. and Mademoiselle Gachet, Landscape at Auvers, L'Eglise d'Auvers,* and perhaps more than 60 others.

No one knows exactly what prompted Van Gogh to kill himself on the evening of July 27, 1890. It's believed that he went into the countryside above the village, leaned his easel against a haystack, and walked behind the Château d'Auvers to shoot himself. Surviving the bullet's impact, he returned to his room, where he was later discovered by the inn's owner, Ravoux. His beloved brother, Thèodore, sped from Paris to his bedside, but Vincent died early on the morning of Tuesday, July 29. The two brothers' graves sit side by side and covered with ivy at the back wall of the town cemetery.

GETTING THERE
By car:
From Paris's Porte de Clignancourt, take highway *A1* north toward Lille and Charles de Gaulle Airport. After a short time, exit for highways *A86* (toward Nanterre) and *A15* (Pontoise). After crossing the Seine, the highway divides. Follow signs to *A15* Pontoise. Just before Pontoise, exit at St.

▼

Ouen L'Aumone onto *rte. N184*. Take this to *rte. N328*, and exit following signs for Auvers. There is parking in the village along the main road.

By train:

Trains to Pontoise depart almost hourly from Paris's Gare du Nord and St-Lazare stations. From Pontoise, one can make convenient train connections to the nearby village of Auvers. The entire trip takes up to 1 1/2 hours.

Walk 1 Directions

TIME: 1 1/2 hours
LEVEL: Easy
DISTANCE: 3 1/2 miles
ACCESS: By car and train

This walk traverses mostly paved village roads and well-used farm tracks. You can pick up provisions for picnics along the main street of Auvers, the *rue de General de Gaulle,* and enjoy a picnic in the fields or on park benches near the church and cemetery.

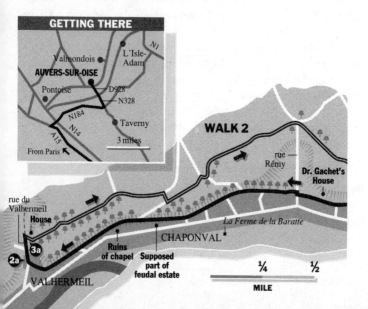

▼

TO BEGIN

After exiting the train station, turn right and follow the main road along the river a short distance to the *rue de Paris.* Turn left and go up the hill toward the church and the *rue Daubigny,* at the foot of the church.

1. Make a left and stroll down the quiet, tree-shaded *rue Daubigny,* following yellow blazes on telephone poles.

2. At a Y in the road at the *rue de Léry,* continue right on the *rue Daubigny* past the studio of Daubigny to your left.

3. In just a few minutes, you'll leave the blazed trails to the left and proceed toward the right on a dirt road leading uphill through a forest. Shortly, it emerges onto a broad, fertile plateau farmed much as it must have been in the time of Van Gogh.

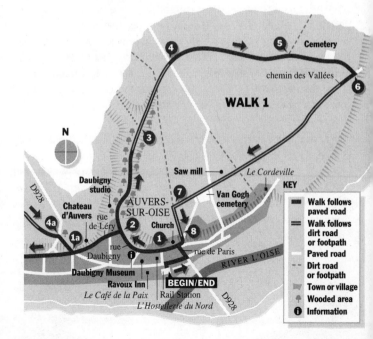

▼

4. At an intersection of farm roads, walk straight and continue on the dirt road across the open fields. To your right there are fine views (disturbed only by a power line) of rolling farmland and the low hills above the river in the distance.

5. In less than ten minutes, you come to a yellow-blazed trail marked by a small wooden footpath sign. Bear right toward and past a walled cemetery. The trail descends into a shallow ravine and arrives at a three-way intersection.

6. Go right onto a dead-end road, the *Chemin des Vallées,* which leads back up a short hill onto the plateau. The church tower will appear in the distance above the trees; the valley of the L'Oise will be below to the left. Another footpath sign will confirm that you're on one of the yellow-blazed circuits.

The farm road leads through fields to a small sawmill. Unfortunately, litter and debris from this operation mar the beauty in this portion of the walk. Proceed on to the cemetery where Van Gogh and his brother are buried. *Their ivy-covered tombs are set against the wall between the two side entrances to the cemetery.* Exit through either of the side entrances and continue beyond the cemetery, passing on your left a paved road leading down to the village.

7. At the first intersection after the paved road, turn left onto another road, back toward the church and village.

Near the intersection, Van Gogh painted Field of Wheat with Crows—*presumed to be his last painting. In one of his last letters, Van Gogh wrote: "It is under these immense stretches of wheat, under these troubled skies, that I am unhindered in expressing deep sorrow and extreme solitude."*

8. The road comes out at the back of the church, where Van Gogh painted *L'Eglise d'Auvers.* Continue back down the hill to the center of town.

▼

Walk 2 Directions

TIME: 3 hours

LEVEL: Easy to moderate

DISTANCE: About 5 1/2 miles

This longer tour takes in the entire length of the town and the neighboring ancient village of Valhermeil, passing by many spots made famous in the paintings of the Impressionists. Famous artists undoubtedly followed this same route, walking from Pontoise to the home of Dr. Gachet and Daubigny.

Afterward, return to the center of Auvers by way of a clearly marked country footpath on the plateau above the town. The local tourist office provides an easy-to-follow English-language printed guide to the village portion of this itinerary. Picnic spots abound along both the village and country sections of this tour.

TO BEGIN

As in the first walking tour, start at the *rue Daubigny* and walk to Point 2, where you make a left onto the *rue de Léry*. Walk along this small road and pass in front of the 17th-century Château d'Auvers.

Somewhere across the rue de Léry on the night on of July 27, 1890, Van Gogh staggered back home after shooting himself, behind the Château d'Auvers.

1A. Cross *rte. D928 (rte. d'Herouville)* onto the *rue Victor Hugo.* The *rue Victor Hugo* shortly becomes the *rue Gachet*. As you walk, you'll pass by several scenes painted by the Impressionists, marked today by encased posters. You'll also pass the home of Dr. Gachet (privately owned) at No. 78.

At the *rue Rémy,* you'll cross the street at a spot once painted by Camille Corot, and then continue straight onto the *rue François Coppée.* At the intersection with the *rue de la Cherielle,* bear left on the *rue des Meulières,* passing en route several prints of paintings by Van Gogh and Cézanne. *The Hanged Man's House,* once painted by Cézanne, was so

▼

known because a local man took his life there, during the same era when the Impressionists flocked to Auvers.

In quick succession, the small village road will change its name to *rue des Ruelles, rue Simone le Danoise,* and *rue des Roches* before it ends in the tiny hamlet of Valhermeil, where Cézanne also painted.

On the rue des Ruelles are the remains of a house said to be part of the village's original feudal estate (note several large stone blocks and an old wall). A little farther along, on the rue Simone Le Danois, you'll find the ruins of the 13th-century St. Nicolas chapel against the hill to your right.

2A. At the end of the *rue des Roches,* turn right on the *rue du Valhermeil,* walking a short distance past a small grocery store.

3A. Soon, you'll notice white-and-red blazes, marking the *GR* trail. Go right, following the blazes up a steep tiny road in front of a house and on up onto the plateau. You'll walk along the edges of fields and farms, crossing small forests and descending several times into shallow ravines before following the blazes back down a well-used farm track toward the village.

4A. When you reach the busy *D928,* go right—still following the blazes—downhill to the Château d'Auvers and the *rue Daubigny.*

PLACES ALONG THE WALK

■ **The studio of Daubigny.** *6 rue Daubigny, tel. 34-48-03-03. Open daily except Mon. 2-6:30 Apr. 10-Sep. 30.*

■ **The Daubigny Museum.** *Manoir des Colombières, rue de la Sansonne, tel. 30-36-80-20. Open Wed., Fri., Sat., and Sun. 2-5:30 in winter and 2-6 in summer. Admission. Located adjacent to the tourist office.*

■ **Auberge Ravoux.** This small inn is where Van Gogh lived and died. It is now open to the public as a restaurant, so that you can soak up the atmosphere while you eat (*see* Dining).

▼

OTHER PLACES NEARBY

■ **Pontoise.** This medieval city on the edge of a large industrial area has managed to preserve a nice promenade above the medieval fortifications and an old cathedral. *12 km. west of Auvers.*

■ **Tavet Museum.** A noteworthy 15th-century building, it displays works of well-known local artists and other temporary exhibits. *4 rue le Mercier, Pontoise 95300, tel. 30-38-02-40 or 34-43-34-77. Open daily except Tue. 10-12 and 2-6. Closed on major holidays.*

■ **The Pissarro Museum.** Located in an annex to the Tavet Museum, it displays some of the works of the great Impressionist painter and houses his archives. *17 rue du Château, Pontoise 95300, tel. 30-32-06-75. Open Wed.-Sun. 2-6; closed on major holidays.*

■ **St. Maclou Cathedral.** This is a historic 15th-century church. *Pontoise. Closed Thu.*

■ **L'Isle Adam.** A tiny town upriver of Auvers, it is known for its old bridges offering views of the L'Oise, a 16th-century church, and an 18th-century Chinese-style building in the park to the northeast of the city. *7 km. northeast of Auvers.*

■ **Museum of Transportation.** At this museum in nearby Valmondois, train buffs can take a half-hour ride on a steam train and visit a museum with over 50 trains of different vintages. *Open Sat. and Sun. 2:30-5:30 year-round. Train runs Apr. 1-Nov. 15, with departures at 3, 4, and 5. Admission.*

DINING & LODGING

The village is a great day-trip from Paris. Here are some restaurants in Auvers near the walking routes.

■ **L'Hostellerie du Nord** (moderate). The most formal restaurant in town—conveniently located near the train station—is a place where locals go for special occasions. You might find *langoustines au coriandre* (prawns grilled with coriander) or *gibelottes d'agneau* (lamb braised in a sauce of butter, egg yolk, and cream) on the menu. *6 rue de General de Gaulle, tel. 30-36-70-74. Closed Sun. eve. and all day Mon.*

■ **Les Canotiers** (moderate). Located in the 17th-century Château

▼

d'Auvers, it offers traditional French cuisine. *Rue de Léry, tel. 30-48-48-56. Closed Mon. and weekdays for dinner.*

■ **Auberge Ravoux** (moderate). Dine on traditional French food in the inn where Van Gogh spent his last days. *8 rue de la Sansonne, tel. 34-48-05-47. Closed Sun. for dinner and Mon.*

■ **La Ferme de la Baratte** (moderate). Farther down the road from the train station and a step down in price and ambience, this restaurant is recommended for a good, simple meal of meats, fish, or game. *5 rue Marceau, tel. 34-48-06-42. Closed Sun. for dinner and Mon.*

■ **Le Café de la Paix** (inexpensive). Brasserie-type food is served in a picturesque old building near the center of town—very casual. *11 rue de General de Gaulle, tel. 30-36-73-23. Open daily except Mon.*

■ **Le Cordeville** (inexpensive). This is for the adventuresome in search of inexpensive home cooking. It's up the river, about 1 km. out of town, in a tiny, charming house along the road. Mrs. Cordeville has no menu and does not speak English. She's open for lunch, but she might serve you dinner if you pass by and the light is still on. Then again, she might not. *18 rue Rajon, tel. 30-36-81-66. No credit cards. Open for lunch.*

FOR MORE INFORMATION
Tourist Office:

Manoir des Colombières. *Rue de la Sansonne, Auvers-sur-Oise 95430, tel. 30-36-10-06. Open daily 9:30-12 and 2-6. Closed Christmas and New Year's.*

For Serious Walkers:

The tourist office sells a packet of numerous day walks in the area. Unfortunately, it's available only in French, but it could be useful to those who also buy IGN map 2313OT.

In the Footsteps of a Poet

EXPERIENCE 2: CHEVREUSE

When you visit the town of Chevreuse and walk the **Chemin de Jean Racine,** you follow in the exact footsteps of this great 17th-century French poet, who more than 300 years ago regularly walked this country path from Chevreuse to the now abandoned Abbaye de Port-Royal. His path is so well known, in fact, that the Touring Club of France has marked the four or so miles with small concrete monuments bearing lines of his verse written about the area. The historic path traverses fields, forests, and a small river valley that probably haven't changed all that much in the last 300 years—if you can ignore the telephone and electric poles and the paved country roads you pass occasionally along the way.

The town of Chevreuse and the surrounding **Parc Naturel de la Haute Vallée de la Chevreuse** (National Park of the High Valley of Chevreuse) comprise a dramatically diverse playground of history and

> **The Highlights:** A country footpath regularly used by French poet Jean Racine in the 1600s, a magnificently restored medieval castle, an ancient abbey.
>
> **Other Places Nearby:** A vast national park; two chateaus with surrounding gardens, one at Breteuil and another at Dampierre; a luxuriously restored abbey where you can dine or spend the night.

▼

nature just 25 minutes southwest of Paris. Much of the land here is protected either by the government or by wealthy Parisians who have made it their country retreat, and so it preserves much medieval and Renaissance character. Large tracts of forest and farmland stand unspoiled; the Château de la Madeleine, which dominates the town of Chevreuse from atop a steep ridge, has been beautifully restored; and the haunting remains of the Abbaye de Port-Royal and other historic ruins evoke a strong sense of the past.

The village of Chevreuse first turns up in historical records in the late 10th century with the founding of a small abbey, **Saint-Saturnin,** of which you'll see a small portion near the town church. Over the next several centuries, however, war and bloodshed cast their shadow over the area. The **Château de la Madeleine,** built in the early 11th century, withstood numerous assaults during the 11th and 12th centuries in battles between the chateau's feudal lords and the French kings.

Perhaps the town's most lasting fame came during the 17th century. The **Abbaye de Port-Royal,** founded as a Cistercian abbey in the 13th century, had declined seriously in the early 1600s and was taken over by a group of monks known as the Messieurs de Port-Royal and later as the Solitaires. They were followers of Dutch theologian Cornelius Jansen, who preached a purified form of Catholicism that was bitterly opposed by the more liberal Jesuit order. While the abbess, Mère Angélique, and her nuns ran the abbey itself, the monks lived in a building known as **Les Granges de Port-Royal** on the hill above, where they ran a school. In October 1655, an orphaned boy named Jean Racine was sent by relatives to attend the school. The Jesuits pressured the Pope to condemn Jansenism, however, and the school was closed in 1656.

Six years later, Racine returned to Chevreuse for several months, filling in for a relative hired to oversee the reconstruction of the castle. Racine seems to have found this period of life boring, and he spent much of his time in a local watering hole, the Cabaret du Lys, where you can stop for a drink today. "I taste the pleasures of solitary life," he

▼

wrote of this period. "I am alone and don't hear the slightest noise; yet it is true that the wind makes a terrible noise to the point of making the house tremble. I read poems, and try to write some."

The struggle between the Jansenists and the Jesuits continued, threatening to tear apart the Catholic church; Racine himself later joined the fray, writing several works in support of Jansenism. But in 1709, by decree of the Pope, the abbey's buildings were disassembled stone by stone. Two years later, the church was destroyed and the remains of the dead moved from the cemetery to another graveyard in nearby St-Lambert.

Today, few ruins near Paris rival those of this site for tranquillity and rural beauty. All that has survived is the abbey's beautiful park, with a pond in the shape of a crucifix, an old tower, a granary, and a row of linden trees marking the former site of the cloisters and the cemetery. Outside the old entrance, you can walk on the same 100 steps the monks used to climb to and from Les Granges. The building itself remains intact despite numerous modifications; today it houses the **Musée Nationale des Granges de Port-Royal,** dedicated to the Jansenist movement.

GETTING THERE

By train:

On the RER (Regional Train Network), take Line B4 from Paris (stations at Luxembourg, St-Michel, Port-Royal, Denfert-Rochereau, and Cité Universitaire) to St-Rémy-les-Chevreuse, a trip of less than 50 minutes, depending on the point of departure from Paris.

By car:

From Paris, exit the *blvd. Péripbèrique* at Porte de St-Cloud, following signs for the *autoroute* to Chartres. After crossing the Seine, exit following signs to Chartres on *N118,* a four-lane highway. Drive about 15 km. and exit at Le Christ-de-Saclay. Follow signs to St-Rémy-les-Chevreuse on *rte. N306,* about 9 km. Take *rte. N306* through St-Rémy, following signs to Chevreuse, about 2 km. farther on. Follow the signs to the tourist office, where you'll find parking in the *pl. Charles-de-Gaulle* near the church.

▼

Walk 1 is specifically designed for those who come by train. Those who come by car should take Walk 2.

Walk 1 Directions

TIME: 1 1/2 hours round-trip
LEVEL: Easy
DISTANCE: Under 3 miles
ACCESS: By RER train

This route takes train travelers from the RER station, just outside of Chevreuse, along a pleasant stroll into town, stopping at several sights. Almost all of this short route follows small paved roads or well-traveled dirt paths. Buy a picnic lunch in Chevreuse, and find wonderful spots to eat at the Château de la Madeleine or in the rural stretch between the RER and Chevreuse.

TO BEGIN

Exit the RER station and walk parallel to the tracks toward a tall blue RER sign at the entrance to the station.

1. When you reach the sign, go right on the main road (away from the train tracks) and then make a quick left following a road sign to Chevreuse. You can walk along a bike path, off the road on your right. You should see white-and-red blazes crossed by a slash, indicating a branch of a long-distance *GR* trail. *Within a few minutes, on your left you'll see the Château de Coubertin, home of the founder of the modern Olympic Games, now open for special exhibitions.*

2. After about ten minutes of walking, just past a small intersection, follow the blazed trail that veers right off the road onto a dirt track marked by a sign prohibiting bicycles. You'll shortly emerge from a copse of trees onto a field offering fine views of Chevreuse and the Château de la Madeleine above.

3. Here the dirt track becomes paved and continues toward the castle (it is still marked with the white-and-red slashed blaze). The trail

▼

crosses a small bridge over the tiny canal of the Yvette river and then turns left onto a picturesque dirt path that runs along the narrow river itself. Shortly after, at a bridge, the white-and-red-blazed trail turns right over the river, but you continue straight along the left side of the river. *You'll see old stone sheds, remnants of ancient leather works.*

4. When you reach a small footbridge, you'll see Chevreuse's old *lavoir,* where local folk washed their laundry before the advent of modern appliances. Go right across the tiny bridge and enter the village by way of a narrow paved path, the *ruelle de Mandar,* which leads between small buildings (look for white-and-red blazes indicating the long-distance *GR 11*).

5. At the main road, the *rue de la Division-Leclerc,* follow the blazes to the right. Then turn left up the *rue Lalande,* named for a 17th-century French astronomer born in Chevreuse. This road, reserved for pedestrians, leads past restaurants and the *Cabaret du Lys, on your right, where the poet Jean Racine frequently came for refreshment.*

6. Enter the triangular *pl. des Halles.* To visit the chateau, go to the top right-hand side of the plaza and find a small cobblestoned alley marked with yellow and white-and-red blazes. Follow the blazes to the top of the hill, where you'll find excellent views and *the entrance to the castle and the information center.*

Retrace your steps down the alley to the *pl. des Halles,* where you turn right onto the *rue de Versailles. You'll pass the town's oldest building, the 15th-century Maison des Bannières (on your right), now a crêperie.*

If you want to follow Walk 2 (below), exit the castle and proceed uphill toward a driveway, which you follow straight for a very short distance. Go left on a white-and-yellow-blazed trail heading downhill. Proceed downhill to the rue de Versailles, where you turn right onto the Chemin de Jean Racine. From here, follow the instructions in Walk 2.

7. A little farther on the *rue de Versailles,* go left on a small one-way road that leads to the tourist office, the *pl. Charles-de-Gaulle,* and

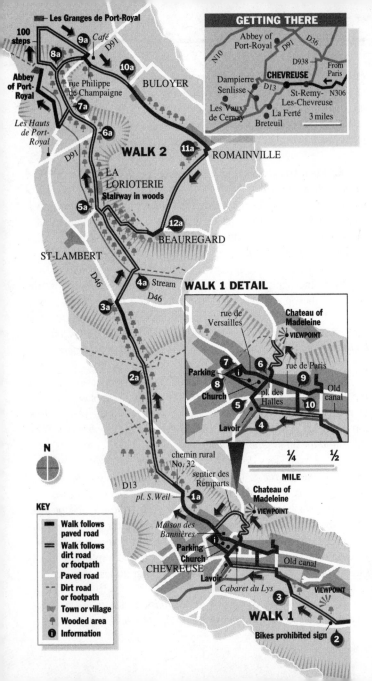

Les Granges de Port-Royal

100 steps

9a Café

8a D91

Abbey of Port-Royal

10a

rue Philippe de Champaigne

BULOYER

Les Hauts de Port-Royal

7a

6a

11a

ROMAINVILLE

D91

WALK 2

LA LORIOTERIE

Stairway in woods

5a

12a

BEAUREGARD

ST-LAMBERT

D46

4a Stream

D46

3a

2a

GETTING THERE

Abbey of Port-Royal

N10

D91

D36

D938

From Paris

CHEVREUSE

Dampierre

D13

Senlisse

St-Remy-Les-Chevreuse

N306

Les Vaux de Cernay

La Ferté

Breteuil

3 miles

WALK 1 DETAIL

rue de Versailles

Chateau of Madeleine

VIEWPOINT

7

6

rue de Paris

Parking

i

9

8

Church

pl. des Halles

Old canal

5

10

4

Lavoir

N

chemin rural No. 32

sentier des Remparts

Chateau of Madeleine

VIEWPOINT

D13

pl. S. Weil

1a

¼

½

MILE

Maison des Bannières

Parking

i

Church

Old canal

Lavoir

VIEWPOINT

CHEVREUSE

Cabaret du Lys

3

WALK 1

KEY

▬ Walk follows paved road

═ Walk follows dirt road or footpath

Paved road

--- Dirt road or footpath

Town or village

Wooded area

ℹ Information

Bikes prohibited sign

2

▼

a public parking area. *At the pl. Charles-de-Gaulle, you will see the town's 12th-century church (which is usually open) and, across from it, the Saint Saturnin priory, founded in the 10th century.*

8. From the parking lot, go to the right of the church and follow the *rue de l'Eglise* to the *pl. des Halles*. Cross the *pl. des Halles* and go downhill on the *rue de Paris*.

9. When you reach the *pl. des Luynes*, continue straight just a few more minutes and bear left onto the *rue de la Division-Leclerc*. Walk a short distance and then make a left on the *rue de la Tour*. In just a few yards, go left into a driveway and walk a short distance to see what remains of the castle's ancient outer wall. Retrace your steps to the *pl. des Luynes* and go left.

10. Cross the the main road and take a small pathway across from the *Mairie* (town hall) back down to the river. Here, turn left onto the trail that brought you into town (marked white and red with a slash) and walk back to the RER station the same way you came.

Walk 2 Directions

TIME:	4 hours
LEVEL:	Difficult
DISTANCE:	8 1/2 miles
ACCESS:	By car or RER train

Walk through woodlands, fields, and meadows to the ancient Abbaye de Port-Royal along the *Chemin de Jean Racine,* the same path used by the poet Jean Racine in the 17th century. A yellow-blazed *PR* trail guides you almost the entire way, although you won't always find the blazes. You may encounter a few muddy or overgrown spots.

TO BEGIN

If you come by car, park in Chevreuse at the *pl. Charles-de-Gaulle* and

L'YVETTE RIVER

RER Station

①

Chateau of
Coubertin

ST-REMY-
LES CHEVREUSE

▼

walk past the tourist office to the *rue de Versailles,* where you turn left. If you come by train, follow the instructions for Walk 1 as far as the *pl. des Halles* (*see* Point 6, above) and turn left on the *rue de Versailles,* following the yellow blazes. In both cases, continue on the *rue de Versailles* straight through the intersection just outside the village and walk to *rte. D13,* where you go straight.

1A. You will shortly reach the *pl. Simone Weil,* occupied by a few park benches and carefully pruned linden trees. Leave *rte. D13,* turning right uphill along a small paved road (*Chemin rural No. 32*) marked with yellow blazes. You'll shortly bear left at a Y. After you pass between three small concrete posts, this becomes a dirt road. It veers to the right up a hill through a deciduous forest between fences and continues on about 1 km. to the *Carrefour de la Madeleine,* a junction with a paved road, where a concrete monument to the *Chemin de Jean Racine* has been erected. (You will see several of these monuments throughout the walk, each one inscribed with several lines of the poet's work.) *If you hear gunshots in this area, don't be concerned; there's a shooting range nearby.*

2A. Continue on the yellow-blazed trail for another ten minutes or so, until you arrive at another intersection, the *Carrefour du Roi de Rome.* Go straight across the intersection, following the trail leading downhill on a semi-paved road (ignore the two trails going off to your right). At the bottom of the wooded hill, you'll come out on a minor road with a few small houses. Continue straight.

3A. Stay on this minor road until it comes out on a larger road, *rte. D46.* Here, you will see a Jean Racine monument that displays this verse: *"There one sees the light-footed deer and her sweet mate of the fields."* Go right about ten feet, then left across the road and onto a trail crossing a field toward the woods.

4A. At the far end of the field, cross a small footbridge. *The plaque on the monument here reads: "There along the numerous forest alleys*

▼

one finds a thousand thick willows." Go left, following the yellow blazes (ignore the blue-blazed trail to your right and another trail that goes straight). Just before you reach the intersection at Point 5A you will see stairs heading up a hill on your right. You will come down these stairs later if you complete the entire circuit.

5A. At an intersection in the tiny hamlet of La Lorioterie, bear right. *Here, a concrete monument tells you, "This is where one hears the murmur of these pleasing streams."*

6A. Follow the yellow-blazed trail for about ten minutes, until you cross a busy road, *rte. D91*. Here, you proceed on the yellow-blazed trail as it reenters the forest at the base of a steep hill.

7A. In just a few more minutes you'll meet a three-way intersection, with a white-and-blue-blazed trail forking off on your left.

If you choose to skip the abbey, continue straight on the yellow-blazed trail. Go left on this trail if you wish to visit the old Abbaye de Port-Royal. It's a short footpath leading to a paved road; turn right on this road to reach the parking lot for the abbey. A clearly marked footpath leads from the parking lot to the entrance. After visiting the abbey, retrace your steps to the three-way intersection with the yellow-blazed Chemin de Jean Racine at Point 7A.

As you proceed toward Point 8A, *the ancient abbey walls appear on your left. Holes provide views of the beautiful property, its crucifix-shaped pond, and what little remains of its once impressive buildings.*

8A. At another three-way intersection, go right up the hill following the yellow-blazed trail. *To take the 100 steps, the stairway used by the monks to reach Les Granges on the hill above, continue straight along the wall at Point 8A. You'll see the stairway in the woods to your right, near the ancient main entrance, now closed. Follow the stairs uphill to a stone gate, which is open everyday except Tuesday. Continue uphill to visit Les Granges, exit the property by way of its main driveway, and follow it to* rte. D91 *and Point 9A.*

▼

9A. At the top of the hill, just past a small old house on your left, the path meets *rte. D91*. There, you can stop for refreshment at a café, the Auberge au Chant des Oiseau. To return to Chevreuse, cross *rte. D91* and go straight on a dead-end paved road, following the yellow blazes. The trail soon leaves the paved road and passes under a green metal barrier; there's a broad field to your left and woods to your right.

10A. After passing through another green barrier, the trail comes out onto a paved road in the tiny hamlet of Buloyer. Follow the blazes straight along the paved country road, which is bordered by fields. In about ten minutes you'll enter the hamlet of Romainville.

11A. At a three-way intersection in tiny Romainville, go straight on a paved road in the direction of Milon-La-Chapelle, indicated by a road sign. After rounding a bend to the right and then left in the road, go right onto a paved road leading past a small country estate on your right. Just beyond, the trail becomes a farm track across a broad field. You'll still be following yellow blazes.

12A. At the far end of the field, at a farm wall, there's a three-way intersection. The yellow-blazed trail goes left, but you turn right on the white-and-blue-blazed trail, walking with the farm wall on your left and the huge expanse of field on your right. At the edge of the walled farmyard, near a new house on your right, a small pictorial sign indicates a horse trail. Follow this trail, keeping the fields on your right and the forest on your left. Take the white-and-blue-blazed trail as it veers left and down into the forest, descending a wooded ridge for about five minutes before you reach the stairway noted in Point 5A. Go down the stairs, turn left, and retrace your route along the yellow-blazed trail to Chevreuse.

PLACES ALONG THE WALK

■ **Château de la Madeleine.** *Tel. 1/30-52-09-09. Open Mon.-Fri. 9-12 and 2-5. Admission charged for castle tour.*

■ **Abbaye de Port-Royal.** *Open daily 10-12 and 2:30-5:30 May 17-Oct. 15 and 10-12 and 2:30-5 Oct. 16-May 16. Closed Tue. and Fri.*

▼

morning. Admission.

■ **Musée National des Granges de Port-Royal.** *Tel. 1/30-43-73-05. Open daily except Tue. 10-12 and 2-5:30 (5 in winter). Admission.*

OTHER PLACES NEARBY

■ **Château de Breteuil.** This impressively restored chateau, originally built as a fortress on the site of a Roman villa, was significantly remodeled and expanded in the 16th and 18th centuries. It's now a museum and a park. *Tel. 1/30-52-05-11. Open Mon.-Sat. 2-5 and Sun. and holidays 11-6. Admission to chateau. Off rte. D41, 5 km. southwest of Chevreuse.*

■ **Château de Dampierre.** This elegant chateau was reconstructed in the Renaissance style under the direction of Jules Mansart in the 17th century. *Tel. 1/30-52-53-24. Chateau interior open daily 2-6:30 Apr.-Oct. 15; 11-6:30 Sun. and holidays. Admission. About 5 km. west of Chevreuse off rte. D91.*

■ **Abbaye des Vaux de Cernay.** A surprisingly intact 12th-century monastery has been painstakingly restored into this luxury hotel with a notable restaurant. Set in a large forest, the Cistercian abbey consists of several buildings and beautiful grounds. *Cernay-la-Ville, Dampierre-en-Yvelines 78720, tel. 1/34-85-23-00. Open Sat., Sun. and holidays 10-6. 8 km. southwest of Chevreuse.*

■ **L'Etang de Cernay.** Near the Abbaye des Vaux de Cernay you can see part of the elaborate waterworks constructed by the monks in its natural, undisturbed setting. *Rte. D24, 7 km. southwest of Chevreuse.*

■ **Parc Naturel Regional de la Haute Vallée de la Chevreuse (Natural Park of the High Valley of the Chevreuse).** Surrounding Chevreuse, this extensive park includes both forestland and historical monuments. The information center *(Maison du Parc, tel. 1/30-52-09-09)* is located in the Château de la Madeleine; stop here for complete information on walking tours and other activities in the area.

DINING

■ **Abbaye des Vaux de Cernay** (very expensive). Near Chevreuse, this famed restaurant enjoys an incomparable setting. Some

▼

locals think the restaurant is overrated, but those who can afford it dine in a magnificently restored Gothic-vaulted room once used by the Cistercian monks. You might find *pavé de filet de truite de mer, fondue de poireau au Noilly* (fillet of sea trout with leeks), or *escalopede filet de boeuf au Madère* (fillet of beef in a wine sauce). *Cernay-la-Ville, Dampierre-en-Yvelines 78720, tel. 1/34-85-23-00, fax 1/34-85-20-95. 8 km. southwest of Chevreuse.*

■ **Les Hauts de Port-Royal** (expensive). Located in an eclectically decorated old home near the Abbaye de Port-Royal, this restaurant has plenty of personality and a highly recommended kitchen. Specials might include *escalope de saumon d'Escosse* (thinly cut Scottish salmon with Burgundy wine) or *emincé de rognon de veau* (slices of veal kidney served with preserved garlic). *2 rue de Vaumurier, St-Lambert-des-Bois, tel. 1/30-44-10-21, fax 1/30-64-44-10. Closed Sun. eve., all day Mon., and Dec. 24-25. Just off rte. D91, 4 km. northwest of Chevreuse.*

■ **Auberge Le Pont Hardi** (expensive). Here's another country gem, located in an old inn in a quiet, deeply wooded valley in the tiny village of Senlisse (near the Dampierre chateau). You may find country favorites such as oven-roasted lamb chops or *poisson du marché* (fresh fish of the day with a fennel purée); for dessert, there might be a *bavaroise aux pommes* (an apple custard) or a hot pear tart with almond cream. *1 rue du Couvent, Senlisse, tel. 1/30-52-50-78, fax 1/30-52-54-72. Closed Mon. 8 km. west of Chevreuse.*

■ **La Tour des Bannières** (inexpensive). Here you get 15th-century atmosphere in one of the oldest buildings in town without the refinement and the expense. Crepes are the specialty. *16 rue de Versailles, Chevreuse, tel. 1/30-52-25-51. Closed Mon. for dinner.*

LODGING

■ **Abbaye des Vaux de Cernay** (very expensive). For the affluent, nothing compares with staying in this lovingly converted 12th-century abbey, now part of the Relais & Chateau hotel network. The old building has spectacular rooms on the first floor and almost equally impressive accommodations on the second floor, all discreetly integrating antique decor with modern conveniences. In the main building,

▼

Room 104 on the first floor and Room 207 on the second floor are particularly attractive. A newly restored wing has attractively furnished modern rooms. All guests can enjoy the abbey's beautiful buildings, pastoral setting, and highly praised—but very expensive—cuisine. The hotel also has a pool, tennis courts, and an inspiring network of wooded footpaths. *Cernay-la-Ville, Dampierre-en-Yvelines 78720, tel. 1/34-85-23-00, fax 1/34-85-11-60. 8 km. southwest of Chevreuse.*

■ **Auberge Le Pont Hardi** (expensive). Those of more humble means won't be disappointed by this quiet and attractively furnished tiny retreat near the Dampierre chateau. With only six rooms, almost all overlooking the quiet garden, it has the amenities of a high-class hotel at more reasonable prices, especially when compared with Parisian hotels nearby. Rooms 3, 4, and 5 are the best, with rates that skirt the moderate category. *1 rue du Couvent, Senlisse, tel. 1/30-52-50-78, fax 1/30-52-54-72. 8 km. west of Chevreuse.*

■ **Auberge Le Gros Marronnier** (expensive). This popular spot has the same excellent price-quality ratio as its neighbor, Le Pont Hardi. It's located in a tranquil, tiny village in old buildings that the ownership has tastefully if not luxuriously restored. We liked rooms 1, 4, 14, 15, 16, and 17 the best. All are relatively quiet. *3 pl. de l'Eglise, Senlisse, tel. 1/30-52-51-69, fax 1/30-52-55-91. Open year-round but sometimes closed around Christmas.*

■ **Maison de Fer** (inexpensive). This *gîte d'étape* (hostel) occupies a recently renovated collapsible house designed by Gustave Eiffel, designer of the Eiffel Tower. Convenient for long-distance hikers using the *GR 11,* or for budget travelers who have a car, it offers clean but communal quarters in the woods on a hiking trail just outside of Dampierre. *Contact Maison du Parc, Château de la Madeleine, Chevreuse 78460, tel. 1/30-52-09-09, fax 1/30-52-12-42.*

FOR MORE INFORMATION

Tourist Offices:

    Syndicat d'Initiative. *Pl. Charles-de-Gaulle, Chevreuse 78460, tel. 1/30-52-02-27. Open Wed. and Sat. 10-12 and 2-5; Sun. 10-12.*

    Maison du Parc. In addition to information about walking and

▼

history, this office also administers the park's two *gîtes d'étapes*. *Château de la Madeleine, Chevreuse 78460, tel. 1/30-52-09-09, fax 1/30-52-12-43. Open Mon.-Fri. 2-5:30 and Sun. 10-1 and 2-5:30.*

For Serious Walkers:
Parc Naturel Regional de la Haute Vallée de la Chevreuse. This area has hundreds of kilometers of well-marked long- and short-distance walking trails. Literature (some of it in English) documenting the trails is available at the Maison du Parc in the Château de la Madeleine (see above). IGN map 2215 OT clearly shows the best walking trails.

The Forest of Kings

EXPERIENCE 3: BARBIZON

Handily located near Paris, the **Fontainebleau Forest** for centuries attracted royalty as a prime hunting ground. In the 17th century, the forest was one of the largest in the kingdom, crisscrossed with trails and maintained for the pleasure of kings and aristocrats. Until the 19th century, however, ordinary Europeans viewed forests mostly as a source of food and firewood, or as a hideout from the law. But around 1810, a group of landscape painters from Paris, influenced by the

The Highlights: Dramatic views of boulder-strewn ridges and ancient forests, landscapes painted by artists of the Barbizon school, the studio of Theodore Rousseau, an inn where Robert Louis Stevenson lived.

Other Places Nearby: Fontainebleau and its famous chateau and gardens, the beautiful village of Milly-la-Forêt with its famous 15th-century covered marketplace, and nearby Chapelle St-Blaise-des-Simples.

Romantic movement, "discovered" Fontainebleau as a source of inspiration. The forest's bizarre rock formations—huge piles of split and eroded limestone scattered along and atop the forest's steep ridges—and its thick stands of oak, Scotch pine, beech, and birch trees created a decidedly picturesque sylvan scene. Rather than settle in Fontainebleau, many artists stayed in the village of Barbizon, on the northwestern edge

▼

of the forest, and their work came to be dubbed the Barbizon school of painting, with Theodore Rousseau and Jean-François Millet among its leading lights.

In the 1830s, work began in earnest to open up the forest to tourists, an effort led by a man named Claude-François Denecourt. Having taken up residence in Fontainebleau in 1832, Denecourt set out to catalog the many miles of forest trails, originally made for hunters and people on horseback. Denecourt started publishing brochures called "Guide for Travelers in the Forest of Fontainebleau," in which he described numerous walking itineraries along the old trails; in 1842, Denecourt became even more ambitious, laying out his own walking trails. Soon, his brochures had become a series of books, the world's first walking guides, which remained in publication until 1931.

I n 1853, a small parcel of the Fontainebleau Forest was officially set aside for the pleasure of visitors, thus becoming the world's first forest reserve. (The United States did not establish the world's first national park, Yellowstone, until 1872.) Today the expanded Fontainebleau park attracts lots of French people during warm-weather months, although its extensive trail system provides plenty of opportunity to escape from the crowds. Abandoned during World War II and for several years thereafter, the Denecourt trails were restored by hardy volunteers during the 1950s. There are now hundreds of miles of blazed trails, along with some well-paved roads, exploring every corner of the forest and its varied terrain.

Today, the tiny village of Barbizon remains relatively unscathed by tourism, although tour buses driving from Fontainebleau to Paris chug along its narrow main street during the summer. It remains a cheerful, relatively quiet village with attractive galleries and antiques stores and a few special places to dine and spend the night. Barbizon is an excellent base of operations for those who want to explore the less traveled sections of the park or to visit the gardens and palace at Fontainebleau.

The **Musée Auberge du Père Ganne,** on the *rue Grande,* the town's main street, displays works of some of the Barbizon artists in an old inn where the artists used to meet to discuss their work. Just down

▼

the street, the **Musée de l'Ecole de Barbizon** displays works of the Barbizon school in what used to be Theodore Rousseau's studio.

Fontainebleau Forest is inviting territory for anything from a casual stroll to a strenuous hike. Our first walking itinerary starts on the valley floor, rises up a short but steep ridge strewn with huge boulders, and loops back to the village. Those who just want a short stroll can easily shorten the walking tour (*see* Walk 2).

GETTING THERE
By car:

Take the *Autoroute du Sud A6,* which begins at the Porte d'Orléan in Paris. Exit the highway at *rte. N37,* following signs for Fontainebleau (just before tolls). About 5 km. after you've exited the autoroute, exit *rte. N37* at *rte. D64* and follow signs to Barbizon. When you get to the main road, the *rue Grande,* make a left onto it to reach the center of town and the starting point of the forest walking tour.

By train:

From Paris's Gare de Lyon, some 20 trains a day go to Fontainebleau, about 10 km. (6 miles) from the town of Barbizon. Buses to Barbizon leave from in front of the main post office in Fontainebleau three times a day.

Walk 1 Directions

TIME: About 2 1/2 hours
LEVEL: Moderate
DISTANCE: About 4 miles
ACCESS: Best by car

This circuit, rambling through the Fontainebleau Forest near the town of Barbizon, presents several ups and downs through rocky, slippery passages and is designed for more experienced walkers who feel comfortable navigating forests and rugged terrain (*see* Walk 2, below, for an easier route). Pick up provisions along the *rue Grande* in Barbizon and picnic at an overlook on one of the forest's wooded ridges.

▼

TO BEGIN

Walk or drive out of town east on the main road, the *rue Grande*, which leads into the forest. If you drive, park at the *Carrefour du Bas Bréau*, a major intersection of trails about 1 km. east of the town.

1. Facing the park's wooden entrance sign, walk down the signposted *rte. des Artistes,* a broad, flat trail that leads diagonally away from the intersection. You'll see a recently cut forest on the left and an old forest on the right.

2. In just a few minutes, you'll reach a trail marked

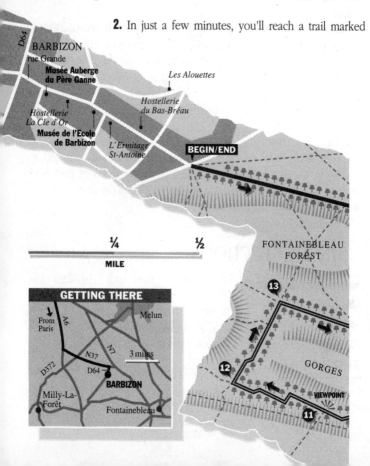

▼

rte. des Peintres. Turn right and follow this trail, which quickly veers right and then left. You'll cross one forest path; continue straight a few more minutes.

3. At the next intersection, turn right on a trail marked first by white-and-blue blazes, then by the white-and-red blazes of a *GR* trail.

4. You quickly reach an intersection with a wide dirt road; go straight, climbing up the ridge. A metal sign will tell you that you're on the *rte. de la Solitude.* As you climb the hill, you will see both white-and-blue and white-and-red blazes. Through this section, you traverse a field of boulders—be aware that the footing can be tricky in wet weather.

5. Near the top of the hill, you'll come to a trail intersection. Follow the white-and-blue blazes to the left (the white-and-red *GR* trail will fork off to your right). You are now on one of the trails laid out by Claude-François Denecourt, the deep blue blazes of which shortly

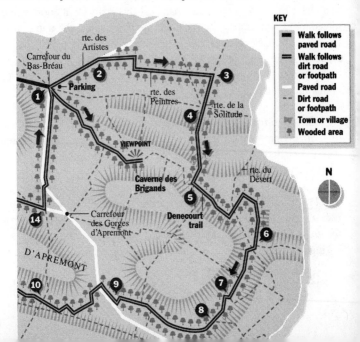

▼

appear. Winding through the boulders along the ridge, this trail offers dramatic views of the rugged ridges and the forest below and passes an intersection with the *rte. du Désert*.

6. About 15 minutes past Point 5, you'll reach a T intersection. Turn right and go uphill on a sandy path, following the deep blue blazes. This is a shortcut connecting two sides of Denecourt loop No. 6.

7. You'll soon arrive at another intersection. Go right, following the blue blazes.

8. At the next intersection, go right, still following the blue blazes. You are now on the other side of Denecourt loop No. 6. After crossing the flat top of the ridge for a few minutes, the trail descends. At a Y in the trail, bear left, going downhill, still following a blue-blazed trail.

9. A small paved road soon appears several dozen feet away on your left. The blue-blazed trail parallels this road for a short while, threading its way among the rocks. At the point where the trail crosses the road, you have *two options:* Either turn right on the paved road to return to your car, a little more than half a mile away in Barbizon, or cross the road and follow the blue-blazed Denecourt trail, bearing left uphill through a forest of old trees and ferns.

10. A short while later, the trail reaches an intersection of a few footpaths. Here you'll pick up a *GR* trail marked by white-and-red blazes. Go straight across the intersection, following both the white-and-red and deep blue blazes up a hill.

11. At another intersection, on top of the ridge, *two benches provide a good stopping place where you can drink in the sweeping view to the north. This is an especially good spot to picnic.* Continue straight, following the white-and-red and blue blazes across the ridge.

12. At the next intersection of blazed trails, turn right, following the white-and-red-blazed trail steeply down the hill. Wet conditions could make this short descent quite tricky: Proceed slowly.

13. In under ten minutes, you'll reach a big intersection on the valley floor. Go right, following the white-and-red-blazed trail through the forest.

14. When you reach a green wooden barrier (just before the *Carrefour des Gorges d'Apremont*), make a left on a dirt road, leaving the white-and-red trail. The dirt road soon joins a paved road; cross to the other side of the paved road and go left on a tiny trail that parallels it back to the *Carrefour du Bas Bréau,* where you parked, or where you go left back to town.

Walk 2 Directions

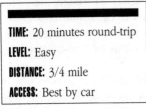

TIME: 20 minutes round-trip

LEVEL: Easy

DISTANCE: 3/4 mile

ACCESS: Best by car

As in the above walk, park at the *Carrefour du Bas Bréau,* just outside Barbizon. From the parking lot, cross the street to enter the grounds of a snack bar and picnic area. A Denecourt trail marked with deep blue blazes heads diagonally up the hill. A 15-minute walk along this trail will take you to *an overlook;* a few more minutes away is the *Caverne des Brigands,* which local tradition says was at one time a hideout for outlaws.

PLACES ALONG THE WALK

■ **Musée Auberge du Père Ganne.** This houses the municipal museum which, of course, focuses on the Barbizon school. It displays furniture and objects decorated by the artists as well as some of the walls they painted. *92 rue Grande. Open daily except Tue. Apr. 1-Sep. 30 10-12:30 and 2-6. Otherwise, it closes at 5.*

■ **La Maison Atelier de Théodore Rousseau.** Open for temporary exhibits. *55 rue Grande, tel. 1/60-66-22-38. Same hours as above. Admission.*

▼

OTHER PLACES NEARBY

■ **Fontainebleau.** Set in an immense garden, this huge Renaissance palace was built by Francis I in the early 16th century on the site of an earlier royal hunting lodge. *10 km. southeast of Barbizon on rte. N7.*

■ **Milly-La-Forêt.** This charming town is known for its elaborate 15th-century covered marketplace. *15 km. southwest of Barbizon.*

■ **Chapel St-Blaise-des-Simples.** Just outside Milly-La-Forêt, this 12th-century chapel was originally dedicated to helping lepers. In the late 1950s it was decorated by Jean Cocteau. *Rte. de la Chapelle-la-Reine, Milly-La-Forêt. Open daily except Tue. 10-12 and 2:30-6 Easter-Oct. 31; Sat., Sun., and holidays only Nov. 1-Easter. Admission.*

DINING

■ **Hostellerie du Bas-Bréau** (very expensive). For a fine meal, no restaurant in Barbizon compares with this charming inn where Robert Louis Stevenson lived for a while. On the day we visited, the dinner featured *poularde de Bresse rôti* (roasted chicken from Bresse) and *petite langouste rose "puce,"* a sumptuous preparation of shrimp served as an appetizer. *22 rue Grande, Barbizon 77630, tel. 1/60-66-40-05, fax 1/60-69-22-89.*

■ **Auberge du Grand-Veneur** (expensive). Right outside town, in an old hunting lodge, this restaurant provides rustic atmosphere, with hunting trophies and related paraphernalia decorating the walls. The menu features such hearty, traditional French food as poached turbot in Hollandaise sauce, grilled pigeon, and pheasant. *Rte. N7, Barbizon 77630, tel. 1/60-66-40-44. Open for lunch daily except Thu.; open for dinner daily except Wed.-Thu. Located 1 km. northeast of Barbizon.*

■ **Hostellerie La Cle d'Or** (moderate to expensive). Located in the old portion of a hotel, the restaurant has an attractive, romantic dining room. In spring, you might find *salade de haricots verts aux langoustines rôties* (an appetizer of tiny string beans and roasted shrimp) and *filet de boeuf en cocotte, au lard et petits oignons,* a cholesterol-laden but delicious offering of fillet mignon in a crock with tiny onions and a dousing of lard. *73 rue Grande, Barbizon 77630, tel. 1/60-66-40-96, fax 1/60-66-42-71.*

▼

■ **Les Alouettes** (moderate). This lovely dining room in an old hotel once frequented by painters is still known for a good meal at a fair price. Specials might include *escalope de saumon rôtie au fumet safrané* (roasted fillet of salmon with saffron) or *papillote de volaille au curry et son riz Indien* (chicken breast in a puff pastry with a curry sauce served with Indian rice). *4 rue Antoine Barye, Barbizon 77630, tel. 1/60-66-41-98, fax 1/60-66-20-69. Closed Sun. dinner.*

■ **Restaurant L'Angélus** (moderate). A charming, almost elegant setting and a focus on simplicity. Specials on our visit included *filet de canard à l'orange* (the classic French preparation of duck) and *brochette de St. Jacques aux filaments de safran*, skewers of scallops spiced with saffron. *31 rue Grande, Barbizon 77630, tel. 1/60-66-40-30, fax 1/60-66-48-62. Open daily for lunch and dinner, except Christmas Eve.*

■ **L'Ermitage St-Antoine** (inexpensive). Popular with the local crowd, this lively brasserie is set in a cellar dining room with a barrel-shaped stone ceiling. The atmosphere is charming yet simple, the prices reasonable. Much of the charcuterie is made on the premises; try the *assiette vigneronne* (the winemaker's plate) if it's available—a combination of ham, sausage, terrine, andouille, cheese, and salad. *51 rue Grande, Barbizon 77630, tel. 1/60-66-48-51, fax 1/60-66-48-62 and 1/60-66-46-21.*

LODGING

As a long-established country retreat, Barbizon has a number of hotels, a few of which offer both rustic charm and quiet.

■ **Hostellerie du Bas-Bréau** (very expensive). At the top of the list in both price and quality, this Relais & Châteaux hotel includes several rooms located in the old home once occupied by the writer Robert Louis Stevenson, but even the rooms in the newer wings are a treat, furnished sumptuously with a combination of antiques and modern conveniences. Room 31 has an especially nice view of the garden, but almost all rooms have quiet and pleasant settings. The hotel's guests have included such world leaders as Margaret Thatcher, François Mitterand, and Helmut Kohl. *22 rue Grande, Barbizon 77630, tel. 1/60-66-40-05, fax 1/60-69-22-89.*

▼

■ **Hostellerie La Cle d'Or** (moderate to expensive). This hotel's modern rooms have no special charm, but they do face a quiet, flower-filled garden. Rooms over the restaurant (*see* Dining, above) have more appeal, with No. 15 being particularly nice, but the noise from down below can be a drawback. At the top of the price range, the best room is a pleasantly furnished modern apartment over a building out back. *73 rue Grande, Barbizon 77630, tel. 1/60-66-40-96, fax 1/60-66-42-71.*

■ **Les Alouettes** (moderate). Travelers on a budget who still want a hotel with character should appreciate this one, situated in an old home that was frequented by artists in the 19th century. Although most of the rooms have no special beauty, they are clean and quiet, with all the basic conveniences plus nice garden views. Note the artwork painted by Barbizon-era artists on doors and wood trim in the hotel's dark-paneled, sinuous hallways. *4 rue Antoine Barye, Barbizon 77630, tel. 1/60-66-41-98, fax 1/60-66-20-69.*

FOR MORE INFORMATION
Tourist Office:
Office de Tourisme. *41 rue Grande, Barbizon 77630, tel. 1/60-66-41-87; fax 1/60-66-42-46.*

For Serious Walkers:
Fontainebleau Forest has one of the most extensive trail networks of any forest in France; most trails are clearly marked and easy to follow with the help of IGN maps 401 or 2417. Experienced walkers can significantly extend the tours with the help of IGN map 2417.

Hills of
the Artist

EXPERIENCE 4: GIVERNY

What brought the Impressionist painter Claude Monet to Giverny? Certainly not the elaborate gardens and lily ponds admired by tourists today. In 1883, when Monet first leased his house in an area still known as Le Pressoir (wine press), nothing but the peaceful course of the tiny Epte river suggested the waterworks and gardens to come. Visiting the area today, however, you can readily imagine why he chose this spot, for in many other respects it has hardly changed in the more than 100 years since.

The Highlights: Sweeping views of Giverny and the idyllic Seine river valley where Monet painted, special picnic spots away from the crowds, the new American Museum of Impressionism, and the house and gardens of Monet.

Other Places Nearby: The medieval town of Vernon, Château de Bizy, and the fortress town of La Roche-Guyon.

As art historians have pointed out, a particular play of light off the Seine here and the interesting alignment of hills on either side of the river may well have struck a chord in the artist's sensibility. On the way to Giverny, an art critic visiting Monet wrote: "It's a delightful road, with its adjacent fields where livestock graze on rich, already nearly Norman, pastures, and with its little stream glimpsed here and

▼

there, animated with washerwomen. On the other side, up on the hill, the open wounds of sandstone quarries plummet down in streams of gray or white. Roofs begin to appear, more and more group themselves together. Walls with moss-grown tops border the road; orchards now surround the dwellings: This is the village of Giverny." The old dirt road that you can follow from Vernon to Giverny offers views much like this today.

Another art critic of the time speaks of an odd "contrast of barrenness and fertility." While on the riverside he sees lush meadows and dense orchards, on the other, "tall chalk cliffs rise, like those of the Normandy coast.... If one were to stop and climb one of these cliffs, one would enjoy the incomparable sight of a valley as grand as it is gentle—a veritable fairyland of tranquillity." This description, too, still applies to the landscape hereabouts.

Today, as in Monet's time, Giverny is little more than a string of houses looping off of a small departmental (provincial) route. Between the village and the Seine lies a small fertile field and the river Epte, from which Monet eventually routed canals to feed his famous Japanese gardens. Behind Giverny a ridge of hills forms a backdrop of woods, fields, and meadows; from there you can take in the dramatic views described by Monet's contemporaries.

In his younger years in Giverny, Monet spent most of his working time painting outdoors, proudly rejecting any need for a studio. From his early paintings, it seems clear that he spent a lot of time around the river, even constructing a barge on which he drifted about to find subjects for his paintings, particularly his morning-time studies of the river and the poplar-lined fields surrounding it. He also wandered away from the river to focus his attention on the fields and haystacks around Giverny. Unlike Auvers-sur-Oise (*see* Experience 1), where you can find the precise locale of many great paintings, Giverny offers few clues to the actual fields of haystacks, oats, and poppies that Monet depicted, but when you follow the walking tours outlined below, you won't have trouble imagining a scene from one of his famous works.

▼

Monet's house and gardens are the chief tourist attraction in Giverny today. The house itself has been restored to Monet's original decor, right down to the Japanese prints he so avidly collected. Although he began planting his gardens almost as soon as he moved in, Monet did not undertake the major waterworks and plant-ings there until the latter part of the 1890s. He gradually concentrated more and more on his garden, with its Japanese bridges, ponds full of water lilies, graceful willow trees, and rhododendrons. As he aged, it became more difficult for him to tramp out along the river and through the surrounding countryside, so he increasingly made his gardens the subject of his paintings. Eventually he built a studio there in which to perfect his studies.

Another reason Monet originally selected Giverny was its proximity to **Vernon,** a town large enough to support decent schools for his numerous children from two marriages. Vernon was easily accessible by train from Paris, where, of course, he sold many of his paintings. Most visitors to Giverny still pass through Vernon, a bustling town that's worth a stop in its own right. Set on the ancient border between Normandy and the Ile de France, it was the scene of frequent con-frontations between the French and the Normans in medieval times. Few of the fortifications from those turbulent years have survived, except for the **Tour des Archives,** the only remnant of the town's 12th-century chateau. In the river Seine just west of Vernon's main bridge, you'll also see the footings of a 12th-century bridge, and, nearby, the remaining towers of a 12th-century castle and the recently restored remains of a 16th-century mill. In the town itself, many half-timbered houses with elaborate plaster facades reflect Vernon's Norman origins. The **Notre-Dame** church, first built in the 12th century and expanded through the Renaissance, is testament to the town's wealth and impor-tance in medieval times.

These walking tours provide options for people of all physical abil-ities. The best views are only a 20-minute walk from Monet's gardens; more ambitious walkers can extend the tour to enjoy dramatic views of Giverny, the winding Seine and its hill-rimmed valley, and the fields, forests, and meadows.

▼

GETTING THERE

By car:

From Paris, take autoroute *A13* toward Rouen; exit at *rte. N15* toward Bonnières and Vernon. At Vernon, cross the Seine toward Veronnet and Giverny. At the other end of the bridge, bear right onto *rte. D5* toward Giverny. Follow signs to the museum and parking, about 8 km. (5 miles) from Vernon.

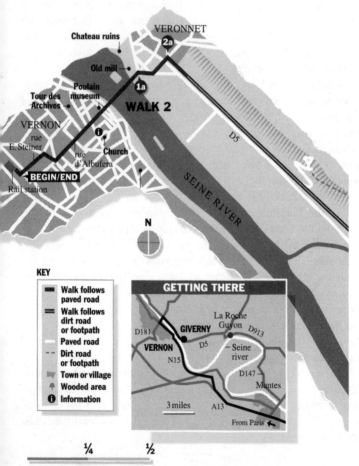

▼

By train:

From Paris's Gare St-Lazare, take a train on the Rouen line to Vernon. Trains run about every hour on weekdays and take about 1 1/4 hours. Train travelers can walk the three miles to Giverny, as Monet himself no doubt did countless times.

Walk 1 Directions

TIME: 1/2 to 2 hours
LEVEL: Easy to moderate
DISTANCE: 1 to 3 miles
ACCESS: By car

This scenic stroll can be tailored to various ability levels with a number of short-cuts and other options. The only challenging stretches are two relatively steep sections that are especially tricky when wet. You'll walk along paved roads, farm tracks, and woodland trails. Beautiful picnic spots adorn the ridge above Giverny, but you have to buy your provisions in Paris or Vernon.

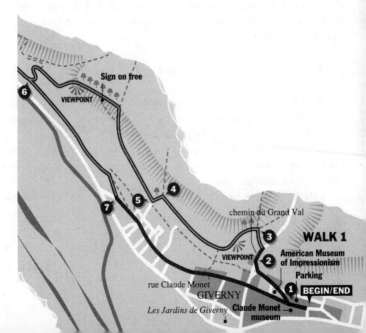

▼

TO BEGIN

Facing the main entrance to the Claude Monet museum (the artist's house and gardens), walk to the right down the *rue Claude Monet* to the first intersection.

1. Turn right on a small road and walk uphill following the white-and-red blazes of a *GR* long-distance route. This small road runs behind the new American Museum of Impressionism.

2. At the next intersection after the museum, turn right on a small road that leads out of the village toward the hills. Walk up the road for about 100 yards to the edge of a field, until you see white-and-red trail markings. Follow them left onto a dirt track going uphill across broad fields that are filled with wildflowers in spring and summer.

3. At the first intersection of dirt tracks, make a left, continuing to follow the white-and-red blazes. You're now on a ridge offering impressive views of the village and the Seine river valley. *If you just want a short stroll or a picnic outing, stop here to enjoy the view and your lunch, then retrace your steps to the museum.*

4. After another 300 yards, the trail goes left and steeply downhill.

5. At the bottom of the hill, at an intersection of farm tracks on the edge of the village, go right, heading uphill following white-and-red blazes. *If you choose to abbreviate the walk, instead go left at the bottom of the hill onto a farm track and back to Point 2. Or you can follow the paved road straight down the hill to the rue Claude Monet, where a left turn will take you back to the museum.*

Otherwise, continue to the top of the hill, where you enter a forest and then quickly emerge into a field. Carefully follow the white-and-red blazes to your left back into the woods. *This trail leads through the forest to a spectacular view of Giverny and the Seine river valley, a spot well marked by a big wooden cross and surely one of the best picnic spots in France.* Continue following the blazed trail downhill through the forest,

▼

eventually passing along the yards of several homes.

6. At the bottom of the hill, you'll reach an abandoned railroad right-of-way. Make a left, leaving the white-and-red-blazed trail, and follow this abandoned railbed back to Giverny and the *rue Claude Monet.*

7. Turn left on the *rue Claude Monet* to return to the museum parking lot.

Walk 2 Directions

TIME: 3 to 4 hours round-trip
LEVEL: Moderate
DISTANCE: 6 1/2 to 7 1/2 miles
ACCESS: By train

This itinerary allows train travelers to visit Vernon and experience the walk to Giverny, little changed from the time of Monet. Because the route follows an abandoned railroad bed on the outskirts of Vernon, you travel quickly into the quiet of the countryside. A slightly longer version, below, permits you to take the ridge-top trail, at least in one direction, to experience the beautiful views.

TO BEGIN

Exit the train station and enter the parking area. Turn left onto a small road, the *rue Emile Steiner.* Walk one block to the *rue Ambroise Bully,* where you turn right. In one more block, you'll reach a traffic circle, where you'll make a left onto a main street, the *rue d'Albufera,* to the bridge crossing the Seine.

1A. On the other side of the bridge, about ten minutes after you started, you'll see the white-and-red blazes of a *GR* trail, which you will follow to the right along a busy road and then quickly past the back of a small apartment building. Continue straight through an intersection with a stop sign and then up a small road, the *rue de la Ravine.*

2A. About 50 feet farther, at a small café, make a right and follow

▼

the white-and-red blazes onto the abandoned railroad right-of-way. Continue on this for about 20 minutes, until you reach Point 6 on Walk 1, above, marked by a pine tree. From here, you have two options. To take the ridge-top trail, make a left on the white-and-red-blazed trail (described in Walk 1, Points 1 through 5). Or, you can continue straight along the abandoned railroad right-of-way to the *rue Claude Monet* (Point 7 in Walk 1), where you turn left to reach the Claude Monet museum. You may wish to take the ridge-top trail to Giverny and then take the *rue Claude Monet* and abandoned railroad track back.

PLACES ALONG THE WALK

■ **Museum and home of Monet.** *rue Claude Monet, tel. 32-51-28-21. Open Tue.-Sun. 10-6.*

■ **American Museum of Impressionism.** A unique collection of American art, much of it by 19th-century American painters who came to France to admire the Impressionists. *99 rue Claude Monet, tel. 32-51-94-65, fax 32-51-94-67. Open Apr.-Oct. 10-6 Tue.-Sun.*

OTHER PLACES NEARBY

■ **Château de Bizy.** This 18th-century estate is known for its Versailles-inspired stables, fountains, wainscoting, and tapestries. *Tel. 32-51-00-82. Guided tours daily except Mon. 10-12 and 2-6 Apr. 1-Nov. 1; Sat.-Sun. 2-5 Nov.-Mar. Closed major holidays. Admission. 2 km. south of Vernon on rte. D181.*

■ **A. G. Poulain Museum.** On display are paintings by local artists—including Claude Monet—as well as archaeological and historical objects from the region. *12 rue du Pont, Vernon, tel. 32-21-28-09. Open Tue.-Fri. 11-1 and 2-8 and Sat.-Sun. 2-6 Apr.-Oct. Open Tue.-Sun. 2-5:30 Nov.-Mar. Closed major holidays. Admission.*

■ **La Roche-Guyon.** This tiny riverside village sits tucked against a dramatic cliff and fortress. Numerous trails crisscross the hilltop and surrounding area. *About 10 km. east of Giverny.*

DINING

■ **Les Jardins de Giverny** (moderate). Don't be daunted by the

▼

somewhat formal dining area in this charming house. You won't feel uncomfortable as long as you're neatly dressed, and you'll eat elbow to elbow with a bustling crowd of locals. On our visit, specials included *sautée de coquille St. Jacques aux champignons* (scallops sauteed with mushrooms) and *filet de canard aux griottes* (duck fillet with cherry sauce). *Chemin du Roy, rte. D5, Giverny 27620, tel. 32-21-60-80, fax 32-51-93-77. Open for lunch daily except Mon.; open for dinner Tue.-Sat.*

■ **Les Nymphéas Giverny** (inexpensive to moderate). Conveniently located adjacent the home of Monet, this garden restaurant fills up with tourists. On our visit, the menu featured *rôti de porc aux pommes* (pork roasted with apples) and *moules marinières* (mussels marinara). *rue Claude Monet, Giverny 27620, tel. 32-21-20-30, fax 32-51-15-75. Open Tue.-Sun. Apr.-Oct.*

LODGING

■ **Château de Brécourt** (expensive). Luxury accommodations in an 18th-century chateau. All the rooms are large and classically decorated. Room 32 is huge and graced with old rafters. There is also an elegant, expensive restaurant on the premises. *Pacy-sur-Eure, tel. 32-52-40-50, fax 32-52-69-65.*

FOR MORE INFORMATION

Tourist Office:

Office de Tourisme. *Le Temps Jadis, 36 rue Carnot, Vernon 27200, tel. 32-51-39-60. Open Tue.-Sat. 10-12 and 2:30-5:30. Closed major holidays.*

For Serious Walkers:

IGN map 21130 (west) covers the region around Giverny and Vernon. Along the Seine river valley run a series of long-distance trails that intrepid walkers can turn into loops by getting on and off trains.

Vineyards of Rome

EXPERIENCE 5: POMMARD

As you drive southwest from Beaune, the wine capital of southern Burgundy, you enter the Côte de Beaune, one of the finest wine-growing regions in France, where vineyards stretch in all directions on either side of the road. In contrast to northern Burgundy, there are few trees on the sun-drenched hillsides—just vineyard after vineyard. Walk above the vineyards into the hills and remote valleys, however, and you'll plunge into the shadowy comfort of a forest.

No one knows for exactly how

The Highlights: A spectacular walk into ancient vineyards and to the top of a ridge offering sweeping views of this famous wine-growing region; local vineyards where you can taste wine made from the fields you've walked through.

Other Places Nearby: The white-wine-growing village of Meursault (*see* Experience 6); the famous wine center of Beaune, a well-preserved medieval city with beautiful old homes and public buildings.

long, but it's a safe bet that vineyards have covered these hillsides for more than 2,000 years, at least since the time of Roman rule. Writings that date back to the 4th and 6th centuries mention the vineyards of Burgundy, and monastic movements centered in Cluny and Cîteaux brought the same entrepreneurial skills to medieval wine production and

▼

marketing as they did to all their thriving enterprises. Not until the 17th and 18th centuries, however, did Burgundy wines really gain the favor of royal connoisseurs, and it wasn't until the 19th century that serious exportation to the outside world began. Today, Burgundy's various soil types, micro-climates, and wine-making techniques yield a rich assortment of wines ranging from table varieties to world-renowned reds and whites that rank just one level below the great Bordeaux (well-known Burgundys include Chablis, Côte de Nuits, Côte Chalonnaise, and Côte de Beaune). While Burgundy wines are produced in a region stretching more than 100 miles, from Chablis in the north to Macon in the south, three of the best wine-making villages in the region are clustered together here, in Pommard, Volnay, and nearby Meursault (*see* Experience 6). Pommard and Volnay produce strong, heady reds based on the pinot noir grape; white wines take over just south of here, in Meursault.

As you tramp around the vineyards on the walking tour outlined below, you can see close up the distinctive quirks of Burgundy wine growing. Wine producers here rarely own a single, discrete property but rather a collection of small parcels in different vineyards, so they can take advantage of each plot's specific growing conditions. While summers are generally hot and winters cold, each bit of land has its own micro-climate, affected by its particular elevation and the amount of sun and wind there; local soil conditions also vary, with different proportions of clay, limestone, and silica affecting the taste of the grape. As you walk around the vineyards, you'll notice stone walls and fences dividing the parcels; within each grow rows of grapes owned by several wine growers.

Growing grapes is a year-round affair, and on your walk you'll see quite different activities depending upon the season in which you visit. In early spring, workers plant new cuttings, and oddly shaped tractors lumber through the vineyards turning the soil. In late spring, you may notice workers preparing for an unseasonal frost by pushing soil against the roots; in summer, they spray and weed the fields and trim back new shoots. In early autumn, when the wine grower decides that the sugar content and other factors are right, harvest begins. During this busy time, you'll have to make your way carefully along tiny vineyard roads bustling with

▼

people and equipment. Following the harvest, the strange-looking tractors fertilize the vines, and in the last few months of one year and the beginning of the next, you'll see lots of pruning and cutting; you may also see workers clambering up the slopes, hauling soil that had eroded to the bottom.

O f course, the wine maker plays a big role in the final outcome of the wine, too, making key decisions: how long to let the grapes ferment and at what temperature, how much anticontaminant to add, how long to leave the wine in the cask, what sort of cask to use, etc. Since the vineyard walking tour takes no more than a few hours, you'll have time to visit local wine makers who will show you the complete process and let you taste the distinctive wines grown in the area you've walked (a tasting is called a *dégustation*). You don't have to be a connoisseur to appreciate the experience. In fact, tastings also provide an opportunity to talk with the locals and learn about how wine is produced. The tourist board at Beaune (*see* For More Information, below) will send you the multilingual "Guide de Visites & Dégustation," which lists addresses and hours of operation and indicates whether or not personnel speak some English. Generally speaking, you can have a simple tasting at no charge, but there is a fee if you try a number of wines. **Château de Pommard,** which produces well-regarded village appellations (although no *premiers crus*), offers a relaxed wine tasting and tour. **Les Domaines de Pommard,** a cooperative wine-tasting center in a storefront in Pommard, offers free tastings of 16 producers but no winery tour. You'll pass several places open for wine tastings along the walk.

The French classify wine according to four basic categories, from the inexpensive *vin de table* and *vin de pays* to the better-quality *vin delimité de qualité supérieure* and the best, the so-called *appellation controlée.* A wine with the appellation Burgundy could have been produced anywhere in the region; an appellation Côte de Beaune must contain grapes grown only in that area, and one called Pommard comes exclusively from the grapes of that village. The top two rungs of the *appellation controllé* category are *premier cru* appellations—which carry the name of the village and the vineyard,

▼

such as Pommard Premier Cru Les Rugiens—and *grands crus,* which carry only the name of the vineyard, such as the Corton Grand Cru. About ten percent of Burgundy's wine production is *premier cru,* and three percent is *grand cru.* Pommard, Volnay, and Meursault produce several *premiers crus* but no *grands crus* (although some locals and wine experts believe that Les Rugiens, which you'll visit on the walking tour below, merits this exalted designation). Volnay has a reputation for careful wine making, and its village appellations are of more consistent quality than those of Pommard, with more elegance and subtlety. Some of the best-known Pommard vineyards are Les Rugiens, Les Clos des Epeneaux, Les Epenots, Les Charmots, Les Vignots, and Clos de la Commaraine. Among the many Volnay *premiers crus* are Les Santenots, Les Champans, Les Mitans, Les Caillerets, Taillepieds, and Les Clos des Chênes, which is especially highly regarded. The best recent vintages are 1988, 1989, 1990, 1992, and 1993.

While you probably don't want to go through the hassle of exporting wine in bulk to the United States, after a wine tasting you may want to buy a couple of bottles (depending on the exchange rate, local wines at the chateaus start at about $7). You will often see wine for sale at stands along the road. Local growers recommend you drink the light red Burgundies, such as the Volnays, with white meat and poultry and the heavier reds, such as the Pommards, with red meat, heavily spiced chicken, and game. Burgundy wine goes best with milder cheeses, although the older Pommard reds can stand up to strong cheeses such as Gruyère and Brie.

GETTING THERE

By car:

The *A31* expressway leads south from Dijon 40 km. (25 miles) to Beaune; a more scenic but slower parallel drive follows *rte. D122* and *rte. N74* through several small wine-growing villages. From Beaune, follow signs to Chagny by way of route *N74.* Just outside Beaune, go right on *D973* toward Pommard. In Pommard make a right turn to the town's main square, where you can park.

▼

Walk Directions

TIME: 1 1/2 hours

LEVEL: Easy to moderate

DISTANCE: 3 1/2 miles

ACCESS: By car

This walking tour takes you along small paved roads, up through the most famous vineyards of Pommard and onto a hilltop featuring beautiful views and good picnic spots, then down through the vineyards of Volnay. A wonderful tree-shaded spot with a bench is about 2 km. (1 1/4 miles), or 40 minutes or so, into the walk. You can buy picnic foods in Beaune or Meursault. The walk is best done in cool weather or in the early morning or evening, when you won't be as likely to work up a sweat—the first 1/2 mile runs mostly uphill, and the rest of the route passes through mostly treeless vineyards.

TO BEGIN

From the main square, proceed into the village on the *Grande Rue*.

1. When the *Grande Rue* veers abruptly right, go left onto the small road leading toward the vineyards.

2. In a few minutes, at the edge of town, continue straight uphill on the small country road, following the white-and-red blazes (if you can find them) of a long-distance *GR* trail. To your left as you go uphill, you'll see the vineyards of the *premier cru* Pommards known as Les Rugiens-Hauts. Just beyond, you enter the vines of Pommard's *appellation d'origine controlé*. Both have pinot noir grapes. On your right you'll see first the vineyards of La

KEY

▬▬ Walk follows paved road

═══ Walk follows dirt road or footpath

▭ Paved road

- - - Dirt road or footpath

⋔ Town or village

🌲 Wooded area

▼

Combotte and then, to your left and right, *Les Vaumuriens-Hauts and Bas, respectively.*

3. Near the top of the hill, go left, following the blazes along the ridge. *There are fine views of the valley and the town of Beaune beyond. You may see Mont Blanc from here on a clear day.*

4. Go left again onto a dirt road, still following the white-and-red blazes.

5. At the next intersection of roads, bear left and away from the blazed trail. Follow a paved road downhill into the vineyards of Volnay, where there are more beautiful views.

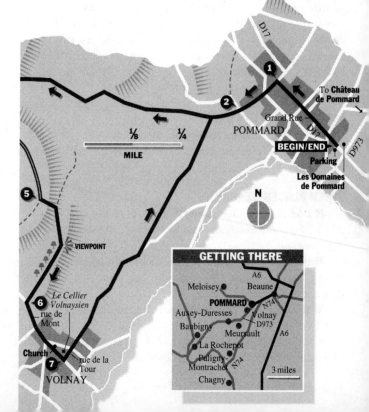

▼

Eventually you will reach a picnic bench under a grove of trees; there's no view here, but the shade may be welcome.

6. Continue on to the edge of the village of Volnay and turn left at the *rue de Mont,* which leads to the heart of the village. At a Y in the road, bear right onto the road leading around to the church. (If you bear left, you'll end up nearly at the same place.) Just a little farther on, just beyond the church, *is the restaurant and wine-tasting center Le Cellier Volnaysian (see* Dining, below).

7. Turn left at the *rue de la Tour,* just beyond the church, for the walk back to Pommard. Follow this road to Pommard, ignoring a country road on your right (although it also leads back to Pommard). The road you're on goes through the vineyards where several Volnay and Pommard *premiers crus*—including Les Chanlins, Les Jarolières, and Fremiets—are grown. Turn right onto the same village road that you took out of Pommard and walk back to the *Grande Rue,* making a right to return to your car.

PLACES ALONG THE WALK
■ **Les Domaines de Pommard.** *Pommard 21630, tel. 80-24-17-20. Open daily 9:30-12:30 and 2:30-7. Closed Dec. 25-Jan. 1. No charge for a basic tasting.*

OTHER PLACES NEARBY
■ **Domaine du Château de Pommard.** *Pommard 21630, tel. 80-22-07-99, fax 80-24-65-88. Open daily 8:30-6:30. Closed Nov. 23-Mar. 30. Admission.*
■ **Beaune.** Once the seat of the Dukes of Burgundy, this charming old town 3 km. east of Meursault by way of *rte. D973* is a center of wine and architecture.
■ **Musée du Vin de Bourgogne (Museum of Wine).** A history of wine from antiquity to the 20th century is displayed in a 14th-to-16th-century hotel once owned by the Dukes of Burgundy. *Rue d'Enfer, Beaune, tel. 80-22-08-19. Open daily 9:30-6. Closed Tue. Dec.-Mar. Admission.*

▼

■ **The Notre-Dame Basilica.** The highlight of this 12th-century Romanesque church is a set of 15th-century Flemish tapestries. *Just off ave. de la République, Beaune.*

■ **Hospices de Beaune.** This charitable organization, founded in 1443 as a hospital, owns prized vineyards in the region; its annual wine auction draws thousands to Beaune during the third weekend of November. The flamboyantly tiled roof of this Gothic-Flemish-style hospital has few parallels in Europe. The museum inside displays some medieval medical instruments as well as paintings and tapestries. *Rue de l'Hôtel-Dieu, tel. 80-24-45-00. Open daily 9-6:30 Mar.-Sep.; 9-11:30 and 2-5:30 Oct.-Apr. Admission.*

■ **La Rochepot.** An ancient Burgundian village set on a plush hillside, it is dominated by a multiturreted castle. Located along an important prehistoric trail (later a medieval road) about 13 km. west of Pommard by way of *rte. D973,* the village has been occupied since Neolithic times. Note the well-preserved 12th-century Romanesque church.

■ **Le Château de la Rochepot.** Built first in the 12th century, this pretty chateau was rebuilt 300 or so years later. *La Rochepot, tel. 80-21-71-37. Open daily except Tue. 10-11:30 and 2-5:30 Palm Sun.-May 31; 9:30-11:30 and 2:30-6:30 Jun.-Oct. Admission.*

DINING

■ **Le Cellier Volnaysien** (moderate). Drink in the atmosphere in this wine-tasting center and restaurant in the heart of the wine-growing village of Volnay. The menu features basic Burgundian offerings such as escargot, *jambon persillé Bourguignon* (Burgundy ham), *oeufs en Meurette* (eggs in a red wine sauce), *fondue Bourguignonne* (a local fondue), and for dessert, *soufflé glacé au Marc* (a soufflé glazed with pure spirits). You can also taste wines grown in the vineyards you walked through. *Rue de la Tour, Volnay, Meursault 21190, tel. 80-21-61-04, fax 80-21-21-95. Open 9-5 except Wed. Next to the church in Volnay, 2 km. west of Pommard on the walk or by way of rte. 973.*

■ **Le Bénaton** (moderate). This Beaune restaurant offers a particularly fine blend of creativity, value, and attentive service. On our visit, the menu featured *estouffade de boeuf Bourguignon et pâtes fraîches*

▼

(Burgundian beef stew with fresh pasta). *25 Faubourg Bretonnière, Beaune 21200, tel. 80-22-00-26. Open every day except lunch Wed.-Thu.*

■ **Le Relais de la Diligence** (inexpensive). Also in the heart of the wine-growing region, this restaurant attracts local crowds, probably in part for its low prices and country location, although some people find the place too big. All of the set meals offer an ample choice. On our visit, the menu featured *médaillon de mignon de porc à la crème de moutarde* (medallions of pork in a mustard sauce) and *faux-filet au poivre vert* (steak with peppercorns). *23 rue de la Gare, Meursault 21190, tel. 80-21-21-32, fax 80-21-64-69. Closed Tue. eve. and Wed. and mid-Dec.-early Feb. Located just south of town on rte. D23.*

LODGING

■ **Hotel Les Magnolias** (expensive). Beautifully created out of an 18th-century home in the heart of Meursault, this hotel has generally cheerful rooms, many of which are larger than you'll find in the average small hotel. Try to get a room facing the courtyard, since rooms overlooking the adjacent road get traffic noise during the day. Room 6 seems the best buy, with a pleasant exposure. There are no rooms with a view here, but you're compensated with very subdued, tasteful decor combined with modern comforts. *8 rue Pierre Joigneaux, Meursault 21190, tel. 80-21-23-23, fax 80-21-29-10. Closed Nov. 20-Dec. 1.*

■ **Hotel Les Charmes** (expensive). This small hotel has plenty of charm and quiet rooms overlooking a courtyard. *10 pl. du Murger, Meursault 21190, tel. 80-21-63-53, fax 80-21-62-89.*

■ **La Rochepot** (moderate). For a perfect escape, try this very picturesque two-bedroom bed and breakfast in an old home in the medieval village of La Rochepot, 13 km. west of Pommard. You'll experience life in a tiny village, the pleasant company of your hostess, and two very comfortable, authentically decorated rooms with private baths. *Madame Fouquerand, La Rochepot 21340, tel. 80-21-72-80. No credit cards are accepted. Located about 13 km. west of Pommard by way of rte. D973. You'll see a Gîtes de France sign.*

▼

■ **Chez Mme. Marie Fussi** (inexpensive). You're right near Meursault, but this small lodging in a modern house feels like it's in the middle of nowhere, set on a hillside with a broad view of hills and valleys. Two of the four well-maintained rooms have their own bathrooms; all are decorated in a pleasant country motif. *Baubigny 21340, tel. 80-21-84-66. Open Apr.-Sep. Located 10 km. west of Pommard off rte. 973. You'll see a Gîtes de France sign.*

FOR MORE INFORMATION
Tourist Office:

Office de Tourisme. *Pl. de la Halle, Beaune 21200, tel. 80-26-21-30, fax 80-26-21-39. Open daily 9-8 in summer; otherwise 9-6. Closed Christmas and New Year's.*

For Serious Walkers:

Several French-language walking books and maps detail numerous walks in the region; look for them in bookstores or at the tourist office in Beaune. IGN map 3024O (west) covers Pommard. Using this map, you can extend the walking tour to the old town of Meloisey as well as to a Roman-built bridge and a Celtic dolmen.

The Ancient Outpost

EXPERIENCE 6: AUXEY-DURESSES

All who see the aqueduct Le Pont du Gard or the great coliseums of Nîmes, Orange, or Arles will understand the importance of ancient Rome in early French history. These architectural feats bear witness to a centuries-long occupation in which the Romans successfully subdued and then mingled peacefully with the conquered populace.

> **The Highlights:** Secluded hilltop vestiges of a Roman garrison, great picnic spots, special views of a picture-perfect village, and a world-famous wine-growing region.
>
> **Other Places Nearby:** The white-wine-growing village of Meursault; Pommard (*see* Experience 5); the famous wine center of Beaune, a well-preserved medieval city with beautiful old homes and public buildings.

But the famous ruins tell only one side of the story. To experience the dark side of history, you must escape to such rarely visited places as **Le Mont Milan,** where the crumbled ruins of an ancient fort lie half-buried in the forest, undisturbed by parking lots or ticket booths. Here, alone on this quiet hilltop near Meursault, you can sense what it might have looked and felt like for the warriors manning this lonely outpost so long ago, always on the lookout for raiding parties of rebellious natives or Germanic invaders.

▼

Little is known about the precise nature of the pre-Roman inhabitants of France, since no written records have survived. The Celts left the most noticeable signs—megaliths, armor, tools, and decorations. Numerous other tribes fought amongst themselves and with the Celts, and the Romans called all of these people Gauls.

Romans began entering Gaul at least several hundred years before Christ, some as mercenaries protecting Greek outposts in such cities as Nice and Antibes. By the beginning of the last century before Christ, they had established colonies as far north as Vienne on the Rhône river. The Romans brought relative prosperity and advanced technology, constructing elaborate road and water systems in the cities of Arles, Nîmes, Aix-en-Provence, and others. But their hold was at times perilous, especially in the early years. The local peoples often rebelled, and there were frequent incursions by tribes from the north, posing a real threat to the fringes of the empire. It was Julius Caesar who finally conquered Gaul 60 or so years before the birth of Christ, by deftly playing the various warring parties one against the other.

By any standard, Caesar ruled firmly, using brutal means to put down local revolts. The Celts resisted, however, and under the leadership of one of their chiefs, Vercingétorix, they used guerrilla tactics to wear down the Roman occupiers. The hilltop fort of Le Mont Milan played a part in this struggle, though the precise events are not known. The Romans unleashed their forces to subdue the Celts, who withdrew to a fortress in the Gallic town of Alésia, today Alise-Ste-Reine, in northern Burgundy not far from Fontenay (*see* Experience 8). Caesar followed and laid siege to the fortress. Other Gauls rallied to the cause, attacking the Romans from behind, but after fierce fighting, the Romans prevailed, and Vercingétorix surrendered—to his regret, undoubtedly, since the Romans hauled him off to Rome and had him publicly dragged behind a chariot and strangled. The famous leader, France's first patriot, is now the hero in a popular French comic book series.

Caesar brutally punished the population as well, slaughtering thousands, chopping off hands, and making it clear that he would tolerate

▼

no further troubles. Then, in a strategy with considerable long-term success, he reduced taxes, actively encouraged economic recovery, and liberally allowed Gauls access to Roman citizenship and the privileges of aristocracy. This led to a golden age of Roman occupation: Latin replaced Celtic as the language of the local aristocracy, many Roman-style cities were built (Paris, Toulouse, and Bordeaux, among others), education flourished, and a certain degree of peace prevailed until the collapse of Rome in the 4th and 5th centuries, when the reign of the Romans in Gaul ended forever.

A short but steep ascent up a hillside leads today's visitor to beautiful views at the now-peaceful ruins of the Roman garrison on Le Mont Milan. If you want to enjoy the same views but prefer to skip the steep climb, you can drive along a small, hard-to-find country road out of Meursault to the Statue de St-Christophe, a dramatic overlook above the village—although those who drive miss the full haunting encounter with the distant past.

Looking down from the Statue of St. Christophe, however, you do behold one of the legendary white-wine-making villages of France—Meursault, which has a worldwide reputation for high quality and huge production. The white-wine-growing region of southern Burgundy begins in Meursault, where the soil changes to a lighter, rockier composition more conducive to producing white wine (the only red wine produced hereabouts is a little-known wine sold under the name of Volnay and made in the area's northern reaches). The best vineyards lie north and south of the village. From the Statue of St. Christophe, you directly overlook the good-quality but lesser-known vineyards of Les Tessons, Les Tillets, and Les Meix Chavaux, among others. A little to the south grow the best known: Les Génèvrières, Les Charmes, and Les Perrières Dessous. To the north, toward Volnay, you'll see Les Santenot, which has the only pinot noir grapes in the region. Probably no winery in Meursault is more popular for wine tastings than the Château de Meursault, which makes high-quality village appellations (a designation of the French wine-rating system) based on grapes from Les Charmes and Les Perrières. True wine-lovers will gravitate toward the chateaus making some of the best wines, known as *premiers crus,* including

▼

Comte Lafon, J. F. Coche-Dury, Louis Jadot, and others.

Meursault is just a short distance from the lovely wine-growing village of Pommard (*see* Experience 5); you can comfortably combine visits to the two villages, with the same hotels and restaurants being convenient to both.

GETTING THERE
By car:

The *A31* expressway leads south from Dijon 40 km. (25 miles) to Beaune; a more scenic but slower parallel drive follows *rte. D122* and *rte. N74* through several small wine-growing villages. From Beaune, take *rte. D973* south through Pommard, following signs to Auxey-Duresses. As you go through the small village of Auxey-Duresses, bear left onto a village lane *(rue de l'Arbre d'Or)* at the point where the main road veers sharply right. Follow this village lane around to the left, passing a small square and the church on the right. Cross a tiny stream and turn right on a country road, *Chemin des Fontaines,* where you'll notice white-and-red blazes marking a long-distance *GR* walking trail. In a moment, the road forks. Here, you can park or continue by car uphill to the left, following

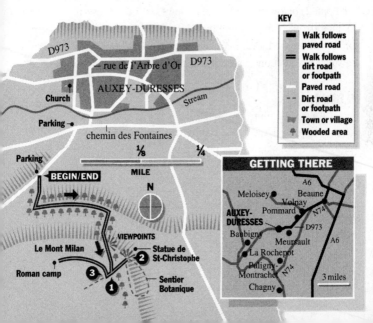

▼

the blazes and the small paved farm road. About 100 yards up the hill, the blazed trail turns sharply left uphill into the forest; you can park along the side of the road here or at the base of the hill.

Walk Directions

TIME: 1 1/4 hours round-trip
LEVEL: Moderate
DISTANCE: 1 mile
ACCESS: By car

This very short walk would have an easy rating except for a short but steep climb up a hillside. However, even those who are out of shape can manage the trail if a recent rain hasn't made it too slippery. A dense canopy of forest provides welcome shade all day. When you get to the top of the hill, note the hidden overlooks to your left through the trees. Both these and the tranquil ruins afford excellent picnic spots. Your best bet for picking up picnic supplies is in Meursault or Beaune. The overlook at the Statue of St. Christophe (*see* Point 2, below) provides great views but not necessarily tranquillity, since people can get there by car. If you want to drive to the statue, you'll need a good local map and a strong sense of direction, because the small paved country road that leads to it can be difficult to find.

TO BEGIN

Follow the white-and-red blazes from your parking spot on the small paved farm road into the forest and up a steep hill (depending on where you parked, you'll walk for about 15 to 20 minutes). *At the top of the hill, look for viewpoints through the brush to your left.*

1. Come out of the forest onto a larger dirt road. Turn left, heading toward an overlook.

2. In just a minute, you'll reach the *Statue of St. Christophe, where*

▼

you'll find a fine view of Meursault and its vineyards, with Beaune visible in the distance on a clear day.

Here you can follow the short Sentier Botanique, designed to give people of all physical strengths easy access to the forest and meadows of this Burgundy hilltop that has been traversed by people for thousands of years.

Retrace your steps to Point 1. From here, you can go back down the hill to the village on the white-and-red-blazed trail or proceed to the Roman ruins by continuing to walk straight along the dirt road away from the statue.

3. In just a few yards, make the next right on a well-worn path, the old Roman road. Follow this a short distance until you see piles of rock and glimpses of walls.

As you approach, you'll notice the clear traces of the ancient road leading into the encampment. An impressive line of stone ruins cutting across the hilltop of Mont Milan is all that remains of the ancient Roman fort.

To return, walk back down the trail from the ruins to Point 3 and turn left. Make another left at Point 1 and follow the white-and-red-blazed trail back to your car.

OTHER PLACES NEARBY

See Experience 5, Pommard.

DINING & LODGING

See Experience 5, Pommard.

FOR MORE INFORMATION
Tourist Office:

Office de Tourisme. You can obtain a booklet here in English that provides a comprehensive guide to the region's wineries. *Pl. de la Halle, Beaune 21200, tel. 80-26-21-30, fax 80-26-21-39. Open daily 9-8 in summer; otherwise 9-6. Closed Christmas and New Year's.*

▼

For Serious Walkers:

Several French-language walking books and maps detail numerous walks in the region; look for them in bookstores or at the tourist office in Beaune. IGN map 3024O (west) covers this itinerary and Pommard (*see* Experience 5).

Rural Exodus

EXPERIENCE 7: VEZELAY

The wooded hills, farmland, and tiny villages surrounding the town of Vézelay barely betray the great movement of peoples that marks the history of this quiet place. In medieval times, kings, saints, and people from all walks of life made pilgrimages to Vézelay, to atone for their sins or to

The Highlights: Old farms, magnificent landscapes, villages, an 18th-century bridge, a natural bridge, and Gallic-Roman ruins.

Other Places Nearby: The historic town of Vézelay and its famous basilica, St-Père-sous-Vézelay and its Gothic church, the ancient city of Avallon.

launch a Crusade. Today, the area's diminishing farm acreage and quiet villages are signs of a different sort of movement: the rural exodus, a huge event in contemporary French history.

This walking tour takes you away from the famous (and often crowded) walled town of Vézelay to peaceful rural villages and farms that have maintained their character despite the dramatic flight from French farmland. At one point you'll be able to visit **La Roche Percée,** a natural bridge along the Cure river; at another point you'll cross the river on an 18th-century bridge built by French engineer Sebastien Vauban who, among other major accomplishments, revolutionized French military defenses. At still another point in the walk you'll see **Vauban's home.** Legend has it that the bells of a nearby church lie buried in the river's waters, beneath the old bridge.

You'll also visit the earliest signs of human habitation in the area,

▼

on the outskirts of **St-Père-sous-Vézelay** in a field along the Cure river. There, a spring of mineral water foams to the surface—**Les Fontaines Salées** (Salted Fountains). Vestiges of huge hollowed-out stumps suggest that, thousands of years before Christ, residents funneled the water for extensive use. The place must have had religious significance, for signs of a small circular sanctuary and monetary offerings have turned up. Archaeologists believe a Roman bath prospered on the site in the 1st century A.D., benefitting from its location near a Roman road.

In the 17th century, royal authorities filled in the spring as part of a new system of taxation on salt. Locals continued to take water from the spring, however, despite the risk of severe punishment, and there were sporadic altercations between locals and authorities until the French Revolution, when the onerous laws governing salt were repealed.

The walk below provides unspoiled views of Vézelay and its wondrous basilica. Vézelay sprang from a 10th-century settlement in the valley near St-Père, formed by a group of monks supported by a local count and his wife. The monks quickly moved their location up to the hilltop for better protection from marauders, despite the lack of water. The town's fortunes suddenly changed in 1050, when the abbot Geoffroy convinced Pope Leon IX to authorize Vézelay as a place of pilgrimage, on the basis that it possessed relics of Mary Magdalene. Making a long, arduous journey to a holy place was certainly a dangerous affair in those unlawful times, so pilgrimages were considered an extreme act of penitence to make up for sins—those atoning for the worst sins had to make the most difficult journeys. While this sounds very noble, the reality was that towns that found a good reason to attract pilgrims profited handsomely, as the prosperity of medieval Vézelay clearly demonstrates. With pilgrims came markets to sell them products, inns and restaurants to house and feed them, money changers, vineyards, and plenty of money to expand the church, which in turn provided work for skilled laborers.

In the 12th century a local chaplain recommended Vézelay in France's most famous medieval tour guide, the *Guide for Pilgrims,* suggesting that miracles regularly took place there, and it became a fre-

▼

quent stop for penitents making the even longer trip to St. Jacques of Compostelle in Spain. In 1146 St. Bernard (*see* Experience 8) came here to announce the second Crusade to Jerusalem; in 1190 King Phillip-Augustus and King Richard the Lionhearted met here to begin their Crusade. Despite its cherished place in the world of religion, however, the town suffered its share of attacks. In fact, its great wealth attracted armed bands and jealous neighbors, forcing the town to construct double rows of ramparts surrounding the hilltop.

Pilgrims coming to Vézelay from the north commonly approached by way of what today is *rte. D957* from **Avallon,** the road travelers to Vézelay usually take when coming from Paris. From the suburb of Fontette, at a spot marked by a cross, you can get a beautiful view of hilltop Vézelay. Today's motorists all too often race past this spot, which for many medieval travelers represented a high point in the long journey. Another nearby town, Asquins, was a stopover for pilgrims on their way to Vézelay (2 km. to the south) and St. Jacques of Compostelle. Although medieval beliefs brought great wealth to Vézelay, the Renaissance brought an end to the mass pilgrimages, and agriculture sustained the area from then on. Modern times, however, have brought about a decline in traditional agricultural life. Since World War II, French farmers in huge numbers have abandoned the countryside—in some places emptying entire villages, in others giving way to city folk in search of country retreats. Between World War II and the mid-1980s, the number of French men in farming dropped from nearly 4 million to little more than 1 million, out of a population of 55 million. Throughout the 1960s, thousands of rural schools closed each year. The average age of the farmer increased; one study showed that only about ten percent of farmers' children wanted to keep their family farms going. When you get stuck in the punishing traffic jams of the sprawling Parisian suburbs, you get a pretty good idea of where all these people have gone.

What drove people in such great numbers from the land? Some attribute it to farm mechanization: While tractors dramatically increased productivity after World War II, there was less need for manpower, and all this favored larger farms that could benefit from economies of scale.

▼

Others aren't so sure: Did the purchase of a tractor cause family members to leave, or did farmers buy tractors to replace departed helpers? At any rate, greater productivity and larger farms led to a long-term decline in farm prices, which probably forced at least some farmers to seek better wages among the ranks of unionized workers or management.

In some parts of France, near-empty villages starkly tell the story of this great exodus of people. The area around Vézelay tells another part of the tale. In the countryside here, you will still see smaller farms—many well below the national average in size—and intermingled with them come signs of a new migration, urbanites escaping from the city to country homes and rural vacations. Slowly, old farms are giving way to houses, lawns, and gardens, or to large agricultural operations.

On one hillside in this itinerary you'll cross pastureland that has changed little over the centuries; on another you'll walk through broad fields of grain farmed by large-scale farming operations.

Experiencing this beautiful countryside and the peaceful lifestyle of its inhabitants, you may better understand the fear and anger that drives French farmers to blockade major highways or the entrance to EuroDisney and to oppose trade pacts that reduce farm subsidies. At stake for them is not just a way of making a living but a cherished way of life.

GETTING THERE
By car:

From *A6 (Autoroute du Soleil),* which links Paris, Lyon, and the south of France, exit for Avallon by way of *rte. N146.* At the junction with *N6,* follow signs to Avallon. Follow *rte. N6* through town, then turn left onto *rte. D957* following signs to Vézelay. In St-Père, cross the tiny river in the heart of town and make a left in front of the Gothic church onto *rte. D958.* (You should see a sign for the ruins of Les Fontaines Salées.)

One km. beyond the entrance to Les Fontaines Salées (about 2 km. out of St-Père), you'll come upon *rte. D53,* where you'll turn right following signs to Foissy-les-Vézelay. After about 1 km. you will reach the village, where you can park in front of the church.

▼

Walk Directions

TIME: 2 1/2 hours
LEVEL: Easy
DISTANCE: 5 miles
ACCESS: By car

This walking tour follows paved and unpaved farm roads through farmlands, villages, and forests. Pretty picnic spots abound, especially on a hillside offering beautiful views of the Cure river valley and Vézelay beyond. You can pick up provisions for your picnic in St-Père or Vézelay.

TO BEGIN

Facing the church, make a right on *rte. D53,* the main road leading out of town. You'll soon pick up the white-and-red blazes of a long-distance *GR* trail, which comes in from the right; continue straight, following it up the paved road.

1. In a few minutes, you'll see an old stone granary in a field to your left. At an intersection, follow the blazes left onto a farm road. The blazed route heads uphill into the farmland, crosses a small paved road, follows a short dirt section, and then rejoins the paved road, where you continue straight.

2. Shortly, at the point where a dirt road comes in from the right, bear left following the blazes. *As you bear left, look out to the fields on your right—there's a remarkably undisturbed view of farms and forests and a castle in the distance, a landscape that probably hasn't changed much for hundreds of years.* You'll soon cross another farm track and continue straight, still following the blazes.

3. The white-and-red-blazed trail will lead you down the hill to *rte. D958.* Cross *rte. D958* and walk onto a small paved road *(D353)* leading toward the hamlet of Pierre-Perthuis. *Still following the white-and-red blazes, you'll walk through the ruined remains of a 12th-century castle gate and around a bend to a beautiful turreted house once owned by the 18th-century engineer Sebastien Vauban and now privately owned.*

▼

4. Just beyond the house, the white-and-red trail goes right, leaving the road; walk sharply downhill on a footpath.

5. At the bottom of the hill, you reach the Cure river and *a bridge built by Vauban in 1770,* which now carries the *GR* trail you are walking on. Above the old bridge looms a more modern one, built as part of the departmental road (*rte. D353*). Retrace your steps up the hill to Point 4, where you rejoin the road. Turn right, leaving the blazed trail.

6. The road goes straight over the modern bridge across the Cure river. *At the other end of the modern bridge, on a bluff to your left, there's a wonderful picnic spot offering dramatic views of the river valley, farmland, and Vézelay in the distance.* Follow the road to the turnoff for *La Roche Percée, a natural bridge along the Cure river* that's just a short detour away. Afterward, continue on the road, passing through the tiny hamlet of *Prècy-le-Moult.* Bear left at the village's sole intersection.

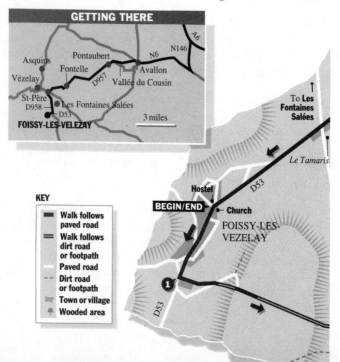

GETTING THERE

Asquins · Pontaubert · Fontelle · Avallon · N6 · N146 · A6
Vézelay · D957 · Vallée du Cousin
St-Père · D958 · Les Fontaines Salées · D53
FOISSY-LES-VELEZAY

3 miles

To **Les Fontaines Salées**

Le Tamaris

D53

Hostel

BEGIN/END · Church

FOISSY-LES-VEZELAY

KEY

▬ Walk follows paved road
═ Walk follows dirt road or footpath
▭ Paved road
╌╌ Dirt road or footpath
🛖 Town or village
🌲 Wooded area

D53

❶

▼

7. Just on the outskirts of the village, at the corner of a barn on your left, a farm track goes left, blazed with yellow on a telephone pole. The trail quickly takes you into broad, cultivated fields on a hilltop offering *views of the countryside and Vézelay* before you. Follow this trail straight across the field in the general direction of the town, disregarding other farm trails going off to your left and right.

8. In a short while, you'll reach a paved road, *rte. D53.* Turn left onto this road. Follow it back to and across *rte. D958. Just a few dozen feet to your left is Le Tamaris, a restaurant offering a unique combination of Mexican, Brazilian, and basic French food. Or, you may want to turn right for the ten-minute walk along rte. D958 to reach the ruins of Les Fontaines Salées.* Otherwise, continue straight on *rte. D53,* back 1/2 mile to the hamlet of Foissy-les-Vézelay and your car.

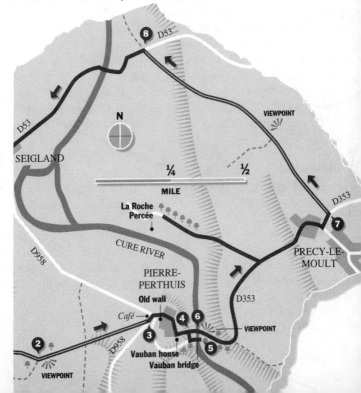

▼

PLACES ALONG THE WALK

■ **Les Fontaines Salées.** This Roman vestige and associated museum is just a short walk from the itinerary. *Tel. 86-33-26-62. Open 9:30-12:30 and 2:30-6:30 Mar. 14-Nov. Closed Wed. and Nov.-Mar. 15.*

OTHER PLACES NEARBY

■ **Vézelay.** Well-conserved, this medieval town is crowned by a remarkable Romanesque basilica and ancient homes from the 15th to the 18th centuries. *Open every day. Basilica open for guided tours on demand at the premises. 6 km. west of Foissy-les-Vézelay.*

■ **St-Père-sous-Vézelay.** This tiny village has a beautiful 13th-century Gothic church with a unique covered entryway. *4 km. west of Foissy.*

■ **Avallon.** Old homes and a 12th-century church adorn this bustling town. *15 km. east of Vézelay on rte. D957.*

■ **Parc Naturel Régional du Morvan.** An enormous park now protects a wild plateau still covered by deep forests. The region was never prosperous—for centuries, the men made their living in logging while the women were known as excellent wet nurses. Today, it's prime terrain for rugged walks and remote picnics. *Maison du Parc, St-Brisson 58230, tel. 86-78-70-16, fax 86-78-74-22. Open Mon.-Fri. 8:30-12:00 and 1:30-6. During summer, daily 10-6. 40 km. southeast of Vézelay.*

DINING

■ **L'Esperance** (very expensive). Some people might not consider this world-acclaimed restaurant an escape. Jacket and tie are required at this top-rated establishment in St-Père-sous-Vézelay, run by the well-known M. and Mme. Méneau. It's an elegant gourmet country dining experience with lots of fashionable, wealthy customers. When we visited, the menu included *huîtres à la gelée d'eau de mer* (oysters in an aspic of seawater), *artichaut en soufflé de melle* (artichoke in a soufflé of beef marrow), and *homard risolé aux gousses d'ail* (lobster browned with garlic cloves). *St-Père-sous-Vézelay 89450, tel. 86-33-39-10, fax 86-33-26-15. Closed Feb. and Tue. and Wed. lunch.*

▼

■ **Moulin des Ruats** (moderate). This converted mill in a secluded spot outside Vézelay offers an idyllic setting for a distinctive meal. On our visit, the menu offered *magret de canard aux champignons des bois* (sliced duck with wild mushrooms) and *spirale de saumon à la réduction de vin rouge et crustacés* (salmon filet with a reduction of wine and shellfish). *Vallée du Cousin, Avallon 89200, tel. 86-34-07-14, fax 86-31-65-47. Open daily during season. Open Sun. and holidays only mid-Nov.-mid-Feb. From Vézelay, take rte. D957 toward Avallon. Just after passing through the village of Pontaubert and crossing a small river, make a right onto a small country road following signs to Vallée du Cousin. The inn will appear soon on your right.*

■ **A La Fortune du Pot** (inexpensive). Don't go for the decor. This tiny restaurant off the main square of Vézelay is popular among locals for its family-style food and low prices. The menu offerings range from *côtes de porc* (pork chops) to *cuisse de canard* (duck thighs). *Pl. du Champ du Foire, Vézelay 89450, tel. 86-33-32-56. Closed mid-Dec.-early Jan. No credit cards.*

■ **Le Tamaris** (inexpensive). Tacos in France? This eclectic countryside restaurant, run by a Brazilian and his French wife, is located right along the itinerary and makes a great place to take a break. It offers an unusual assortment of Brazilian, Mexican, and French foods, including empanadas (meat pastries), chili, ribs, and crepes. *Rte. D958, Seigland 89450, tel. 86-33-23-07. Open evenings except Wed. and for lunch and dinner on weekends; open Thu.-Sun. Oct.-Nov. Closed Dec.-Feb.*

LODGING

■ **L'Esperance** (very expensive). You'll find beautiful rooms and luxury—and fashionable crowds—in this bustling, successful enterprise that seems to be taking over the tiny village it occupies. All rooms have upscale amenities and decor. *St-Père-sous-Vézelay 89450, tel. 86-33-39-10, fax 86-33-26-15. Open all year. Located in the heart of St-Père.*

■ **Hostellerie du Moulin des Ruats** (moderate to expensive). The gurgling river will help lull you to sleep in this exceptionally quiet riverside inn. All rooms have plenty of charm; those in the front face the road, but all are quiet. *Vallée du Cousin, Avallon*

▼

89200, tel. 86-34-07-14, fax 86-31-65-47. Closed mid-Nov.-mid-Feb. From Vézelay, take rte. D957 toward Avallon. Just after passing through the village of Pontaubert, make a right onto a small country road following signs to Vallée du Cousin. The inn will appear soon on your right.

■ **Moulin des Templiers** (moderate). The river rushes by, the forest surrounds you, and the silence is exceptional in this converted old mill. The rooms, however, are generally small and in some cases dark, despite cheerful, tasteful decor. *Vallée du Cousin, Pontaubert 89200, tel. 86-34-10-80. Open all year. From Vézelay, take rte. D957 toward Avallon. Just after passing through the village of Pontaubert and crossing a small river, make a right onto a small country road following signs to Vallée du Cousin. The mill will appear soon on your right.*

■ **Le Petit Clèret** (inexpensive). Set in a garden overlooking Vézelay but a few kilometers away is this peaceful bed and breakfast. Rooms are in a detached house that's part of an old farm and share a bathroom. You can take dinner with your hostess, Mireille Demeule, for about 100 francs, including wine. *St-Père-sous-Vézelay 89450, tel. 86-33-25-87. Open late Mar.-late Sep. No credit cards.*

■ **Gîte d'Etape** (very inexpensive). This small center for horseback riding also has rustic dormitories for hikers. Horseback tours for small groups are possible. You might be able to join a group going out for a single day. *M. Tastu, Foissy-les-Vézelay 89450, tel. 86-33-28-40. Located in front of the church where you park in Foissy.*

FOR MORE INFORMATION
Tourist Office:
Syndicat d'Initiative. *Rue St-Pierre, Vézelay 89450, tel. 86-33-23-69, fax 86-33-34-00. Open daily except Wed. and Thu. 10-1 and 2-6 Oct.-May and daily Jun.-Aug. Closed Feb. Responds to faxes all year.*

For Serious Walkers:
An extensive network of trails depart from the center of Vézelay, documented in a free guide available from the tourist office. IGN maps 2722O (west) and 2722E (east) greatly facilitate navigation.

An Enterprising Order of Monks

EXPERIENCE 8: FONTENAY

"To understand Fontenay in what is her essence and power of beauty, you have to approach step by step, by the forest trails, in an October rain...."

With these words begins the guidebook welcoming you to the renowned Cistercian complex, the **Abbey of Fontenay.** Probably the best-maintained abbey of its time—it

> **The Highlights:** A beautifully restored Cistercian abbey in a rural setting unchanged for centuries, flower-filled meadows, an ancient fish farm, a medieval iron mine.
>
> **Other Places Nearby:**
> Castles, a Gallic-Roman battle site, ancient villages, the Burgundy canal.

dates to the 12th century—it stands a remarkably faithful monument to medieval religious life. Of even greater appeal, it lies in a peaceful Burgundian valley filled in summer with the gurgle of rippling water and a multicolored tapestry of wildflowers—a setting that undoubtedly attracted the monks almost 900 years ago.

The abbey guidebook laments: "The car or bus drops you in front of the door. Without transition, one passes in several minutes from the 20th to the 12th century." You don't have to make such an abrupt transition, however—the easy walking tour below takes you from the village of Montbard over the same country footpath the monks probably used, up the wooded

▼

river valley, past an abandoned fish farm. Tens of thousands of travelers make the journey to this beautifully preserved pastoral setting, but few approach it step by step through the forest as the guidebook suggests.

The Cistercian order was founded early in the 12th century in reaction to the more opulent lifestyle of the predominant Benedictine order. Seeking to establish an ascetic way of life far from the corrupting influence of neighboring communities, the monks built their first monastery, known as Cîteaux, in the remote wilderness of Burgundy, south of Dijon. But it was not until 1112 and the arrival of a 22-year-old nobleman, Bernard de Fontaine, that this new religious order really began to take shape. Known today as St. Bernard, this Cistercian monk eventually helped the austere religious order dominate 12th-century France in the realms of religion, politics, and industry.

Cîteaux's abbot, an Englishman named Etienne Harding, quickly recognized Bernard's talents and sent him off to establish a new abbey at Clairvaux in Champagne. Then, in late October 1118, about a dozen monks from Clairvaux set off to found the abbey at Fontenay, personally led, it is said, by Bernard. It is believed that they settled near a small pond, which you can see and which bears the name of the saint. About a dozen years later, they moved to better quarters a few hundred yards down the road.

Austerity and simplicity were ostensibly the watchwords of the Cistercian order. "Flee this Babylon," St. Bernard once told students in Paris. "Fly to the monasteries of the wilderness, where solitary rocks and forests teach more piety than mortal masters." The early Cistercian monks followed a rigorous existence dominated by prayer; they rejected worldly pleasures, wearing the same coarse robe day after day. But they also created a thriving commercial enterprise, evidence of which is all around you at the abbey today. Although the order did not technically hire lay workers, a lesser rank of monk was employed to labor on the monastery's vast projects. On a large network of waterworks, they raised trout renowned for their quality. They produced their own wine, experimented with new planting techniques in the fertile soil, and mined ore in the hills above the abbey, which they smelted in the abbey's forges.

▼

If you believe that commercialism corrupts, it won't surprise you that the Cistercians apparently fell victim to their own success. Wealth and the commercial orientation, as well as the increasing involvement of nonmonastic interests, led to a decline of the monastery. During the Revolution it eventually was sold, and it even served as a paper factory for a while. Careful work has restored the abbey and its rural setting, however. Today it's a frequent backdrop for movies (it appeared in the popular French film *Cyrano de Bergerac,* starring Gérard Depardieu).

As you follow the walking tour around the abbey, you'll see the monks' waterworks as well as an abandoned building associated with a 19th-century fish farm. Near the abbey, on a hilltop now cleared of dense forest, you'll see where the medieval monks dug into the limestone rock to reach natural galleries containing an ore of nearly 50 percent iron.

The longer version of this walking tour starts at the Montbard train station; those who come by car can skip the first mile or so of this tour, parking at a convenient spot along the way. You'll walk from Montbard to Fontenay, along footpaths that have been in use for hundreds of years.

GETTING THERE

By car:

Montbard lies 30 km. north of the *Autoroute du Sud (A6)* by way of Semur-en-Auxois and *rte. D980.* Take *rte. D980* through the town, following signs toward Châtillon-sur-Seine. Just after leaving town, the road goes up a long hill, through fields, and comes to a parking and picnic area on the right less than 2 km. from the center of town. Enter the road that loops through the small area, and park just before it rejoins the main road.

By train:

Montbard has frequent service from Paris as a stop on both the TGV and the conventional train line between Paris and Dijon departing from the Gare-de-Lyon. It's about 2 1/4 hours by conventional train from Paris and about 1 hour by TGV. From Dijon, it's about an hour by conventional train and about 35 minutes by TGV.

▼

Walk 1 Directions

> **TIME:** 2 to 3 1/2 hours round-trip
> **LEVEL:** Easy to moderate
> **DISTANCE:** 2 1/2 to 6 miles
> **ACCESS:** By car and train

The route you take depends on your mode of transportation. For those who come by train, the directions begin at the train station in the south part of town. Those who come by car can cut 2 1/2 miles out of the round-trip by parking at Point 1. You can get provisions for a picnic at Montbard, and you will find beautiful spots along the route to the abbey.

Experienced walkers with a compass and an IGN map can find an alternative return path, making this a loop, but the landscape is so beautiful and tranquil that you won't be bored retracing your steps.

TO BEGIN

For those who arrive by train, exit the train station and cross the Burgundy canal onto the *rue d'Abrantes*. Walk through the town for about ten min-

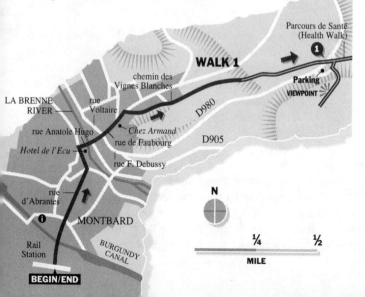

▼

utes, until the road ends. Bear left a short distance to a big intersection (marked by a statue of Buffon and the Hotel Buffon), and go right over a small bridge across the La Brenne river. Continue straight, crossing a main road (the one on the left is named the *rue Voltaire,* the one on the right the *rue F. Debussy*). The road you're walking on becomes the *rue de Faubourg.* Just across from No. 125 (beyond the restaurant Chez Armand), turn right onto the *chemin des*

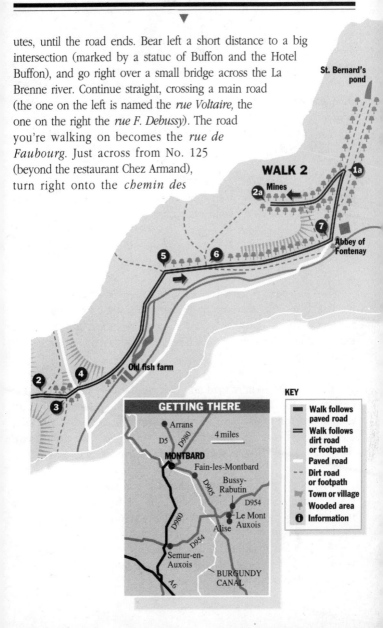

WALK 2

St. Bernard's pond

Mines

1a

2a

7

Abbey of Fontenay

5

6

Old fish farm

2

4

3

GETTING THERE

Arrans

D5 D980

MONTBARD

Fain-les-Montbard

D905

Bussy-Rabutin

D954

Le Mont Auxois

Alise

D980

D954

Semur-en-Auxois

A6

BURGUNDY CANAL

4 miles

KEY

■ Walk follows paved road

= Walk follows dirt road or footpath

— Paved road

- - - Dirt road or footpath

🌲 Town or village

🌲 Wooded area

ⓘ Information

▼

Vignes Blanches. This is a paved street at first; walk on until it becomes a dirt road. At the top of the hill, after 40 minutes of walking, cross *rte. D980* into a small picnic area where car travelers park (Point 1).

To take in a view of Montbard, walk a short distance down a dirt road that leads away from the picnic area from the middle of the picnic-area loop road. On your right, through a break in the trees, you'll come upon a commanding view of the old town and the industrial area beyond. From this point, retrace your steps to the parking lot.

1. On the small driveway that loops uphill through the picnic area, just before it rejoins the main road, you'll see a sign marked "Parcours de Santé" (Health Walk). Follow this grassy track downhill.

2. Within a few minutes, at the entrance to the forest, you go right on an unmarked but well-worn trail veering downhill.

3. A few minutes later, you reach an intersection. Bear left, leaving the Health Walk, which goes off to the right. After a few minutes, the trail goes sharply downhill (note the old stone steps), across a small field, and through a fence. You will notice the white-and-red blazes of a *GR* hiking trail.

4. Cross the country road and pick up the dirt farm road on the other side. *You'll soon see the ruins of a building associated with an abandoned fish farm. A recent wood-clearing project has disturbed a portion of this otherwise beautiful setting, but a season or two will heal the damage. You will continue to see white-and-red blazes.*

5. The dirt road intersects another dirt road going left into the forest. Bear right, continuing along a dirt path that follows the river in the meadow to the right, which you parallel all the way to the abbey.

6. Just a few minutes later, you'll reach another intersection, with a tangle of trails leading off to your left in the forest. Bear right along the path you've been following.

▼

7. The trail comes out at the abbey's front entrance and parking lot, about 40 minutes from Point 1. To return to Montbard, retrace your steps.

Walk 2 Directions

<table>
<tr><td>

TIME: 1/2 hour round-trip

LEVEL: Easy

DISTANCE: 1 mile

</td><td>

This extra round-trip walk takes you to the site of the medieval mines above the Abbey of Fontenay. An optional quick sidetrip visits the pond where St. Bernard and the other monks first lived when they founded the abbey.

</td></tr>
</table>

TO BEGIN

Follow Walk 1 up to Point 7. Facing the abbey's entrance, turn left on the small road leading up a tiny river valley toward the L'Etang St-Bernard (St. Bernard's Pond), where the abbey was first established. A sign across from the entrance to the abbey points to the start of this Sentier de Nature (Nature Trail), the route to the mines.

1A. Before the pond, a wooden sign on your left points to a well-worn dirt trail leading to the mines. *Before you follow it, you might want to proceed a little farther along the small road, to see the quiet spot where St. Bernard and his followers first lived when they founded the abbey in the 12th century. The setting has hardly changed in the centuries since.* As you proceed up to the mines, a few signs along the way will keep you on the Nature Trail for the short walk through the dense forest.

2A. The entrance to the area of the mines is marked by a clearing in the woods and a wooden explanatory sign (in French). The hilltop provides a few views of distant hills over the surrounding treetops. In the clearing, you'll see open shafts protected by metal nets and flimsy railings—be careful. You cannot enter the mines, but the quiet setting deep in the woods evokes a sense of how the landscape might have been when these mines were worked centuries ago. Retrace your steps to the car.

▼

PLACES ALONG THE WALK

■ **Abbaye de Fontenay.** *Tel. 80-92-15-00. Open all year, with hourly guided tours 9-12 and 2-5; every half hour in the afternoon Jul.-Aug. Admission. Walk less than 5 km. east of Montbard.*

OTHER PLACES NEARBY

■ **Musée des Beaux-Arts.** *Rue Piron, Montbard, tel. 80-92-09-02. Open daily except Tue. 3-6. Apr.-Oct.*

■ **Parc Buffon.** *Montbard. Park open daily.*

■ **Château de Bussy-Rabutin.** This magnificent 15th-century Renaissance-style chateau has a stunning interior and period furniture. *Tel. 80-96-00-03. Open daily, with guided tours at 10, 11, 2, 3, 4, 5, and 6 Apr.-Sep.; at 10, 11, 2, and 3 Oct.-Mar. Closed Tue. and Wed. Admission. 20 km. southeast of Montbard off rte. D954.*

■ **Le Mont Auxois.** A famous battle between Caesar and Vercingétorix was fought here in the year 52 B.C. Some traces remain of the ancient Roman and Gallic town. *Alise-Ste-Reine. Tel. 80-96-10-95. Open daily 9-7 Jul. 1-Sep. 10; daily 10-6 Apr.-Jun. and Sep. 11-Nov. 11. Admission. 21 km. southeast of Montbard, also off rte. D954.*

■ **Semur-en-Auxois.** In this beautifully intact riverside town, you can see a noteworthy church and remnants of once-elaborate ramparts. *18 km. south of Montbard on rte. D980.*

■ **Les Forges de Buffon.** Built by the Count of Buffon in the 1700s, this forge has been restored to demonstrate 18th-century industrial techniques. *Tel. 80-89-40-30. Open daily except Tue. 2:30-6 Jun.-Sep. and 10-noon Wed.-Fri. Jul.-Aug. 6 km. northwest of Montbard on rte. D905.*

DINING

■ **Château de Malaisy** (moderate). For a luxurious country dining experience at reasonable prices, try the dining room of this hotel in a beautifully maintained 17th-century chateau. On our visit, specials included *oeuf poché en salade Baltique* (poached egg on a bed of spicey salad), *côtelette de saumon aux fines herbes et beurre Nantais* (a salmon steak with herbs and Nantes butter), and coq au vin. *Fain-Les-Montbard (off rte. D905), Montbard 21500, tel. 80-89-46-54, fax 80-92-*

▼

30-16. Open daily except Christmas Eve.

■ **Hotel/Restaurant de l'Ecu** (moderate). Not really a country restaurant, this hotel dining room has a quiet location off the main road in town. There's a courtyard open for dining in summer. A good local crowd is attracted by simple but creative offerings such as *petit ballotin d'escargots au chou* (tiny meatloaf of snails and cabbage), *gigot d'agneau sauté aux légumes printaniers* (leg of lamb sautéed with spring vegetables), and *chaud froid de pommes sauce Anglais* (a dessert of chilled apples with a warm English egg-based sauce). *7 rue A. Carre, Montbard 21500, tel. 80-92-11-66, fax 80-92-14-13. Open daily.*

■ **Chez Armand** (inexpensive). You get lots of atmosphere, hefty portions of bistro-type food, and cheap prices. It's not the place for a quiet romantic dinner, but it's great for seeing how the locals entertain themselves. *106 rue de Faubourg, Montbard 21500, tel. 80-92-09-46. Open daily for lunch; Mon.-Sat. for dinner.*

LODGING

■ **Château de Malaisy** (moderate). Enjoy the quiet of Burgundy's countryside in this impeccably restored 17th-century chateau complete with such modern comforts as a swimming pool. Rooms are spacious, with charming decor, and all have pleasant views of well-maintained gardens away from the road. *Fain-Les-Montbard (off rte. D905), Montbard 21500, tel. 80-89-46-54, fax 80-92-30-16.*

■ **L'Enclos** (moderate). You'll sleep in peace at this small, charming bed and breakfast in the country hamlet of Arrans, about 11 km. north of Montbard. The Clergets speak no English and don't accept credit cards, but they're used to hosting people from all over the world. *Tel. 80-92-16-12. Closed Dec. 20-Mar. 20. Arrans, Montbard 21500. 9 km. north of Montbard on rte. D5.*

■ **Hotel de L'Ecu** (moderate). Convenient for train travelers, this downtown hotel is located away from the noise and commotion of Montbard's main street. It offers clean rooms and a little charm, though it's not really an escape by the standards of this book. *7 rue A. Carre, Montbard 21500, tel. 80-92-11-66, fax 80-92-14-13.*

■ **Chez Dufour** (moderate). A nice bed and breakfast in a charm-

▼

ing farm village. There's one big room with a private bath, and two smaller rooms that share one. English is spoken. *Le Village, Montigny-Montfort 21500, tel. 80-92-44-16, fax 80-92-44-93. 3 km. south of Montbard off rte. D980.*

FOR MORE INFORMATION
Tourist Office:

Office de Tourisme. *In the Pavillon Carnot on the rue Carnot, Montbard, tel. 80-92-03-75. Open daily 9-12 and 2-7 Apr. 15-Oct.; Mon.-Sat. 9:30-12 and 2-6 and Sun. 10-noon Nov.-Apr. 14. Closed Christmas and New Year's.*

For Serious Walkers:

IGN map 2921O (west) covers the walking tours described in this chapter. The tourist office sells a book of local walking tours that is available only in French.

A Town Built on a Rock

EXPERIENCE 9: GORDES

The modernist artist Victor Vasarely, well known for his geometric paintings, found the rugged, rocky terrain around Gordes a revelation. "It was, in the daytime and by moonlight, a permanent, obsessive but ever so fertile a spectacle," he wrote. "Leaving aside the history and the beauty of the old stones, it was the plasticity of the vertical plane that struck me and that engendered a succession of crucial, polychrome works."

The Highlights: Rugged hills and valleys, ancient stone sheds, fields of lavender, a magnificent Cistercian monastery, a museum dedicated to the artist Vasarely.

Other Places Nearby: The ocher hills of Rouissillon, a village of *bories,* the mysterious graves of St-Pantaléon, the canyon of Véroncle (*see* Experience 10), the cedar forest of the Luberon (*see* Experience 11).

Today, tourists pile out of buses to see this perfectly intact medieval hilltop town, with its **Renaissance castle** housing the **Musée Didactique Gordes** (Didactic Museum of Gordes, also called the Vasarely Museum) and labyrinthine old streets. The castle has a beautiful 16th-century mantlepiece, and the museum displays Vasarely's geometric works in an apt setting of stone walls. But day-tripping tourists to Gordes cannot really experience the extravagant rhythms of the region's

▼

rock—for that, you must escape into the countryside.

From what little is known of Gordes's origins, it seems to have followed the same pattern of development as dozens of other hilltop towns in the region. These rocky promontories attracted prehistoric people because they allowed them to watch over the comings and goings of enemies and defend themselves. Signs of Neolithic workshops that manufactured flint weapons have been found north of the current town and primitive Neolithic tools in the town itself. Shepherds or nomadic peoples could also have used such tools, however, so experts can't assume that Gordes was actually settled that early. Nearby, traces of a Neolithic village have been found in a rugged ravine near the hamlet of Les Dilais, just to the south of Sénanque.

On the plains below Gordes, in an area known as Carcarille, Roman tombs and other traces of habitation have been found, including what may have been an aqueduct. This suggests that the valley was scattered with Roman villas or farms, though the hilltop town of Gordes itself was probably not a Roman settlement. Whatever peace the local inhabitants found during Roman times collapsed along with the empire. By the end of the 5th century, Visigoths had invaded the area, followed a century later by the Lombards.

The first reference to the village of Gordes, then called Vordenses, is found in a 1st-century tomb in the cathedral at Ste-Anne d'Apt. The modern name of Gordes first shows up on November 30, 1031, in a document transferring the properties of one Guillaume d'Agoult. By this time, Gordes seems to have taken on some significance as a fortified town on the hilltop near a frontier fought over for centuries by various invaders and warring nobles.

Gordes as we know it seems to have taken shape in the Hundred Years War, during the 14th century. When marauders of various origins passed through the area pillaging and killing inhabitants, residents built ramparts to protect the homes built against the hilltop fortress. Most of the ramparts were demolished in the 18th and 19th centuries, although traces can still be found in the walls of village homes.

▼

The walking tour outlined below will lead you a short distance away from Gordes to the magnificent **Abbaye de Sénanque,** a perfectly intact Cistercian abbey founded in 1148 in a valley practically unchanged for hundreds of years. One 18th-century dictionary described it thus: "The situation is in terrible isolation, gripped by mountains wild and arid, of a prodigious height." When you come upon the abbey on the walk, you will be struck by how little the setting has changed.

In 1150, the local noblemen Guiran I of Simiane and his brother Bertrant Raimbaud gave this land to Cistercian monks who had come from the Ardeche region to establish a new monastery. The monastery followed a pattern of development similar to that of the abbey at Fontenay (*see* Experience 8); it quickly gained the support of local noblemen and prospered for more than 100 years. But, as at Fontenay, wealth brought corruption, and the monastery went through several cycles of decline and reform until the religious wars of the 16th century, when a band of Protestants hanged several monks and destroyed some buildings.

Spared the ravages of the French Revolution by an enlightened owner, the monastery was restored to religious use in the mid-19th century and has since been occupied, and then abandoned, on several occasions. The monks currently living there returned in 1989. You can visit the grounds and the old buildings and browse around the shop that sells books and local bric-a-brac.

Perhaps the most mysterious legacy of this beautiful rocky terrain are the ancient stone sheds called *bories*—nearly 1,000 of them—scattered around this region. Like the nearby mills of Véroncle (*see* Experience 10), *bories* received little attention from locals until a relatively recent wave of interest in the nation's past. No one knows the exact origins of these structures, and because they bear no inscriptions, it is impossible to precisely date the *bories,* many of which lie nearly hidden in the dense undergrowth of this wild terrain. Some resemble beehives, others anthills or igloos, but all are built without mortar, using flat hand-hewn rocks taken from the surrounding fields. When modern builders have attempted to replicate these sheds, the work has required

▼

considerable time and manpower, so the original builders must have worked in teams moving from site to site.

Several remains of these strange, mostly windowless stone igloos crop up along this itinerary, in various states of repair. Not far from Gordes you can also visit the entirely reconstructed **Village des Bories,** believed to date to the 14th century, with some buildings as recent as the 19th century.

GETTING THERE

By car:

From Avignon, take *rte. D22* east following signs for Apt. About 18 km. after you pass the *Autoroute du Sud,* go left on *rte. D2,* following the signs for Gordes, about 8 km. to the north. Park in the main square.

Walk Directions

TIME: 25 minutes to 3 hours
LEVEL: Easy to difficult
DISTANCE: 1 1/4 to 5 1/2 miles
ACCESS: By car

This tour can be a short stroll, for those who want to take in a wonderful view in a quiet place, while the longer version is a challenge for serious walkers, crossing an isolated, dramatic landscape. The itinerary essentially loops along the outside of a small, steep, mostly uninhabited valley below Gordes. The extended version is difficult, not so much because it's long or because there are a lot of nasty ups and downs but because it's hard to navigate over a tangle of bisecting trails and some confusing trail markings. Most of this walk is marked by blue blazes, but they are not always easy to find. Despite the apparent sense of isolation, you're never more than a mile away from a paved road in any direction. Look out for the remains of *bories* along the way, especially after Point 4.

TO BEGIN

From Gordes's main square, outside the castle, walk a short way down a hill following a sign for the post office that's visible from the

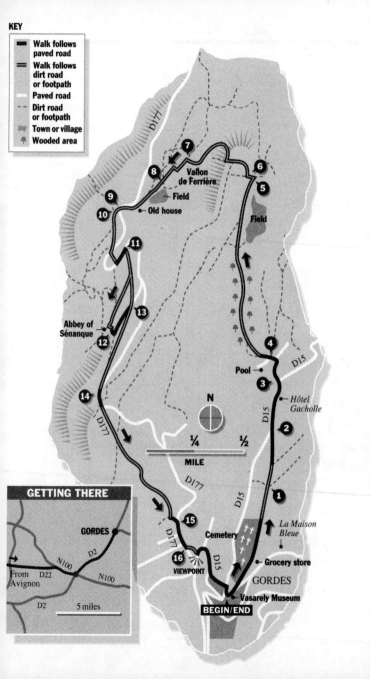

KEY

- Walk follows paved road
- Walk follows dirt road or footpath
- Paved road
- Dirt road or footpath
- Town or village
- Wooded area

D177

7
8
Vallon de Ferrière
Field
9
10 Old house
11
13
Abbey of Sénanque
12
14
D177

6
5
Field
4
D15
Pool
3
Hôtel Gacholle
2
D15

N
1/4 1/2
MILE

D177
D177

1
15
Cemetery
16
VIEWPOINT
La Maison Bleue
Grocery store
GORDES
D15
Vasarely Museum
BEGIN/END

GETTING THERE

GORDES
D2
N100
From Avignon
D22
N100
D2
5 miles

▼

square. Just downhill from the square, bear left onto a tiny road, heading toward a small grocery store and the town cemetery beyond. The road soon narrows, blue blazes begin to mark the route, and beautiful views of the valley below open up on your right. Follow the blue blazes for about 15 minutes.

1. When you reach a three-way intersection, continue straight uphill on a paved road, still following the blazes. This stretch takes you behind village homes on a charming old footpath, beside walls dripping with flowering vines and plants during spring, summer, and fall. A little farther along, bear left and uphill at a Y intersection.

2. The path brings you to *rte. D15*. Turn right, following the blue blazes painted on telephone poles. *Those who want only a short stroll can retrace their steps from here back to town.*

3. A short distance beyond the Hôtel Gacholle, turn left up a small paved road heading toward a campground and pool (signs read "Camping" and "Piscine") and the hamlet of Fontanille. Near the top of the hill, at another Y intersection, bear left, continuing to follow the blue blazes and a sign pointing toward the campground.

4. Just before the entrance to the pool, the road divides. Bear right, following the blue blazes onto a small paved road bordered by walls. Just after the road becomes dirt, it divides; follow the blue blazes straight onto a small dirt road bordered by walls. Follow the blazes straight on the broad path and you will shortly arrive at a meadow. Continue straight; a field of lavender will appear on your right.

5. At the end of the field, you will come to a dirt farm road. Go left, following a wooden sign that says "Abbaye de Sénanque." You'll still be following blue blazes, although blue blazes also mark the trail going to the right. Walk just a very short distance.

6. Make a right on a trail that heads downhill. There should be

▼

another sign for the Abbaye de Sénanque. This trail, which is blazed blue, heads downhill through a pine forest and then across rocks into the Vallon de Ferrière. As you proceed downhill, ignore a trail that comes in to your left. At one point, you will follow the main blazed trail downhill to the right and ignore a path that continues straight. *In this now-silent valley into which you descend, traces have been found of Neolithic enterprises that must once have made the valley ring with noisy activity.*

When you reach the bottom of the valley, cross a streambed, which is often dry, and follow the trail as it veers left and heads uphill parallel to the valley floor. The trail veers sharply to the right.

7. At the top of the hill, you arrive at a T intersection. Go left, following a sign to the Abbaye de Sénanque. The trail heads downhill and veers first to the right and then the left, passing other trails along the way. Continue following the main trail.

8. At the bottom of the hill, you'll reach an intersection. Go straight on a dirt road. You'll see a field and a few houses off through the trees to your left; there will be low shrubs on your right. Before you is a small orchard and a large old house, toward which the trail leads. *This old house, once a hostel for travelers on their way to St. Jacques de Compostelle, belongs to the Abbey of Sénanque and lodges groups of children and adults on church-sponsored retreats.* Bear right past the house and out toward the paved *rte. D177.*

9. Cross *rte. D177* and walk toward a small excavation in the hill on the other side. Head up a trail leading along the spine of land to the left above the shallow ravine. The trail leads into the woods.

10. You'll reach a junction with a long-distance *GR* trail, well marked with white-and-red blazes, just a few minutes' walk from the road. Go left and follow the *GR* trail down toward the valley floor; it will cross the winding *rte. D177* once on the way down. At the valley floor, the *GR* trail goes left following *rte. D177.*

▼

11. Go right on the *GR* trail, following the signs to the Abbaye de Sénanque. Go straight down the broad driveway leading to the abbey, leaving the *GR* trail as it veers off into the woods on your left. *Those wishing to skip the abbey should continue following the white-and-red-blazed GR trail uphill.*

12. After visiting the abbey, make a right outside the entrance, another quick right around the abbey wall, and then a left onto a paved road leading uphill toward *rte. D177.* As you go up the small road, watch out for the white-and-red blazes of the *GR* trail, which crosses the paved road you're on.

13. When you reach the *GR* trail, turn right, following the white-and-red blazes up to the top of the hill.

14. When you reach *rte. D177,* turn right and follow the *GR* trail along the road. After several dozen feet, take it to the right into a recently cut forest. Take the *GR* trail downhill for about 20 minutes, until it meets a small paved road, where you go left.

15. In just a few minutes, you reach *rte. D177.* Make a right and walk a short distance along the road.

16. Turn left on a dirt path that leads to *rte. D15,* where you turn left for the short walk back into town.

PLACES ALONG THE WALK
■ **Musée Didactique de Gordes (Vasarely Museum).** *Pl. du Château, Gordes 84220, tel. 90-72-02-89. Open 10-1 and 2-6. Closed Tue., Christmas, New Year's, May 1. Admission. In the heart of the village.*
■ **Abbaye de Sénanque.** *Rte. D177, Sénanque, Gordes 84220, tel. 90-72-02-05. Open 10-12 and 2-6 Mar.-Oct., except 2-6 Sun. and major religious holidays. Open 2-5 Nov.-Feb. except 2-6 Sat., Sun., holidays; closed Christmas. Less than 3 km. northwest of Gordes by way of rte. D177.*

▼

OTHER PLACES NEARBY

■ **Village des Bories.** *Rte. de Cavaillon, Gordes 84220, tel. 90-72-03-48. Open daily 9-sunset. Take rte. D15 south from Gordes for about 2 km. to the intersection of rte. D2. Quickly follow signs to the right onto a paved road and park.*

■ **Roussillon.** This tiny village occupying a site inhabited for thousands of years sits in the midst of dramatic ocher-colored hills you can walk through. *About 8 km. east of Gordes on rte. D169.*

■ **St-Pantaléon.** In this village, a church built atop a 5th-century sanctuary is surrounded by children's graves carved into the rock. It is thought that people brought dead children to this church believing they could be brought to life just long enough to be baptized. *The church is currently under restoration. To visit it, pick up keys in the nearby auberge on the rte. de Goult. About 4 km. southeast of Gordes on rte. 104.*

DINING

■ **Hostellerie Le Phébus** (very expensive). Luxurious country dining with plush decor and great views of the Luberon and the surrounding *garrigue* (rocky terrain covered with low brush and shrubs). On a given day, you might find *charlotte d'agneau* (a sort of lamb pudding) and *filet de rouget en fondu de poivrons* (fillet of mullet fish with peppers cooked until soft). *Rte. de Murs, Joucas, Gordes 84220, tel. 90-05-78-83, fax 90-05-73-61. Open daily Mar.-Nov. About 8 km. northeast of Gordes on rte. D102 (just north of Joucas on the way to Murs).*

■ **La Gacholle** (expensive). Here you'll enjoy a beautiful view and excellent food served in a refined but casual atmosphere. For a starter, the menu might feature *feuilleté de foie et de poulet* (a flaky pastry of liver and chicken); for the main course, *râble de lapereau aux pommes et aux olives* (the back of young rabbit with apple and olives). *Rte. de Murs, Gordes 84220, tel. 90-72-01-36, fax 90-72-01-81. Open daily for lunch and dinner Jun. 15-Sep. 15; otherwise, dinner only. Closed Nov. 15-Dec. 26 and Jan. 5-Mar. 5. Just north of Gordes center on rte. D15.*

■ **Auberge de la Bartavelle** (inexpensive to moderate). A tiny village restaurant where, depending on the season, you might such memorable dishes as *ravioles de romans, crème de ciboulettes* (ravioli in a

▼

creamy chive sauce), and *alouette sans tête* (actually, beef rolled with mushrooms and cooked with wine). *Rue du Cheval Blanc, Goult 84220, tel. 90-72-33-72. Closed Wed. About 7 km. southeast of Gordes by way of rte. D104.*

■ **La Ferme de la Huppe** (moderate). A charming country restaurant with excellent food, such as a *tourte de pommmes de terre et de hommard* (a sort of potato-and-lobster pie) and *magret de canard, sauce aux jujubes* (cutlet of duck with a sauce made of a datelike fruit). *Rte. D156, Gordes 84220, tel. 90-72-12-25, fax 90-72-01-83. Open for dinner daily except Thu.; for lunch on weekends only. Closed Nov. 5-Apr. 1. About 3 km. east of Gordes village on rte. D156 toward Goult.*

LODGING

■ **Hostellerie Le Phébus** (very expensive). Enjoy luxurious country comforts with great views, all modern conveniences, pool, and tennis. The rooms have luxurious appointments with updated motifs and are perfect for those who want to combine modern style with country charm. *Rte. de Murs, Joucas, Gordes 84220, tel. 90-05-78-83, fax 90-05-73-61. Open Mar.-Nov. About 8 km. northeast of Gordes on rte. D102 (just north of Joucas on the way to Murs).*

■ **Le Gordos** (expensive). Here you'll find another combination of old and new, with the hotel's old stone walls on the outside contrasting with modern comforts and ambience on the inside. There's a sun-drenched private pool, and some rooms have fine views of the Luberon mountains or Mont du Vaucluse. *Rte. de Cavaillon, Gordes 84220, tel. 90-72-00-75. Closed Jan. 15-Feb. 15. Just outside Gordes on rte. D177 toward the Abbaye de Sénanque.*

■ **La Ferme de la Huppe** (expensive). An 18th-century farm restored following traditional local designs. Eight quiet rooms nicely decorated and near a shaded pool. *Rte. D156, Gordes 84220, tel. 90-72-12-25, fax 90-72-01-83. Open for dinner daily except Thu.; for lunch on weekends only. Closed Nov. 5-Apr. 1. About 3 km. east of Gordes village on rte. D156 toward Goult.*

■ **Les Romarins** (expensive). This small pleasant hotel has six rooms with views of Gordes; Room 1 has the best. There's a pool in

▼

season. *Rte. de Cavaillon, Gordes 84220, tel. 90-72-00-75. Just outside Gordes on rte. D2 toward Cavaillon.*

■ **La Gacholle** (expensive). Located just outside Gordes, in its own quiet garden, this hotel offers breathtaking views, charming (if somewhat small) rooms, a pool, and tennis courts. *Rte. de Murs, Gordes 84220, tel. 90-72-01-36, fax 90-72-01-81. Closed Nov. 15-Dec. 26 and Jan. 5-Mar. 5. Just north of Gordes center on rte. D15.*

■ **La Maison Bleue** (moderate). This bed and breakfast offers one nicely decorated bedroom with a modern bath adjacent to the owner's home. The house is in an exquisite location on the hillside below Gordes, with beautiful views from the pool deck and the room. The owner speaks excellent English and can provide recommendations and even guided tours for serious hikers. *Rte. Neuve, Gordes 84220, tel. 90-72-12-56, fax 90-72-05-85. Just outside the town walls on the road toward rte. D2 and Rouissillon.*

FOR MORE INFORMATION

Tourist Office:

Office de Tourisme. *Pl. du Château, Gordes 84220, tel. 90-72-02-75. Open daily 9-12 and 2-6:30.*

For Serious Walkers:

IGN maps 3141O (west) and 3142O (west) cover the area of the walking tour.

Medieval Mills

EXPERIENCE 10: MURS

You won't find this place in most guidebooks—even the tourist office in nearby Gordes hardly mentions it—but that should not deter you. Those who visit this rugged hidden canyon outside the tiny village of Murs, just 7 km. north of Gordes, will be thankful that it remains unknown to most travelers. The solitude is part of the beauty.

The Highlights: Ruins of medieval mills, dams, and canals; flower-filled meadows; an astonishing canyon.

Other Places Nearby: A well-preserved medieval village at Vénasque, the old monastery at Gordes (*see* Experience 9), the cedar forest of Luberon (*see* Experience 11).

The **Canyon of Véroncle** provides more than an exhilarating walk into a dramatic natural setting: It gives visitors a rare, undisturbed encounter with medieval industry—an ancient dam, ten or so ruined stone mills, and a dizzying array of canals and artificial ponds still visible beneath centuries-old undergrowth. You'll have to use your imagination to picture this now-silent canyon as it was some 500 years ago, when it was filled with the sounds of huge stone grinding mills, rushing water, and turning gears.

While the mills are the main reason for a visit, you'll also be deep in a beautiful natural canyon with sheer rock walls. Around you are signs of a once-roaring river, patches of almost junglelike undergrowth, and a sense of wilderness rare in France. The most impressive sights lie about 1 1/2 miles into the walk, but those who take a shorter option

▼

can still walk only 100 yards to the 16th-century dam and mill, where a lush meadow is alive with songbirds and butterflies.

Local authorities have done surprisingly little to uncover this stunning testament to medieval ingenuity. Only in 1986 did local organizations join together to study these ruins, undertaking a preliminary survey of the site and an inventory of the ruins and searching local documents for references that might yield insight into the origins of the place. The project uncovered a striking array of waterworks, starting with a dam and a pond. When you come upon this spot about 100 yards into the walk, you'll notice a tall stone wall standing to your right, partially obscured by brush. Upon closer examination, you'll see that the dam is actually made of a mix of stones, branches, and earth. This dam, together with the **Moulin des Etangs,** a mill of unknown origin, marked the entrance to what was in essence a huge outdoor factory.

This abandoned industrial site fills half of the 4 1/2-mile-long canyon. As you progress down the canyon, you will pass the ruins of one mill and then another, usually less than 1/4 mile apart. At some mills, almost all of the walls remain, as with the **Moulin Jean de Mare** 1 1/4 miles into the walk. You can examine the grinding wheel, untouched by time, and the remains of the wooden gears. Other mills, however, survive only as bare traces under the thick undergrowth. The elaborate network of aqueducts, canals, and ponds connected each mill, regulating the flow of water throughout the dry and wet seasons.

So far, no one knows the exact origin of the mills. The first written record appears in a local document of 1508, in which the lord of Murs, Jean d'Astouaud, grants residents of the village the right to "grind their grain at the mills," which must have already been in operation.

Experts date most of the architectural features to the 16th century or later. Although the date 1584 is engraved on a stone in the dam, the structure was not necessarily new at the time—it could have been rebuilt over an older one washed away or destroyed in an earthquake.

It is known that the three mills in the northern portion of the canyon belonged to the D'Astouaud family until the French Revolution.

▼

Over the centuries, the family granted exclusive management rights to various local inhabitants. In return, the renter had to maintain the locks, canals, and mills. Even less is known about the mills in Gordes, the southern zone of the canyon. One of the most impressive of these remaining mills, the Jean de Mare, was probably built in the 16th century and expanded later. The others seem more recent, perhaps of the 17th and 18th centuries.

The mills all employed a similar method of operation. Canals dug into the earth allowed the water to circulate and feed the water wheels turning the grinding stone. Behind each mill, a reservoir held water. To activate the mill, a gate opened to a shaft, which dropped the water down onto a horizontally placed water wheel. This wheel turned huge grinding stones above.

Most of the mills functioned until the 19th century, when seismic activity caused a fundamental shift in water flow, emptying the canyon. After that, locals apparently just forgot about them. Today, with a rebirth of interest in France's patrimony, local authorities have expressed an interest in developing the site. Now is the time to see these ruins, in their current undisturbed state.

Just to the north of the canyon, the tiny village of **Murs** makes a pretty stop, with a 15th-century castle graced with fairy-tale towers built on the site of an earlier fortress. About 1 km. north of the village, between *rte. D4* and *rte. D15,* lie the **ruins of an ancient wall** built by locals in the early 18th century in a futile attempt to prevent the spread of the plague into the region.

GETTING THERE

By car:

From Avignon, take *rte. N7* southeast, then *rte. D22* east, following signs for Apt. About 18 km. after you pass the *Autoroute du Sud,* go left on *rte. D2,* following signs for Gordes, about 8 km. north. From the main square at Gordes, go north about 7 km. on *rte. D15* toward Murs, and just after a long bend in the road, turn right onto a tiny paved road. (You will see a round white-and-red sign indicating a limited truck weight. You've gone too far if you see a turnoff to your left for *rte.*

▼

D15a.) After about 3/4 km., make the first right turn. Go about 1/4 km. and make the next right. Follow this road about 1 km., noticing blue blazes on telephone poles, until you reach an intersection where a footpath heads diagonally off to the right into the forest. Park along the side of the road.

Walk Directions

TIME: 1/2 to 3 hours
LEVEL: Easy to moderate
DISTANCE: 1/8 to 3 miles
ACCESS: By car

This route takes you down the canyon, past the ancient industrial sites, and back along the same path, although the return walk provides an entirely different perspective of the canyon. You can easily tailor this walk to your own time frame and abilities—simply go as far as you feel comfortable and then retrace your steps. At times, thick underbrush narrows the trail, and about 1 km. into the walk, you face a short but steep drop down to the canyon floor that some people may not want to negotiate, especially in wet weather.

Picnic spots abound, with one about 100 yards from your car, at the sight of the old dam. Otherwise, find a place among the ruins of mills or against the steep canyons you traverse as part of the walk.

Throughout its entire length, the trail is blazed blue, even when joined with a yellow blaze later on. Should you get a little confused at the tangle of trails surrounding the ruins, just look around until you find the blue blazes. However, it's difficult to get lost, as long as you stay in the bottom of the canyon.

TO BEGIN

Head down the trail leading into the woods away from the road.

1. In a few minutes, you reach the first visible mill, the *Moulin des Etangs, with its associated dam. The grassy meadow near the old mill and dam makes an excellent place to picnic, but keep away from the still-occupied home nearby.* Continue on the trail.

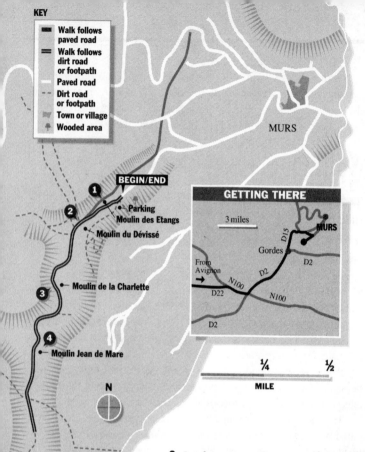

KEY

- Walk follows paved road
- Walk follows dirt road or footpath
- Paved road
- Dirt road or footpath
- Town or village
- Wooded area

MURS

BEGIN/END

1

2
● Parking
Moulin des Etangs

● Moulin du Dévissé

3 ● Moulin de la Charlette

4
● Moulin Jean de Mare

N

GETTING THERE

3 miles

MURS

Gordes

D15

D2

D2

From Avignon →

N100

N100

D2

D22

D2

¼   ½

MILE

2. In about ten minutes, you'll find the ruins of *Moulin du Dévissé*.

3. Another ten minutes or so brings you to the *Moulin de la Charlette*. As you proceed from there, avoid the trail that comes in from the left— it goes back up onto the eastern side of the canyon.

4. You soon arrive at the *Moulin Jean de Mare*. Proceed just a little farther into the canyon, where it reaches its most impressive part, with

▼

steep walls towering around you. When you've gone far enough, simply retrace your steps, following the blue blazes back along the valley floor.

OTHER PLACES NEARBY

See Experience 9, Gordes.

■ **Vénasque.** One of the best-preserved medieval villages in the region, Vénasque has a 7th-century baptistery, three Moorish towers, and an impressive cliffside location. *14 km. northwest of Murs on rte. D4.*

DINING & LODGING

See Experience 9, Gordes.

FOR MORE INFORMATION

Tourist Office:

Office de Tourisme. *Pl. Château, Gordes 84220, tel. 90-72-02-75. Open daily 9-12 and 2-6:30.*

For Serious Walkers:

French-language walk books available in local bookstores and at Au Vieux Campeur (*see* How to Use Short Escapes) suggest much longer loop walks encompassing the plateau above as well as other walks in the region. IGN map 3141E (east) and 3142E (east) detail the area around the mills.

Toujours Luberon

EXPERIENCE 11:
FOREST OF CEDARS

If you're among the millions who have read Peter Mayle's *A Year in Provence* and *Toujours Provence,* you already know about the Luberon, an immensely rich landscape of mountains, farms, ancient villages, and hidden relics of the past less than 50 miles southwest of Avignon.

The Highlights: A remarkable cedar forest; majestic views of rivers, mountains, and hilltop villages.

Other Places Nearby: The charming villages of Bonnieux, Ménerbes, Lacoste, and Oppède-le-Vieux; ancient castles and churches; the old monastery at Gordes (*see* Experience 9); the canyon of Véroncle (*see* Experience 10).

Although this is an extremely popular summer and winter retreat for Parisians and sophisticated European travelers—French President François Mitterand had a home near Gordes—there really aren't any major monuments here, and there are better known tourist spots nearby. As a result, this traveler's paradise is a sort of backwater for American travelers in France, who usually bypass it on the high-speed highway or train on their way to the Riviera.

Peter Mayle has helped changed that, whether he wanted to or not. A former British advertising executive who cashed in his chips and moved to France, Mayle wrote two very personal guides to this minute

▼

but fascinating corner of France. Now, local residents speak with amusement of travelers—mostly British or Americans—who ask about the whereabouts of the author or the places he mentions in his best-selling books. Mayle has since moved away.

Mayle's book titles mislead you, for the area of which he writes is actually the Luberon—certainly part of Provence, but with a geographic, historic, and cultural character all its own. It takes its name from a mountain range called the Luberon, one of several east-west ranges in the southeast of France (Mont Ste-Baume is another—*see* Experience 12) that rose under the pressure of the colliding tectonic plates of Africa and Europe. Only about 3,500 feet at its highest point, this range has two major mountains, Le Petit Luberon and Le Grand Luberon. Together they form a roughly 40-mile wall, from near the town of Cavaillon in the west to Manosque in the east. Here lies a boundary between the dry, hot Mediterranean climate on the south slope and the cooler, moister, more alpine influence on the north side.

Mayle's books describe life in the communities along the northern slope of the mountain: **Ménerbes** (where he lives), **Lacoste, Oppède-le-Vieux,** and **Bonnieux,** four old villages perched on the rocky tops of foothills beneath the main mountain. These villages probably grew out of ancient forts protecting an east-west Roman road connecting Italy and Spain. Above the nearby village of Buoux, you can still see the ruins of the ancient **Fort de Buoux,** which once protected settlements of Ligurians and Romans and later figured in wars between Catholics and Protestants. Just east of Bonnieux, the Roman road probably intersected with the Combe de Loumarain, a river valley that has served since prehistoric times as a north-south route through the mountain range. The four northern-slope villages have preserved their wonderful architecture and traditional way of life, and their rural setting is still unspoiled by miles of modern homes, shopping centers, and the unpleasant distractions you'll encounter in the tourist areas farther to the south.

This itinerary takes you to the top of the Petit Luberon and one of

▼

the forests described by Mayle, himself a regular walker in the area. His book *A Year in Provence* describes what you will see on the mountaintops: "Cedars and pines and scrub oak keep them perpetually green and provide cover for boar, rabbits, and game birds. Wild flowers, thyme, lavender, and mushrooms grow between the rocks and under the trees, and on a clear day the view is of the Basse-Alpes [Alps foothills] on one side and the Mediterranean on the other."

Our walk follows the **Sentier Découverte Nature de la Forêt des Cèdres** (Nature Discovery Path in the Forest of Cedars), a specially marked nature trail running through national park land on the Petit Luberon. Along the path, numbered signposts provide a brief description (in French) of what you're seeing, giving you a mini-seminar in mountain botany while you enjoy the scenery. For example, Markers 1, 2, and 3 point out three different species of trees that dominate the landscape—the *cèdre d'atlas* (atlas cedar), the *chêne vert* (green oak), and the *chêne blanc* or *pubescent* (white oak).

Cedars, which were introduced as part of a reforestation effort in the 1860s, do well at the higher altitudes but generally fail to make it below 2,000 feet, especially on southern-facing slopes. The green oaks, however, thrive on the hot, arid south-facing slopes thanks to the water-retentive qualities of their small waxy year-round leaves. (That's why you'll see green oaks frequently the farther south you go in France.)

In contrast, the white oak, a deciduous tree whose large oval leaves have numerous irregularities, thrives on the cooler, more humid northern slopes. The difference between them is most apparent in autumn when the white oak drops its leaves and the green oak does not. On the trail, you can see how the cedar groves grow outward in concentric circles, so that the oldest trees are always found in the center of the grove. In this mountaintop region live the Bonelli eagle, the eagle-owl, the Percnoptere vulture, and the Jean Le Blanc eagle, as well as beavers, wild boar, fox, stone martens, weasels, and various lizards and snakes, including the aspic viper.

Walking this trail, you'll also learn ways in which rural people have used the resources of these mountains for thousands of years—

▼

for food, medicine, fuel, and building materials. Around Marker 2, for example, several plants and flowers that have long served local people as food or medicine are identified. *Chevrefeuille d'etrurie* (Etruscan honeysuckle) has yellow flowers that yield an essence used to make perfume; *campanule raiponce* (campanula), with blue, bell-shaped flowers that bloom in June and July, has a flavorful root sometimes used in country salads; two species of *scabieuse* (scabious) owe their name to their use in medieval times as a medicine against skin ailments; *phalangère petit lis,* white-flowered plants that bloom in May and June, were once cultivated to relieve spider bites; *lavande vrai* and *aspic* (lavender), the latter used by Romans in their baths, are flowers that today are usually dried and used to deodorize clothes and protect against mites; *luzerne* (alfalfa) grew from seeds fallen from the carts traveling on this ancient road across the Luberon massif. For centuries, locals burned huge piles of the forest's wood into charcoal, especially during World War II, while barrels, ships, and other products were made from the local trees.

And, like any mountain walk, this one of course offers great views of the surrounding countryside, even before you begin. On the drive up, you'll pass a stone tower on the left, the **Tour Philippe** (closed to the public) built by a local for his wife late in the last century to provide a view of the sea, over 20 miles away. Overlooks provide fantastic views of Bonnieux, Lacoste, Ménerbes, and far beyond, Mont Ventoux.

On the walking tour, the mountaintop view looks out over the valley of the river Durance, which once went straight to the Mediterranean Sea but now flows into the Rhône river. The Durance used to be known for devastating, unpredictable floods—notice how the valley's old towns occupy high spots to avoid the floodwaters. The river's flow is now controlled by a system of dams and a canal diverting some of it into the Crau river.

This nature trail is one of a growing number you'll find in French national parks. (It's one of four in the region—others let you discover the ancient stone sheds called *bories* in Viens, the ocher-colored hills in Rouissillon, and the ancient farmlands near Goult (*see* Experience 9).

▼

GETTING THERE

By car:

From Avignon, take *rte. N7* southeast 11 km. to *rte. D973,* following signs for Apt. Shortly, exit onto *rte. D22,* which becomes *rte. N100.* Exit right on *rte. D36,* following signs to Bonnieux. Go through the village, heading east and then south on *rte. D36* and watching for signs pointing to the Forêt des Cèdres (Forest of Cedars). Just under 2 km. from the village, turn right on a paved road marked with a cul-de-sac sign. Follow this road for about 4 km.—to a parking area, just before a barrier that blocks cars from the road entering the forest. On the way, make sure you bear right at a Y intersection. Watch for the Tour Philippe on your left and beautiful views on your right.

Walk Directions

TIME: 1 1/2 hours

LEVEL: Easy to moderate

DISTANCE: Under 2 miles

ACCESS: By car

This well-marked nature trail has only one short but difficult stretch up a rocky hillside. From the summit you enjoy an awesome view of the Durance river valley and Mont Ste-Victoire, Mont Ste-Baume, and the Alpilles—a perfect spot for a picnic. Since you do most of the uphill climb by car, this walking tour provides a particularly dramatic view with relatively little effort. On weekends and holidays and during vacation periods you're likely to encounter many French people from the surrounding area. Between March and November, watch for vipers along the trail and wherever you sit down or place your hands. You probably won't see one, but it's best to be cautious.

TO BEGIN

From the parking area, walk around a barrier and follow the paved road into the forest. Just about 100 steps into the woods, look for a large but difficult-to-spot wooden sign on the left marking the entrance to the trail. If you reach the park map and information sign, you've gone too far.

▼

1. At the wooden trail sign, go left downhill following the blue and yellow blazes. The trail quickly bears right on an old mule trail heading down toward a wooded hillside. It bears left at the base of this hillside and runs along the bottom of the hill, past the next four markers. Marker 1 points out the stand of *cèdres d'atlas* (atlas cedars) climbing the hillside before you. These are gradually encroaching upon the *chênes verts* (green oaks) below, described in Marker 2. In the area

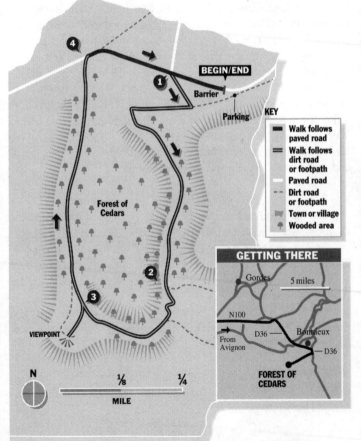

▼

near this sign, you'll also find more than a dozen species of plants and flowers, some of which are described above. Marker 3 indicates the *chênes blancs* or *pubescents* (white oaks), which grow on the northern slopes in the region. At Marker 4, *you stand on an old platform once used to make charcoal, one of five along this walk.* A little beyond Marker 4, you might notice thyme and wild strawberries (*fraisers*), both of which are quite popular in the local cuisine.

2. At the base of a hill, at Marker 5, a rocky trail marked with blue-and-yellow blazes leads uphill to your right. You're leaving the old mule trail to climb the mountain. *This is a good spot to study the difference between the north- and south-facing hillsides around you. On the north-facing hill thrives the white oak; on the southern hillside, the green oak.* Up the hill, Marker 6 elaborates on this difference. Continue on the trail uphill to Marker 7, which describes the *garrigue*—an upland area of low, sparse shrubs and grasses. This area resulted from a fire that destroyed the stand of pines. The sign also cautions you to keep to the trail, which abuts a steep hillside. Just below the top of the hill, Marker 8 points out *le brachypode rameux,* a rugged, spiny grass, and *l'ail à la tête ronde,* a species of wild garlic.

3. In less than ten minutes, the trail intersects a broad trail. Turn left onto the broad trail and head toward a clearing on the crest of the mountain, where you'll find Marker 9 and an excellent place to picnic.

From here you get a spectacular view south encompassing the Durance river valley and several mountains in the distance. You'll see Mont Ste-Victoire and Mont Ste-Baume to the south and east and Les Alpilles (on your right) to the west.

Once you've taken in the view, walk back out the way you came—past Point 3—and continue straight through the lush cedar forest on a broad, flat easy-to-follow trail.

4. When you reach a paved road, turn right. Follow this road straight for about ten minutes, past the trail's entrance, around the barrier, and back to your car.

▼

OTHER PLACES NEARBY

■ **Bonnieux.** The ramparts around this ancient hilltop village are still visible. There's also a 12th-century church displaying 15th-century paintings of the German school. Beautiful views extend from the terrace beside the church. The village also contains the Musée de la Boulangerie (Museum of Bread-Making), displaying bread varieties, utensils, and other bread-making equipment. *Bonnieux 84480, tel. 90-75-88-34. Open daily 10-12 and 3-6:30 except Tue. Apr.-Sep. and Oct.-May. Admission.*

■ **Fort de Buoux.** Old walls, houses, and silos, a sacrificial altar, and other intriguing remains of Ligurians, Romans, Protestants, and Catholics mark this ancient hilltop fort offering fine views. *5 km. east of Bonnieux off rte. D113. Open daily all year. Admission.*

■ **Lacoste.** The impressive ruins of the Marquis de Sade's castle dominate this hill village. *5 km. west of Bonnieux on rte. D109.*

■ **Ménerbes.** This charming hilltop village has a 13th-century fortress (closed to the public) and a 14th-century church. *12 km. west of Bonnieux by way of rte. D109 and rte. D3.*

■ **Oppède-le-Vieux.** Once almost abandoned, this village has now been revived, because of the beauty of its ancient homes and its hilltop site. *16 km. west of Bonnieux by way of rte. D109.*

DINING

For more dining and lodging, see Experience 9, Gordes.

■ **Le Fournil** (moderate). The lovely dining room puts out a cuisine recommended by locals. Specialties might include *lapin roulé aux aubergines* (rabbit prepared with eggplant) and *selle d'agneau, caillette d'abats, jus au basilic, taboulé de légumes* (lamb with a pork sausage served in a sauce spiced with basil and a vegetable taboule). *5 pl. Carnot, Bonnieux 84480, tel. 90-75-83-62. Closed Tue. Located next to the tourist office.*

■ **Chez César** (inexpensive to moderate). This picturesque café and restaurant in the heart of Bonnieux has an authentic Provençal atmosphere, even though local food-lovers do not include it among their recommendations. Stick to basic French offerings such as *soupe de*

▼

poisson and *entrecôte de boeuf, sauce au vin* (rib steak with wine sauce), have some wine, and soak up the atmosphere. *Pl. de la Liberté, Bonnieux 84480, tel. 90-75-80-18. Open daily except Thu. Closed Nov. 12-Dec. 20 and Jan. 5-Feb., but may open if the weather is good.*

■ **Le Simiane** (inexpensive to moderate). Peter Mayle tells the story of a dinner at this restaurant in the shadow of the Marquis de Sade's castle in Lacoste. It has since moved to a location nearby. Offers could still include a *foie gras au torchon* (a terrine prepared with a cloth) or *hommard grillé* (grilled lobster). *Rue Sous Barri, Lacoste 84480, tel. 90-75-83-31. Open for dinner except Wed. Closed for lunch except Sun. and major holidays. In the heart of Lacoste, 5 km. west of Bonnieux by way of rte. D109.*

LODGING

■ **Hostellerie du Prieuré** (expensive). Although it's located in the village, most of the inn's rooms face a garden and the valley. Room 9 has a terrace and a view of the valley; all have refined decor and private bath. Rooms 1, 3, 6, 7, and 8 look out on a garden. *Bonnieux 84480, tel. 90-75-80-78. Open Feb. 15-Nov. 5. Located at the base of the village ramparts.*

■ **Relais du Procureur** (expensive). Five rooms in a 17th-century village home, all with private bath and access to a private pool, are charming, with those on the upper floor having views. You might hear a little noise from the village. *Rue Basse, Lacoste 84710, tel. 90-75-82-28, fax 90-75-86-94. In Lacoste village, 5 km. west of Bonnieux.*

■ **Bonne Terre** (expensive). This modern home has panoramic views, a pretty setting in a shaded park with a private pool, and comfortable, nicely decorated rooms. *84480 Lacoste, tel. 90-75-85-53. Credit cards accepted. Open all year. Off rte. D106, outside the village.*

■ **Le Jas des Fourants** (inexpensive). This funky hostel is for budget travelers only, but the location on the mountainside above Bonnieux, on the edge of the Luberon summits, is perfect for hikers. Inexpensive meals available. *Rte. des Cèdres, Bonnieux 84480, tel. 90-75-91-94. No credit cards. Located on approach road to the Forest of Cedars walk, about 3 km. before the parking barrier.*

▼

FOR MORE INFORMATION

Tourist Offices:

Syndicat d'Initiative. *Pl. Carnot, Bonnieux 84480, tel. 90-75-91-90, fax 90-75-92-94. Open Tue.-Sat. 9-12 and 2-6; Tue.-Sat. 2-6 Nov.-Mar. Closed major holidays.*

For Serious Walkers:

The region has an enormous variety of well-marked walking trails documented in French-language guidebooks available in local bookstores and in hiking shops. IGN map 3142E (east) includes the complete area covered by the Forest of Cedars trail.

Pilgrimage to a Holy Mountain

EXPERIENCE 12: MONT STE-BAUME

For travelers who wish to walk in the footsteps of Jesus Christ and his disciples, France does not seem a likely destination. After all, it is thousands of miles from the Holy Land, and no one—even the fiercest Francophile—has ever claimed that Christ set foot in Gaul.

Yet a centuries-old legend persists, claiming that one of Christ's closest fol-

The Highlights: Incomparable views of the coastal mountains of Provence, a visit to an ancient mountaintop shrine, diverse landscapes of thick forest and low scrubby brush.

Other Places Nearby: Aubagne, the childhood home of Marcel Pagnol; Marseille; Toulon.

lowers, Mary Magdalene, landed on the shores of France after his death and lived for some time as a hermit on a mountaintop cliff not far from Marseille. Many medieval kings and popes walked the same trail you'll walk and visited the same grotto chapel, the **Grotte de Ste-Marie-Madeleine,** a place that had religious importance even before Christ.

In the 20th century, the region has attracted a more secular kind of pilgrim. If you're a film-lover, you may want to visit the locations used in the popular French films *Jean de Florette* and *Manon des Sources* by director Claude Berri. Based on the stories of Marcel Pagnol, these films were shot on the flanks of Mont Ste-Baume near a small hamlet,

▼

Riboux, tucked away in a valley high in the foothills of the mountain. Berri undoubtedly chose this area because it is as wild and empty as Marcel Pagnol's boyhood weekend home, actually located near **Aubagne.** If you're an experienced walker and a Pagnol devotee, you might want to pick up maps provided by the tourist office in Aubagne to discover some of the special little places featured in his books.

Mary Magdalene's history is sketchy—she's variously pictured in the Bible as the woman from whom Jesus expelled seven demons and the one who burst from a crowd and fell to his feet, anointing them with her tears. Whatever the case, for Catholics she is a symbol of passionate penitence, of someone who earned forgiveness for her sins. A loyal follower of Christ, she was one of the few who stayed at his side while he died on the cross; she accompanied his body to the tomb and was the first to learn of his resurrection. Following the resurrection, the legend goes, Mary Magdalene left Palestine and embarked on a boat without sails or oars with two other followers of Christ. Under the watchful eye of Jesus, she floated to the shores of Gaul at Les-Stes-Maries-de-la-Mer. She went first to Aix-en-Provence and then to a cave high on a cliff, on what is now Mont Ste-Baume, where she spent the rest of her life in penitence.

This cave was already a site holy to pagan worshippers. A Roman writer of the 1st century referred to a forest there, "a sacred wood, which, since very ancient times, has never been profaned. It is surrounded by great boughs, a tenebrous air and icy shadows, impenetrable to the sun." It is said that Caesar had his soldiers knock down some of that forest during the siege of Marseille in the year 49 B.C. Today, on the north slope of Ste-Baume, travelers still find a surprisingly thick forest of tall trees in this otherwise arid, scrubby southern Provence terrain. In this deep, moist forest you'll find beech, willow, oak, maple, poplar, Scotch pine, and sycamore and rich undergrowth.

In the middle of the 5th century, Jean Cassien established small monasteries in Provence, at one time drawing as many as 5,000 men and women to his sect, many of whom lived on the mountain of Ste-Baume. Cassien himself came each year in pilgrimage to the grotto of

▼

Mary Magdalene, as did popes, warriors, kings, and other believers.

Sometime in the 6th or 7th century, a basilica was supposedly built over Mary Magdalene's crypt, but fear of Saracen invasions caused the Cassien monks to switch her remains with someone else's. Only after the Saracens were defeated in the late 10th century did a semblance of peace finally return to this part of Provence, and the monks formally returned to Ste-Baume.

The site reached the height of its importance during the 11th and 12th centuries. One Italian visitor of that era described the site: It "is situated in a high rock and is vast enough to hold 1,000 people ... And, as all of the country is uninhabited and desert, the women of Marseille, when they come by devotion, make sure to bring with them donkeys that carry bread, wine, fish and other provisions."

In 1254 on his way back from the Crusades, the revered 13th-century French king St. Louis came here to recover from his voyage. The Italian poet Petrarch was a frequent visitor in the 15th century. And over the next few hundred years such luminaries as Marie de Medicis, Pope Urban VIII, and King Louis XIV visited the shrine. During periods of pilgrimage, thousands took communion at a single Mass—an incredible number for a spot high on a mountain and far from any population center. But like other religious sites, Ste-Baume dwindled in importance during the Enlightenment, and it was sacked and burned at the height of the French Revolution. In the 1850s, however, it was fully reestablished as a religious center, and today it is maintained by a prosperous-looking order of Dominican brothers who benefit from the site's popularity. Large numbers of the faithful still visit the holy grotto, following the main trail from Nazareth, on the other side of the mountain.

Over the years, wealthy people who came to do penance donated funds to build the main church in Nazareth or the sanctuary at Ste-Baume. In the 17th century, a Parisian doctor underwrote the construction of a small chapel still visible today on the trail between the grotto and the mountaintop. Another 17th-century chapel was built on the summit of **St-Pilon,** from which you will get on your walk fine views of Mont St-Victoire to the north, the ridge of Mont Ste-Baume to the east and west, the mountains of Toulon to the south, and beyond that, on

▼

clear days, the Iles (islands) des Embiers. Nearby, an orientation table points out the major mountains. Somewhere in this area, it is said, Mary Magdalene was whisked to the mountaintop by angels and would sit contemplating the view.

Most worshippers who visit the shrine approach the mountain from the north, from the Hôtellerie at La Ste-Baume. Walk 1, outlined below, approaches instead from the south and is more accessible from Marseille and the highways leading north, east, and west; it's also closer to the sites filmed in *Jean de Florette* and *Manon des Sources*. Although both of the Berri movies are supposedly set in one tiny village, they were actually filmed in several parts of France. If you saw the movies, though, you'll probably recognize the home of the *bossu* (hunchback), played by Gérard Depardieu, the location of one of the springs, and many of the landscapes. The hunchback's home is on private property in a place called Château Renard and is closed to visitors, but locals will gladly point out the property on a map. Walk 2 brings you to an overlook that takes in the valley where the house stands and that served as a backdrop for the panoramic shots in the films.

The filming left its mark on the tiny village, where locals boast about having spent considerable time with the stars, waiting around between scenes. One rather offbeat villager, proprietor of the curious Auberge le Solitaire (*see* Dining, below), claims he was almost selected to play the role of half-wit Ugolin. Other restaurant owners will point to a table and tell you that one of the famous actors "sat right there."

Serious walkers with IGN map 3345O (west) can visit places in the film by following some more difficult walking routes. Crude maps outlining such walks have been created by the Mairie (town hall) in the nearby village of **Cuges-les-Pins.**

GETTING THERE

By car:

From Marseille, take *Autoroute A50* east for 17 km. to Aubagne. Exit at Aubagne for *rte. N8,* the old two-lane highway to Le Beausset and Toulon. About 12 km. later, shortly after the village of Cuges-les-Pins, turn left on *rte. D601* at the O.K. Corral theme park. It's about 6 km. to Riboux.

▼

Walk 1 Directions

TIME: 1 1/2 to 3 hours round-trip
LEVEL: Moderate
DISTANCE: 2 1/2 to 3 1/2 miles
ACCESS: By car

This walking tour avoids the weekend and vacation crowds by going up the rugged south face of the mountain through a region of low brush known locally as *garrigue*. As you climb, you get progressively more dramatic views of the still undeveloped mountains of south Provence and of Mont Ste-Baume's impressive chalk-white facade. You can follow the trail into the dense forest that leads to the grotto or walk up to the Chapel of St-Pilon, with its mountaintop view. In both cases, retrace your steps down the mountain and back to your car.

Although this is a short, relatively easy-to-follow walking tour, it is only for regular walkers or those in reasonably good shape. The trail climbs abruptly up the southern face of the mountain for a little over a mile. Periodic copses of low trees offer shade from time to time in the 1 1/4-mile climb, but special care should be taken on hot sunny days. Bring a hat and plenty of water. Pick up picnic supplies in Cuges-les-Pins or in Aubagne.

TO BEGIN

Across from the small group of houses that make up the tiny hamlet of Riboux, you'll see a telephone booth and a small concrete pumping station. From there, drive 3 km. on the small dirt road until you see a trail going up a hill to the left. This trail begins about 100 yards after the paved road ends and becomes dirt. It has a chain across it and is marked with a white can top painted with the words *St.-Pilon* in red letters. It is blazed yellow all the way to the top of the mountain, but the blazes can be difficult to find at times. Park along the road.

1. Just beyond a faint trail on the left and another on the right, the blazed trail goes right off the dirt road onto a small trail leading uphill through a dense low forest.

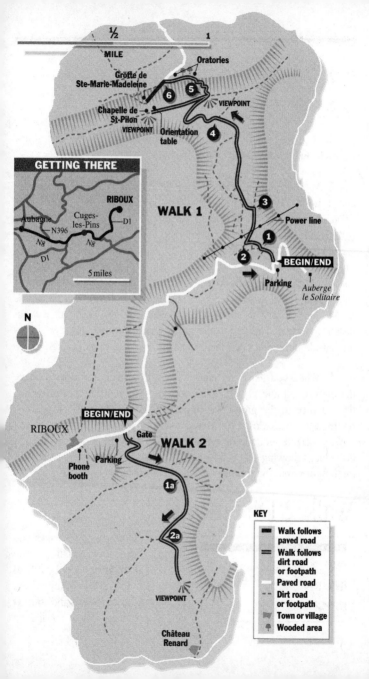

½   1

MILE

Oratories

Grôtte de
Ste-Marie-Madeleine

6   5

VIEWPOINT

Chapelle de
St-Pilon

VIEWPOINT

Orientation
table

4

WALK 1

3

Power line

1

2

BEGIN/END

Parking

*Auberge
le Solitaire*

GETTING THERE

RIBOUX

Aubagne

Cuges-
les-Pins

D1

N396

N8

N8

D1

5 miles

N

RIBOUX

BEGIN/END

Gate

Parking   WALK 2

Phone
booth

1a

2a

VIEWPOINT

Château
Renard

KEY

▬ Walk follows
paved road

▬ Walk follows
dirt road
or footpath

▭ Paved road

- - Dirt road
or footpath

⌂ Town or village

♣ Wooded area

▼

2. Turn right on a broad path heading uphill under a power line.

3. Shortly afterwards, the trail turns left uphill.

4. Near the top of the mountain, in a clear area, the trail splits. Bear left, still following the yellow blazes.

5. At the top of the ridge, the Col de St-Pilon, you reach a four-way intersection. Go left and walk for about ten minutes to the *Chapel of St-Pilon, a small chapel built in the 17th century on the platform of a statue of Mary Magdalene. From an orientation table near the chapel, you can see St-Victoire mountain to the north, the mountains of coastal Provence to the south, and on a clear day the islands off the coast.* From the chapel, retrace your steps to Point 5. Turn right to follow the yellow-blazed trail downhill and back to your car, or turn left to visit the *Grotte de Ste-Marie-Madeleine*, following the white-and-red blazes of a long-distance *GR* trail. The trail to the grotto leads downhill and then across the hillside through a deep, rich forest and past old chapels.

6. When you reach an intersection with a small paved road, leave the blazed trail and go left uphill on the paved road. In a short while, the entrance to the grotto will appear in the cliff face above you. To return, walk back down the paved road, turning right onto the white-and-red-blazed *GR* trail. Take that trail back to Point 5, then go straight downhill, following the yellow-blazed footpath to your car. Watch for the left turn onto the footpath at Point 2 under the power line.

Walk 2 Directions

TIME: 1 hour round-trip
LEVEL: Easy
DISTANCE: 2 miles

This very short, easy walk takes you through the low brush of the Provençal uplands to a beautiful viewpoint above the valley where parts of *Jean de Florette* and *Manon de la Source* were filmed. You'll get a

▼

striking view of *Mont Ste-Baume* and the mountains leading south to the sea.

TO BEGIN

From the phone booth in the hamlet of Riboux, drive straight on the small dirt road 0.4 km. to a big green tank and a small sign that says "La Sauvagère U41," where you park. Walk through a gate and follow a well-worn dirt road. This area is prone to brushfires, so be careful if you smoke, and do not build any fires.

1A. At a Y in the dirt road, bear right. The trail goes around a ridge and then begins to descend.

2A. At the next Y in the road, go left on a trail leading up to the top of a hill, where you'll get a great view. *Not far away in the valley below is the house featured in the Berri films, where the hunchback (played by Gérard Depardieu) lived. The isolated house is now private property, and the owners apparently do not appreciate onlookers.* To return, retrace your steps.

PLACES ALONG THE WALK

■ **Grotte de Ste-Marie-Madeleine.** *Mont Ste-Baume. Open daily year-round.*

OTHER PLACES NEARBY

■ **Aubagne.** Best known as the boyhood home of writer Marcel Pagnol, Aubagne pays tribute to Pagnol with an exhibition in the tourist office called "Le Petit Monde du Marcel Pagnol." *Esplanade de Gaulle, Aubagne 13400, tel. 42-03-49-98. Open daily 9-12 and 2-6. 35 km. west of Riboux by way of rte. N8.*

DINING & LODGING

A few tiny cafés and restaurants in Riboux do a highly erratic seasonal business. If they're open, you can eat inexpensively at the restaurants **Au Rendez-Vous des Chasseurs** (in the village) and **Auberge le**

▼

Solitaire (a well-signposted spot in the forest just east of the starting point of Walk 1). Otherwise, there's a shortage of the kind of restaurants and accommodations we like to recommend. You'd be better off visiting Riboux as a side-trip from Marseille or Aix-en-Provence, or on a spare afternoon while heading through the region toward another part of France.

■ **Le Relais de la Magdeleine** (expensive). This lovely retreat on the edge of the town of Gémenos brings you into the tree-shaded calm of a two-centuries-old home and park. Here you can sleep in large, beautiful rooms with all the comforts of a luxury hotel. The kitchen (moderately priced) mingles local favorites like *filet de rouget au romarin avec ratatouille Provençal* (red mullet fish with rosemary and ratatouille) with its own creations, such as *pavé de canard à l'éventail de poires* (a large cut of duck served with an array of pears). *13420 Gémenos, tel. 42-32-20-16, fax 42-32-02-26. Closed Dec. 1-Mar. 15, Sun. eve., and all day Mon. in winter. Located on the western edge of Gémenos off rte. N396, 5 km. east of Aubagne by way of rte. D2.*

FOR MORE INFORMATION
Tourist Offices:

Aubagne Syndicat d'Initiative. *Esplanade de Gaulle, Aubagne 13400, tel. 42-03-49-98, fax 42-03-83-62. Open daily 9-12 and 2-6. Closed May 1.*

La Mairie of Cuges-les-Pins. *Pl. S. Fabre, Cuges-les-Pins 13780, tel. 42-73-80-11, fax 42-73-81-10. Open Mon., Wed., Fri. 8-12 and 1:30-4:30 and Tue. and Thu. 1:30-4:30.*

For Serious Walkers:

This region presents a spectacular variety of rugged and historic walks through mountains and forests. IGN map 3245E (east), along with a guide available at the Aubagne tourist office, lets you explore up close the world of Marcel Pagnol. With a crude map available from La Mairie of Cuges-les-Pins and IGN map 3345O (west), you can do a walk that takes in some of the famous places in the Jean de Florette films.

Spirit of Somerset Maugham

EXPERIENCE 13:
ST-JEAN-CAP-FERRAT

The Highlights: An untouched seaside resort, a spectacular cliff walk, beautiful beaches and special hotels.

Other Places Nearby: The bustling cities of Nice and Monte Carlo, the captivating village of Eze and its spectacular vistas.

Tucked quietly between bustling Nice and glamorous Monte Carlo, St-Jean-Cap-Ferrat defies time. Although rapid development has gobbled up nearly every inch of available land along the Côte d'Azur, the narrow peninsula of Cap Ferrat and its tiny town of St-Jean have held back the final advance of mass development. For most of this century and much of the last, St-Jean-Cap-Ferrat has served as a seaside escape for nobility and the rich and famous. No one better embodied the languorous, opulently decadent mood of this resort than British writer Somerset Maugham, who made St-Jean-Cap-Ferrat his home for more than 30 years, leaving only for a short time during World War II. This tranquil seaside resort seems to have changed little since the 1930s, when Maugham entertained everybody who was anybody.

In 1928, Maugham bought a former bishop's residence and restored and expanded it. He named it the Villa Mauresque and branded an odd cone-shaped symbol on the front gate, where you can still see it.

▼

Maugham and his companion, Gerald Haxton, relished their social lives. Guests included such celebrities as the Duke of Windsor, Aga Khan, Winston Churchill, H. G. Wells, and Rudyard Kipling. Maugham and Haxton were lavish hosts, and their cook, Annette, was known as one of the best in private service in all of France.

We don't know exactly what these notable guests did with their time—beyond swimming, playing tennis, and socializing—but they certainly didn't have to think about personal details. Maugham assigned each guest a valet and a maid, and he took pleasure in providing appropriate flowers and reading material in their rooms. Guests might stay up to two weeks before wearing out their welcome. Maugham worked each morning in his study and blocked off the view to avoid distractions.

The property suffered considerable damage during the German occupation in World War II, but Maugham returned after the war and quickly restored it to its former glory. Although he continued to travel well into his later years, he always returned to the Villa Mauresque, in the company of his new secretary and companion, Alan Searle. (Haxton died in 1944 of tuberculosis.) Today, Maugham's villa is a private residence and the original property has been subdivided, but the mood of his time lives on in the quiet streets.

If the western side of the peninsula was known for its celebrated residents, the eastern side has a special place in religious history as the burial place of St. Hospice, an early Christian hermit who lived in what is today Nice. Near the chapel dedicated to St. Hospice loomed a fortress protecting the entrance into Nice's harbor. In 778, the Saracens took over the area, staying until the 11th century, when local forces finally defeated them and killed all who couldn't get away.

At Cap Ferrat, rugged cliffs drop abruptly to the sea. Two stunning footpaths follow the face of these cliffs and the rocky shoreline above the frothing sea, permitting you to see the neighborhood of Somerset Maugham, the **chapel of St. Hospice,** and fine views of Nice, the Esterel coast, and the mountains of southern Provence and Italy beyond.

▼

GETTING THERE

By car:

From Nice, the easiest route follows the coastal road, *rte. N98,* 10 km. to the well-marked turnoff to St-Jean. As you enter Cap Ferrat, turn right just after the tourist office, onto the *chemin de Passable,* following the signs to the Plage de Passable. At an intersection, bear right to the beach; park in any of the available spots.

By train:

Trains run regularly between Nice and Beaulieu, from where you can take a taxi to St-Jean.

Walk 1 Directions

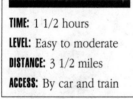

TIME: 1 1/2 hours
LEVEL: Easy to moderate
DISTANCE: 3 1/2 miles
ACCESS: By car and train

Although this loop makes for a relatively long walk, you'll encounter surprisingly few ups and downs considering the terrain. You can significantly shorten the distance by driving to the lighthouse *(phare,* in French) by way of the *blvd. Général de Gaulle* and the *chemin du Phare.* Park at the lighthouse *(see* Point 3, below), and walk down to the cliffside trail above the sea; turn right to walk along the cliffs and get views of Nice and the Esterel coast, or turn left for views of Italy. Those who want to take along a picnic can pick up supplies in the town of St-Jean, in shops on and around the *ave. D. Semeria.*

TO BEGIN

From your parking space at the Plage de Passable (a beach), walk up the *chemin de Passable* toward town.

1. Quickly bear right onto the *chemin du Roy,* leaving the *chemin de Passable* to your left.

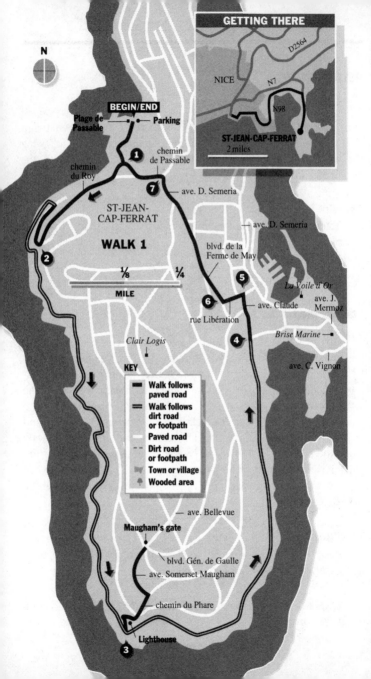

GETTING THERE

D2564

NICE

N7

N98

ST-JEAN-CAP-FERRAT

2 miles

BEGIN/END

Plage de Passable

Parking

① chemin de Passable

chemin du Roy

⑦ ave. D. Semeria

ST-JEAN-CAP-FERRAT

ave. D. Semeria

WALK 1

blvd. de la Ferme de May

②

⑤

La Voile d'Or

⅛   ¼

MILE

⑥   ave. Claude

ave. J. Mermoz

rue Libération

Brise Marine

④

Clair Logis

ave. C. Vignon

KEY

▬▬ Walk follows paved road

═══ Walk follows dirt road or footpath

Paved road

--- Dirt road or footpath

Town or village

Wooded area

— ave. Bellevue

Maugham's gate

blvd. Gén. de Gaulle

ave. Somerset Maugham

chemin du Phare

③ **Lighthouse**

▼

2. When the *chemin du Roy* loops uphill to your left, go straight through the gate and down a seemingly private road. The road loops and goes downhill to a parking area. From here, a small path goes left and left again to reach the cliffside trail. Follow the clearly marked trail along the cliff, taking in dramatic views to the west of Nice and the coastal mountains of the Esterel coast.

3. About 20 minutes beyond Point 2, you reach the lighthouse at the Pointe Malalongue, the southernmost tip of the peninsula. *From here, you can walk up to see the famous gate marking the entrance to Somerset Maugham's former home. Walk uphill two blocks on the chemin du Phare. Make a left on the ave. Somerset Maugham. You will see the gate with Maugham's symbol between the intersections of the blvd. Général de Gaulle and the ave. Bellevue.* Retrace your steps, and go left on the coastal trail. If you opt not to see Maugham's home, continue on the coastal trail and walk for about 20 minutes.

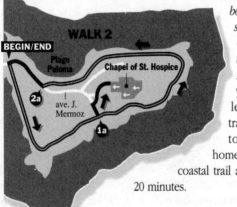

4. On the edge of town, the trail ends in a small private road open to pedestrians. A gate leads onto the *ave. Claude.* Follow this road for two short blocks.

5. *The ave. Claude* ends at the *rue de la Libération,* where you turn left and walk another short distance.

6. *The Rue de la Libération* quickly ends at the *blvd. de la Ferme de May,* where you go right. This road quickly intersects with the *ave. des Etats-Unis,*

▼

where you bear right again. In a few minutes, bear left on *ave. D. Semeria.*

7. When you reach another intersection, bear left on the *chemin de Passable,* following signs to the Plage de Passable. Go down the hill on the *chemin de Passable* and bear right onto a narrow path leading down toward the beach. When you get to the bottom, turn right onto the paved road back to the beach parking lot.

Walk 2 Directions

TIME: 1 hour
LEVEL: Easy
DISTANCE: 1 1/2 miles

This is a shorter route than Walk 1, exploring the headland that juts east out of the main peninsula of St-Jean-Cap-Ferrat. This peaceful walk was the scene of fierce fighting during the time of the Saracens in the 11th century.

TO BEGIN

Walk to or park at the intersection of the *ave. Jean Mermoz* and the *ave. Claude Vignon.* You'll see the clearly marked sign for the Sentier Touristique (Tourist Footpath), a path going off toward the shore and facing the open sea. Follow the path.

1A. About ten minutes into your walk, a road goes left uphill. Make a left and then a quick right to the chapel of St. Hospice and a hilltop view, about a ten-minute walk from the seaside path. To resume the walk, retrace your steps to Point 1A. Turn left onto the coastal trail. In less than 20 minutes you'll reach the Plage Paloma.

2A. A few minutes beyond the Plage Paloma, you arrive at the *ave. Jean Mermoz;* turn right and walk five minutes to your starting point.

OTHER PLACES NEARBY

■ **Ephrussi de Rothschild Foundation.** The former estate of the Rothschilds occupies a beautiful setting with spectacular views and love-

▼

ly gardens. *Ave. D. Semeria, tel. 93-01-33-09, fax 93-01-31-10. Open daily 10-6. Take rte. D25 about 1 km. north from the town of St-Jean.*

■ **Nice.** This large, bustling city has several points of interest: a charming historic center, cathedrals, the elegant *blvd. des Anglais,* Roman ruins, and the Marc Chagall and other notable museums. *6 km. west of St-Jean.*

■ **Monaco.** This tiny but glamorous principality is the place to visit a famous casino, tropical gardens, museums, and the old town and palace at Monte Carlo. *11 km. east of St-Jean.*

■ **Eze.** There's a spectacular view, old streets, a cactus garden, and the remains of a 14th-century castle in this old town. Walk the *Sentier Frédéric-Nietzsche*, a path on which the great German philosopher conceived *Thus Spake Zarathustra. 10 km. northeast of St-Jean.*

DINING

For all its charm, St-Jean-Cap-Ferrat is in one of the most congested parts of France, so do not expect a rustic dining experience. We mention here the most highly recommended restaurants in town; most offer views of the port or the sea, but their relatively high prices reflect the area's popularity with out-of-town visitors.

■ **Voile d'Or** (expensive). An outdoor terrace and a striking view add to the appeal of what is probably the most refined dining experience in town. The general emphasis is on fresh fish, with such offerings as *primeurs de saison de grosses crevettes en salade* (fresh fruits and vegetables in a salad of prawns flavored with coriander), *soupe de poisson de roche* (a soup of rockfish with a light Rouille sauce and croutons), and *jambalaya de crustaces et coquillages comme à Key West* (jambalaya of shellfish Key West style). *Port de St-Jean-Cap-Ferrat 06230, tel. 93-01-13-13, fax 93-76-11-17. Open daily Mar.-Oct. Closed Nov.-Feb.*

■ **Le Provencal** (expensive). An elegant highly rated restaurant with views of the port. Expect haute cuisine with an emphasis on seafood. *Ave. D. Semeria, Port de St-Jean-Cap-Ferrat 06230; tel. 93-76-03-97; fax 93-76-05-39.*

■ **Le Sloop** (moderate). Come here for well-presented local fare at relatively low prices. The portside location and terrace enable patrons

▼

to enjoy a refreshing sea breeze. On our visit, specials included *soupe de poissons du pays* (soup of local fish) and *saumon frais rôti* (roasted salmon in a tomato-basil sauce). *Port de Plaisance, St-Jean-Cap-Ferrat 06320, tel. 93-01-48-63. Open daily Apr.-Sep. Closed Wed. Oct.-mid-Nov. and mid-Dec.-Mar.; closed mid-Nov. to mid-Dec.*

■ **Pizzéria le Saint-Jean** (inexpensive). Capture the sea breezes at this popular local spot, featuring pretty views of the bay and the town. Typical fare includes crisp wood-fired pizzas, salads, seafood, hamburgers, beer, and wine; try a plateful of steaming mussels. *7 pl. Clémenceau, St-Jean-Cap-Ferrat 06230, tel. 93-76-04-75. Open daily except Wed.*

LODGING

■ **Voile d'Or** (very expensive). Luxury amenities, a swimming pool, beautiful room decor, and views of the port compensate for this hotel's central location and nondescript architecture. No credit cards accepted. *Port de St-Jean-Cap-Ferrat 06230, tel. 93-01-13-13, fax 93-76-11-17.*

■ **Hotel Brise Marine** (expensive). Experience St-Jean-Cap-Ferrat the way it must have been during Maugham's time in this old villa converted into a tiny hotel. The charming rooms have beautiful views of the sea and of a lovingly arranged terrace garden below. The location assures absolute quiet, marred only by the sounds of your neighbors (if you're unlucky) through the somewhat thin walls. *58 ave. Jean Mermoz, St-Jean-Cap-Ferrat 06230, tel. 93-76-04-36, fax 93-76-11-49. Open Feb. 1-early Nov.*

■ **Clair Logis** (moderate). In a surprisingly quiet garden location, near the top of the hill outside of the town, the Clair Logis exudes a sleepy Mediterranean charm. The guest rooms are cheerful, clean, and well-maintained, especially for the price. *12 ave. Centrale, St-Jean-Cap-Ferrat 06230, tel. 93-76-04-57, fax 93-76-11-85. Closed Nov.-Feb. 15, except for two weeks at end of Dec.*

FOR MORE INFORMATION

Tourist Office:

Office de Tourisme-Syndicat d'Initiative. *59 ave. D. Semeria, St-Jean-Cap-Ferrat 06230, tel. 93-76-08-90, fax 93-76-16-67. Open weekdays 8:30-12 and 1-5.*

Bridge to Another Time

EXPERIENCE 14:
GRAND CANYON OF VERDON

I f you've spent a couple of days on the congested Riviera, you'll long for an escape to the countryside. Heading north from the coast, you won't have far to go to discover a rugged landscape of intriguing diversity—mountains, plateaus, and valleys verdant with fields and forests.

> **The Highlights:** Remarkable views of one of Europe's deepest canyons, an ancient bridge and footpath, tunnels to walk through, a ghost town.
>
> **Other Places Nearby:** Remote medieval villages, a fortified monastery converted into a luxury hotel.

Just about a two-hour drive north of Nice, near the historic route of Napoleon's triumphant return to France in 1814, you'll find the most dramatic natural feature of this wild region—the **Grand Canyon of Verdon.** It's not big by American standards—the Arizona Grand Canyon is almost twice as deep—but its wild and remote terrain, unchanged for centuries, evokes a mood quite distinct from the modern hubbub of the Riviera. In the 30 km. (18 miles) between Castellane, on the eastern side of the Grand Canyon, and Lac de Ste-Croix to the west, roads follow a winding, vertiginous route through the mountains, passing through only a few small villages.

Many peoples have crisscrossed this canyon since before the time

▼

of Christ; although the region had little importance in terms of mineral or agricultural wealth, it lay at a crossroads of travelers heading in all directions. On Walk 1, when you cross the ancient **Pont du Tusset,** a bridge over the raging Verdon river, you can imagine the Romans, Celts, Vandals, Visigoths, Burgonds, Ostrogoths, French, and Arabs who undoubtedly crossed the original version of this bridge. While most of these travelers rarely stayed for long in this forlorn region, a small local population has eked a living out of this tormented landscape, precariously close to a sky that seems perpetually changing.

Geologists don't agree on the exact cause of the Grand Canyon. Its topsy-turvy terrain—towering mountains of uplifted sedimentary rock, huge cliffs thrust up in every direction, massive piles of rock, and rugged plateaus—suggests a dizzying display of geologic possibilities. The Verdon river rises in the Alps and carves its route down through the foothills and a huge upland area of limestone formed by a prehistoric ocean that covered the area. The jade-colored water slices its way through the limestone to a maximum depth of 2,400 feet at a mountain called La Dent d'Aire before reaching a vast reservoir, the Lac de Ste-Croix.

Mediterranean and sub-Alpine climates meet here, yielding a variety of plant life, from desertlike plateaus to rich forests. In more rugged areas, you may see lavender, astragalus, thyme, rosemary, and sage. In the forests, you'll find oak, hazel, cherry, juniper, sumac, beech, maple, Scotch pine, larch, raspberry bushes, and elderberries.

It is believed that people inhabited the area as early as 10,000 B.C. and that the earliest residents were of Ligurian origin. These early peoples built small forts, called *oppidum,* on rocky summits suitable for defense, near which they lived. They built terraces to shore up their fields, and then against those terraces they leaned their homes, which were usually low, with stone walls and a sloping roof. Subtle traces of this past habitation can still be seen in ancient bridges, footpaths, collapsed wells, rock walls, and caves once carved out as crude dwellings.

In Walk 1, below, you'll traverse the ruins of **Encastel,** a village of unknown origin abandoned by the end of World War I, when the last

▼

of its youths were killed. Some Roman traces found near the sight suggest that people could have lived there thousands of years ago.

In later centuries, the canyon was home to a motley crew of bandits, counterfeiters, Protestants escaping the authorities, and farmers trying to eke out a meager existence in remote agricultural areas. The Grand Canyon region contains little in the way of mineral wealth, so it has produced mostly farm products, including lavender, barley, wheat, and rye grown on terraced fields. You'll find a few fertile fields still farmed to this day, but to a much smaller extent than in the 19th century, when the region's population probably reached its apex. Until then, residents raised sheep to support a local cloth-making industry, and a few continue to raise sheep or keep bees. But even when farmers, hunters, fishermen, and honey gatherers succeeded in producing their goods, they faced the daunting task of getting them to market through the region's rugged geography. The footpath followed on Walk 1 is one of the routes taken by farmers bringing their products to market.

The main population center near the canyon is **Castellane**—a medieval village perched against an imposing cliff topped by a chapel and surrounded by mountains. One of its great families, the Castellanes, ruled it for several hundred years at the beginning of this millennium. The noblemen of Castellane also built a fortress outpost in the tiny town of **Rougon,** standing on the eastern end of the canyon. From there you can still look out on the same view of the canyon seen by the castle's guardians hundreds of years before.

The 20th century has brought with it probably the region's most successful industry of all, tourism. Tens of thousands of people visit the area each year, despite its lack of hotels and restaurants. Those exploring the canyon on foot use trails created by Isidore Blanc, a teacher from Rougon who loved walking in the region. Blanc helped the famous French spelunker Edouard Martel explore and map the area in the early 20th century.

At the beginning of this century, engineers began an effort to divert the waters of the Verdon to generate electricity. They hollowed out tunnels in the cliff face near the water's edge in the now famous **Couloir de Samson** (Samson Corridor), where the water was to be diverted.

▼

Financial troubles ended the project, but today the tunnels are part of the long-distance *GR* trail running the length of the canyon floor.

GETTING THERE

By car:

From Cannes, take the famous *rte. Napoléan, rte. N85,* through Grasse all the way to Castellane. From Castellane, take *D952* west. A few minutes after a turnoff for *rte. D955,* you'll go through a small tunnel and see a turnoff on the left for the Couloir de Samson. Make a left, and go downhill less than 1/2 km. to a parking area. (Careful observers will see the white-on-red blazes of a *GR* trail cross the road.) Park along the road or at the edge of the campground.

Walk 1 Directions

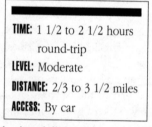

TIME: 1 1/2 to 2 1/2 hours
round-trip
LEVEL: Moderate
DISTANCE: 2/3 to 3 1/2 miles
ACCESS: By car

You only have to walk a short distance downhill to reach a beautiful spot by the rushing turquoise waters of the Verdon and the Pont du Tusset. An optional longer route climbs up to the ruins of an old village, Encastel, and a dramatic view of the canyon, then returns along the same route. The trail leads uphill through a dense forest for most of the way, making this an enjoyable walking tour even on hot days, despite the gain in elevation. You can pick up picnic provisions in Castellane.

TO BEGIN

Walk away from the road to the back of the campground and into the woods, where you go immediately right on a white-on-red-blazed *GR* trail heading steeply downhill for about ten minutes.

1. Cross the Pont du Tusset, *an old bridge built on the site of an even older one dating to Roman times. Those looking for a picnic spot in*

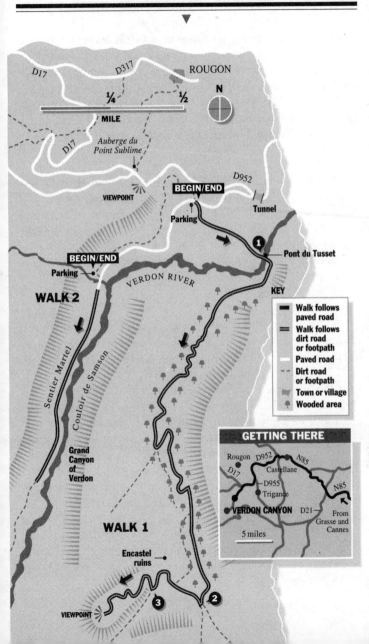

N

¼   ½

MILE

ROUGON

D17   D317

D17

Auberge du Point Sublime

VIEWPOINT

D952

BEGIN/END

Parking

Tunnel

1 — Pont du Tusset

BEGIN/END

Parking

VERDON RIVER

KEY

WALK 2

Sentier Martel

Couloir de Samson

Grand Canyon of Verdon

WALK 1

- ▬▬ Walk follows paved road
- ═══ Walk follows dirt road or footpath
- ▬▬ Paved road
- - - Dirt road or footpath
- 🌲 Town or village
- 🌲 Wooded area

Encastel ruins

3

VIEWPOINT

2

GETTING THERE

Rougon   D952   N85

D17   Castellane

D955

Trigance

VERDON CANYON   D21

From Grasse and Cannes

N85

5 miles

▼

a dramatic setting need go no farther than the old bridge, which strad-
dles the river at one of its narrowest and fastest-moving points, at the
entrance to the deepest portion of the gorge. Once over the bridge, go
right on the well-marked narrow trail going up the hill (huge cliffs
will be to your left). You will be following the white-on-red blazes of
the long-distance *GR* trail and the yellow blazes of a *PR* trail. Ignore
several paths that lead off into the woods to your right as you proceed uphill.

2. After over one mile of walking uphill (slow walkers could take
45 minutes), you reach a broad road. The white-on-red *GR* trail goes
uphill to your left, but you go to the right, following a broad road
downhill. *You'll notice the ruins of Encastel to your right in the fertile*
meadow between the forest and the surrounding cliffs. Either now or on
your way back, you might want to wander through the ruins, an isolated
rural village of the past. Walk downhill for about five minutes. You'll
still be on the *PR* trail.

3. Just before the broad trail winds downhill to the left and
toward the woods, you'll go right on a small path that leads
toward a low rocky ridge rising up to the left of the ancient village. Follow the trail up the short but steep climb to the ridgetop,
with the site of Encastel to your right and the steep cliff of a
mountain behind and to your left. The trail follows the ridgetop,
and you walk along it until you can go no farther (about five minutes or less.) *A breathtaking view of the canyon and its famous*
Couloir de Samson rewards your effort. Directly above the opposite
riverbank in the canyon below, you may make out the brown trace
of the Sentier Martel (Martel Path), snaking its way above the
river's edge.

To return, retrace your steps down the ridge and then uphill on the
road that leads back to the white-on-red- and yellow-blazed trails. Go
left downhill, following the dual blazes of the *GR* and *PR* trail you took
on the way up. These blazes will lead you right back over the bridge
and to your car.

▼

Walk 2 Directions

TIME: 1/2 hour or more round-trip
LEVEL: Easy to moderate
DISTANCE: Your discretion

This well-known excursion represents one of the most unique canyon walks anywhere: through the tunnels of the Couloir de Samson. Although there may be a lot of other visitors here, the sensation of burrowing through solid rock is so memorable you may not even notice the company. Bring at least one flashlight to light your way through the two lengthy tunnels. Go as far as you like and then retrace your steps to your car; the trail goes almost the entire length of the canyon. You encounter relatively few ups or down, but some people might find the footing tricky at times, since you have to negotiate a small ladder and rocky trails.

Begin by proceeding along the same access road taken to reach Walk 1. Go past the parking area used in Walk 1 and on to another at the end of the road. A round parking lot and a national park sign indicate where to stop. A posted map clearly shows the route leading through the Samson Corridor. Go along the trail as far as you want and then turn back. You'll have no sense of monotony, since you will get yet another perspective—this time from the bottom of this tortuous river canyon.

OTHER PLACES NEARBY

■ **Castellane.** This medieval village surrounded by mountains is the chief town of the region. *East of the canyon on rte. D952.*

■ **Rougon.** Perched on the eastern end of the Grand Canyon of Verdon, this tiny town grew around a medieval fortress. *From Castellane, take rte. D952 to Rougon, then go right on rte. D17 toward Rougon.*

■ **Trigance.** Yet another medieval hamlet, this village is the site of the fortified castle Château de Trigance, a former monastery turned into a luxury hotel (*see* Dining and Lodging, below). *From Castellane, take rte. D952, then rte. D955.*

▼

DINING & LODGING

This remote and desolate region does not present a great number of alternatives for overnight visitors. The lack of any big population center, and the highly seasonal tourist trade, have discouraged hoteliers, so most of your choices consist of simple restaurants in the region's small towns. There are three hotels in the area that also offer the best dining options (listed below). In the vicinity of the canyon itself you'll find mostly small seasonal snack bars with sporadic hours. Many visitors here come to camp, and there are abundant facilities for doing so.

■ **Château de Trigance** (moderate to expensive). Here's your chance to stay in a fortified castle, one that once served as a place of meditation for monks above the tiny village of Trigance. The ancient walls, dramatic hilltop setting, and ancient-style rooms with modern conveniences combine to create a unique hotel experience. Almost all of the rooms in this Relais & Châteaux hotel have views, and all are decorated with an emphasis on the hotel's medieval origins; Room 4 has exposed stone walls and offers a stunning panorama. Walkers will delight in a network of trails traversing the hills behind the castle. Within the stone walls of the elegant but expensive restaurant, you'll be served what is undoubtedly the best cuisine in the region. *Trigance 83840, tel. 94-76-91-18, fax 94-47-58-99. Closed mid-Nov. to mid-Mar. From Castellane, take rte. D952 and then rte. D955 to Trigance, where you make a right on the road leading up to the village and the hotel.*

■ **Le Viel Amandier** (moderate). Right below the castle, in the village of Trigance, this small, new hotel offers a pool and a quiet location away from the main road below town. The clean rooms have modern conveniences but a nondescript decor and surprisingly small windows, considering the view. Given the lack of options in the region, this is probably the only choice for those seeking a quiet location at moderate prices. The restaurant, which offers inexpensive to moderate meals, has a wood-and-fern decor, a chef who strives (with some success) for creativity, and plenty of windows overlooking the valley. *Trigance 83840, tel. 94-76-92-92, fax, 94-85-68-65. Closed Tue. except Jun.-Sep., and all of Jan. From Castellane, take rte. D952 and then rte. D955 to Trigance, where you make a right on the road leading up to the village and the*

▼

hotel, located just before the Château de Trigance.

■ **Auberge du Point Sublime** (moderate). This café, restaurant, and hotel is a lively place next to a well-known canyon overlook that's bustling with tourists in season. Certainly not an escape, it nonetheless offers comfortable accommodations and good food and is one of your few options in this desolate region. Specialties on your visit might include *civet d'agneaux* (lamb stew) and *truite meunière* (trout meuniere) as well as lots of homemade pastries. *Rte. D952, Rougon 04120, tel. 92-83-60-35, fax 92-83-74-31. Open daily for lunch and dinner. Closed early Nov.-mid-Mar. Located 17 km. west of Castellane on rte. D952.*

■ **Buvette de Subis** (inexpensive). Talk about a remote location for a *gîte d'étape*—this one is perched above the valley of a tributary of the Verdon, about 10 km. from Rougon. The hostel offers bunk beds, clean bathrooms, and an inexpensive meal if you don't want to cook your own. *Rte. D17, Les Subis, La Palud/Verdon 04120, tel. 92-83-65-34. Open all year. From Castellane, take rte. D952 to Rougon, then go right on rte. D17 toward Rougon. Before the village, make a left and follow signs.*

■ **Gîte d'Etape Trigance** (inexpensive). This tiny village operates a hostel in an old farmhouse on the edge of a small recreation area. *La Mairie, Trigance 93840, tel. 94-76-91-01, fax 94-76-92-44. From Castellane, take rte. D952 and then rte. D955 to Trigance, where you make a right on the road leading to the village. The hostel appears shortly on your left.*

FOR MORE INFORMATION

Tourist Office:

Office de Tourisme. *Rue Nationale, Castellane 04120, tel. 92-83-61-14, fax 92-83-74-36. Open 8:30-7 Jul.-Aug. and 8:30-12 and 1:30-6 Sep.-Jun. Closed Sun., Christmas, and New Year's.*

For Serious Walkers:

IGN map 3442E (east) covers almost the entire area of the Grand Canyon and clearly shows all of the trails described in this experience.

Village in the Forest

EXPERIENCE 15:
ST-SYMPHORIEN

Slow down, traveler, you're going too fast. Often we race around visiting the famous castles, cities, and museums of France, determined to see everything—and we end up seeing nothing. We rush right by tiny villages and forests where

> **The Highlights:** A rich forest of pines and oak, a hidden village, the boyhood stomping grounds of French author François Mauriac.
>
> **Other Places Nearby:** A giant dune, undeveloped beaches and forests, a healing spring in a tiny village (*see* Experience 16, Villandraut, and Experience 17, St-Macaire).

a wealth of knowledge is hidden about the way life once was. Nowhere is this more evident than on this itinerary around St-Symphorien. On this short walk, you'll discover the boyhood playground of the beloved French writer and journalist François Mauriac and learn about customs that may no longer exist by the time today's children reach adulthood.

St-Symphorien is located in what is called the Lande Girondine, in the southwest of France, south of Bordeaux. Although it's covered today with pine and oak forests, until the 19th century it was a landscape of low shrubs, brush, and grasses. The area is so flat and sandy that from ancient times the inhabitants barely supported themselves

▼

with small-scale farming and by raising goats and sheep. To grow grass for grazing, locals would turn the soil, pull out and burn roots and shrubs, and spread the ashes back over the soil, which impeded the growth of forests. By the early 18th century, trees covered only one-fifth of the territory that is woodland today.

P easants lived in tiny villages known as *airials*, small groups of wooden houses with low sloping roofs and broad wooden facades providing enough of an overhang to offer shelter for outdoor dining or relaxing. Near the homes would be a communal bread oven, enclosures for sheep and chickens, a vegetable patch, and, a little farther away, a small wheat field and possibly some beehives. On the walking tour, you'll come upon a still-occupied *airial*, **Lassus,** situated along a forest trail (but accessible by car, too).

The region's character changed in the mid-1800s, when the government determined that the soil was suitable for planting pine forests. Pastureland gradually gave way to pine trees, which locals used to produce turpentine. Most of the *airials* disappeared, with people moving into town or out of the region altogether.

This land, rich with forest, birds, and wildlife, was the boyhood home of French writer François Mauriac, born in 1885 in Bordeaux. Of his childhood, he wrote, "I didn't live in Bordeaux except in body. All the school year, my mind never left the countryside of our vacations and joy.... In the countryside, I found myself. The implacable summers, this forest bristling with cicadas, and a sky sometimes tarnished with the immense cloud of sulfur from fires are impregnated into me forever."

Along the forest walk, you'll visit **Le Moulin de Marian,** an old home, barn, and water mill described in Mauriac's novels *Le Mystère Frontenac (Frontenac Mystery)* and *Un Adolescent d'Autrefois (Adolescent of Another Time)*. Many of the author's boyhood references are centered around the **house at Jouannet,** which you can see along the walk—empty now and not open to the public but still owned by the Mauriac family.

Not far from St-Symphorien is the tiny hamlet of St-Léger-de-Balson, where, just off *rte. D8* on a small dirt road, the **Fontaine de St-**

▼

Clair bubbles up with healing waters for the eyes. Nearby is the charming 15th-century **Church of St. Clair,** where you'll find on the tile floor so-called *pas d'oie* (goose prints) that indicated where lepers were to stand in the church.

Another old-fashioned pastime that survives here is the annual hunt for the *palombe,* or wood pigeon. This is no ordinary hunt but one requiring enormous patience and ingenuity. The hunters set up a system of nets and put a mechanical device attached to live *palombes* high in the trees. Rising before dawn, they hide in sheds or areas of dense underbrush and wait for palombes to pass on their annual migration. When a flock appears—and days can pass without any going overhead—the hunters activate the device to agitate the *palombes* in the tree, hoping to attract the wild *palombes.* When the birds land in the treetops, they see the live bird below and descend to the forest floor, where the hunters hope to capture them in the nets.

To this day, walkers in the region during autumn stay well clear of these hunters, out of respect for the difficult, delicate nature of their hunt. When coming upon a *palombe*-trapping site, walkers are asked to whistle and await a response. If you hear none, stay well clear of the site. (This walking route passes through a known trapping location, which is indicated on the map.)

Ancient ways struggle to survive in spite of the flight of young people from the countryside. The communal life of the *airial* has all but disappeared, but the forests retain that magical mood and the special tranquillity that François Mauriac wrote of fondly.

GETTING THERE
By car:

From Bordeaux, take *autoroute A61* south to the exit for Langon. At a traffic circle shortly after the toll, go right following signs to Bazas. The road ends shortly; make a right on *rte. D932* toward Bazas. Just before Bazas, go right on *rte. D11* toward Villandraut. Go straight through Villandraut, following signs for St-Symphorien by way of *rte. D3.* Park in front of the church in the heart of the village.

▼

Walk Directions

TIME: 2 1/2 hours
LEVEL: Moderate
DISTANCE: 5 1/2 miles
ACCESS: By car

Since the landscape around here is flat, this loop through the forest, past an *airial* and some Mauriac landmarks, is not too strenuous, despite its length. Most of it is along paved roads or dirt paths, and painted wooden posts help you find your way since this is the walking circuit of François Mauriac. This region of France selected its own system of trail-blazes: wooden posts with painted tops. You'll only see the posts at intersections, where they indicate which path you're to take. You might want to picnic near Lassus or Le Moulin de Marian; you can pick up provisions in St-Symphorien.

TO BEGIN

With your back to the front of the church, walk toward a statue and the main road. In front of the statue, go left on a small road leading between houses, the *rue du Lavoir*.

1. Turn left at a T intersection, onto a small paved road that goes over a stream, *blvd. de la Gare*. Continue on this road a few minutes.

2. Make a right onto a small road, *rte. D220E3*. Follow it for about five minutes.

3. When the paved road veers right (near a yield sign), go straight on a dirt road heading toward the forest. You'll notice a yellow-and-green-painted post.

4. When you reach some small pine trees, take the path that bears left. Follow this dirt forest road straight for almost half an hour, noting yellow-and-green posts along the way. *You're in the heart of the pine woods, characteristic of the Landes region marking the Mauriac trail.*

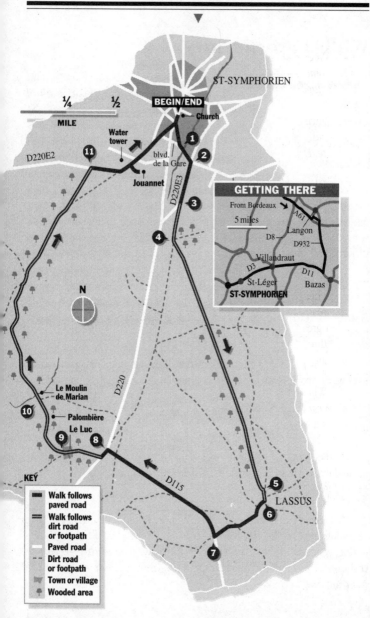

ST-SYMPHORIEN

BEGIN/END
Church
1
2
blvd. de la Gare
Water tower
11
Jouannet
D220E2
D220E3
3
4

1/4   1/2
MILE

N

Le Moulin de Marian
Palombière
Le Luc
10
9
8
D220
D115
5
6
LASSUS
7

GETTING THERE
From Bordeaux → A61
5 miles
Langon
D8
D932
Villandraut
D3
D11
St-Léger
Bazas
ST-SYMPHORIEN

KEY
▬▬ Walk follows paved road
═══ Walk follows dirt road or footpath
━━ Paved road
- - - Dirt road or footpath
🌲 Town or village
🌲 Wooded area

▼

5. You come out in a clearing under oak trees. Turn right on a dirt road between oaks and walk into *Lassus, a typical forest* airial. *You'll see several homes, a communal bread oven and barn, and ruins of part of the old village.*

6. Once you've passed through the tiny hamlet, turn right on a paved road. Follow it around a curve to the left and then to the right, toward *rte. D115.*

7. Make a right onto *rte. D115* and follow it for about 20 minutes, until you reach *rte. D220.*

8. Turn left onto *rte. D220,* cross the road, and follow it for about 20 yards. Across from an electric pole, turn right onto a forest trail under oak trees. Follow this trail for about five minutes.

9. When you reach a clearing, cross a yard by going through a grassy area between a house and an electric pole. Then bear right toward a green post on the edge of the forest. You'll walk for about ten minutes through a forest of silver birch and American oak trees, passing through an area sometimes used by hunters of the *palombe.*

10. When you reach another clearing, *you'll see the old home, barn, and water mill, Le Moulin de Marian, mentioned by Mauriac in his novels.* Cross a tiny stone bridge over a stream. Follow the path that runs between the mill and the barn, heading for a green post. The trail takes you back into the forest. Stay on this main trail, going mostly straight, for a little less than half an hour. Disregard various trails that go off in either direction.

11. The dirt road comes out on *rte. D220E2.* Turn right to head back toward St-Symphorien. After a short distance, turn right down a driveway to look at *Mauriac's childhood home, Jouannet, which sits undisturbed in the forest.* Then go back to *rte. D220E2* and turn right onto it. Follow *rte. D220E2* straight back to the church square and your car.

▼

OTHER PLACES NEARBY

See also Experience 16, Villandraut, and Experience 17, St-Macaire.

■ **Arcachon.** Enjoy an incomparable sunset atop the tallest dune in Europe, the gargantuan Dune du Pilat, 2 3/4 km. long, 1/2 km. wide, and over 300 feet high. The region boasts some of the most scenic, least-developed beaches and forests in France. *About 70 km. west of St-Symphorien by way of rte. 111E to Hostens and Le Graoux; then rte. D3 toward Biganos. Follow signs to Arcachon; the dune is about 5 km. south of Arcachon on rte. D112.*

■ **St-Léger-de-Balson.** Site of the charming old St. Clair Church and adjacent healing fountain as well as the ruins of Castelnau-de-Cernes, a fortified chateau dating to at least the 13th century and covered with underbrush and a stunning stand of bamboo. *Fountain and ruins are off a dirt road to the north of St-Léger. About 2 km. east of St-Symphorien.*

DINING

See also Experience 16, Villandraut, and Experience 17, St-Macaire.

■ **L'Auberge de la Haute Lande** (inexpensive). This favorite of locals is in an *airial* that has maintained much of its rural charm, except for a cluster of rental chalets. The restaurant's cooking is more refined than that of the rustic places listed below. Specials might include *magret de canard au cassis* (breast of duck with a cassis sauce), *coquelet sauce diable* (young chicken cooked in a mustard sauce), or, in winter, local wild boar. You might even find *filet d'autruche* (ostrich.) *Bourideys 33113, tel. 56-25-74-84. Closed Mon. (except in summer) and two weeks in Feb. From St-Symphorien, follow signs south to Bourideys.*

■ **Auberge des Chasseurs** (inexpensive). Although some people might call this a dump, others will enjoy the very rustic atmosphere of this hunters' hangout. You can savor local game and even wild boar (in winter) by a raging fire. Don't miss the apple tarts. *Rte. D3, St-Léger-de-Balson, St-Symphorien 33113, tel. 56-25-71-49. No credit cards. Open every day, except. Wed. in winter. Across from the church, just east of St-Symphorien on the road to Villandraut.*

▼

LODGING

As yet, there are no hotels or bed and breakfasts suitable for *Short Escapes* in this area. Drive a bit farther to the lodgings near Villandraut (*see* Experience 16) or St-Macaire (*see* Experience 17).

FOR MORE INFORMATION

Tourist Offices:

Office de Tourisme de Langon. *11 Allées Jean Jaurès, Langon 33210, tel. 56-62-34-00, fax 56-63-42-46. Open daily, except Sun. in winter.*

Maison de Tourisme de la Gironde. *21 Cours de L'Intendance, Bordeaux 33000, tel. 56-52-61-40, fax 56-81-09-99. Open Mon.-Sat. 9-7. Closed major holidays.*

In conjunction with the regional government, a local resident, Barry Byrne, can assist you with canoe and bike rentals, hiking, nature walks, and guides. Contact *Barry Byrne, Conseil Géneral de la Gironde, Esplanade Charles de Gaulle, Bordeaux 33000, tel. 56-99-33-33, ext. 3611 (during business hours); or La Barthe, Budos, 33720, tel. 56-62-59-48 (Mon.-Fri. 6 p.m-8 p.m.).*

For Serious Walkers:

The regional government has organized the construction of five long but easy walks (coded yellow for the longer walks and green for the local circuits). To obtain a map, contact the Maison de Tourisme de la Gironde. For the walking tour in this experience, use IGN map 1539E (east).

Palaces of the Pope

EXPERIENCE 16: VILLANDRAUT

When people think of the great castles of Europe, the Hautes-Landes hardly comes to mind. Yet buried here in this little-known part of France less than an hour's drive south of Bordeaux are the remains of some of the most authentic and

> **The Highlights:** An authentic medieval castle, a quiet country village, woodland walks along an abandoned railbed, canoeing on a peaceful river.
>
> **Other Places Nearby:** Medieval castles, Sauternes wineries, charming low-priced restaurants and lodgings.

intact castles of medieval times. Most are open to the public and are far from the tourist crowds.

This itinerary lets you explore one of these castles and then walk through a delightful country village along the quiet river Ciron. You'll walk through a forest that marks the transition between the flat pine woods of the Hautes-Landes and the deciduous forests of the Garonne river valley. Afterward, you might even rent a canoe for a peaceful paddle along the river, once teeming with boats laden with materials at the height of castle building during medieval times.

While many of the most famous chateaus of France actually are rebuilt versions of earlier structures, the castles of the Hautes-Landes are

▼

compelling relics of medieval military architecture. Castles in **Villandraut, Budos, Roquetaillade, Cazeneuve,** and **La Trave** were built by the family and friends of Pope Clement V, who was born in Villandraut in 1265. Elected pope in 1305 and installed in Avignon by the French king, he financed the construction of a fortress in Villandraut. It represents a classic version of medieval military architecture, with a good portion of the structure used as living quarters.

Around Villandraut, you'll also discover an element of contemporary history—the struggle to keep France's rural life alive in the face of a huge exodus to the cities (*see* Experience 7, Vézelay, for more on this phenomenon). As French young people abandon the countryside in search of jobs in Paris and other urban centers, local ways of life gradually disappear. Many rural areas have sought industrial investment to create jobs—some without success, others with the inevitable side effects of pollution and unwanted congestion. Yet what seems like a promising alternative—reversing or slowing the rural exodus through development of tourism—actually has been controversial in many communities, and the Hautes-Landes is no exception.

Barry Byrne is one of perhaps thousands of Europeans working in rural communities to develop historical or cultural attractions for tourists, at least on a small scale. An Irishman married to a French woman who teaches in a local school, he began to explore the patchwork of ancient footpaths crossing the forests after they moved to the area. Although maps showed these paths as ancient right-of-ways open to the public, many trails had been blocked by landowners or had become overgrown through neglect. He launched an effort to establish a system of short- and long-distance walking trails linking the region's many areas of natural and historic interest, with brochures and trail signs highlighting local culture and traditions and with canoe and bicycle rentals to help travelers explore the region.

Some landowners feared the effects of walkers and the potential for fire or other damage. Others objected to the idea of having tourists walking around their backyards. But restaurant owners, shopkeepers, and other business people saw this as a potential avenue to prosperity.

▼

Eventually, Byrne and others helped convince the regional government to assist localities in developing a huge regional network of trails—as part of an overall effort to preserve natural areas. A canoe and bicycle center on the Ciron river was set up and a local organization known as Adichats brings in students interested in archaeology to help unearth the region's treasures for scientists and interested travelers.

It's too soon to say what rural tourism will bring to the Gironde, but as you enjoy this escape, look around you for a case study of "green" tourism in the making.

GETTING THERE

By car:

From Bordeaux, take *autoroute A61* south to Langon. At a traffic circle after the toll, go right, following signs to Bazas. When the road ends, go right on *rte. D932* toward Bazas. Just before Bazas, go right on *rte. D11* to Villandraut. Cross the Ciron river and bear right at an intersection. Go left on a road in front of the castle and park in the square.

Walk Directions

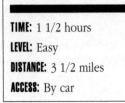

TIME: 1 1/2 hours
LEVEL: Easy
DISTANCE: 3 1/2 miles
ACCESS: By car

You'll follow a local walking trail on a loop out of the village, along the river, through a forest, and back into town. Much of the route is along an abandoned 19th-century railroad bed converted into a bike trail that runs through sandy, pine-wooded terrain and passes some homes. You can find a particularly nice spot for a rest or a picnic on a small bridge in the forest near Point 7.

TO BEGIN

From where you parked, walk toward the castle.

1. Turn right on *rte. D3* and follow it through the heart of the village, bearing left as it leaves town and becomes *rte. D8*.

▼

2. Just before the bridge crossing the Ciron river, bear right into the field by the boat-rental shack. Cross the field to the river. You'll notice a wooden post marking the presence of a local walking trail, the *Boucle Locale de Villandraut*. Follow the trail along the riverbank. You quickly enter the deep shade of the heavily wooded river valley.

3. Just beyond some picnic tables on your right, you reach a field. Bear right along the edge of the field, toward a wooden trail marker. Cross over a low dirt ridge onto a dirt road. Go left, then

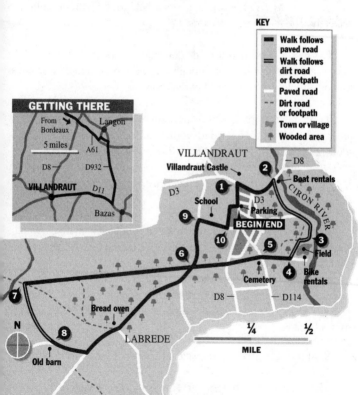

▼

quickly bear left off the dirt road onto a path heading into the forest and marked by a trail post to your left. *You're now following the abandoned bed of the 19th-century railway, running through a forest ravine.*

4. The trail soon comes out on a small paved road and a bike trail, which you follow to the right. A wooden sign on your left reminds you that you're on the local walking trail.

5. Cross *rte. D114.* Proceed across a field to the right of the town cemetery. The trail then crosses *rte. D8.*

6. Cross a small paved road. Continue for about 15 minutes, following the bike trail straight through the pine forest. Ignore any trails leading off into the forest in either direction.

7. At a large intersection marked by wooden posts, make a left on a well-worn dirt road with yellow-orange arrows. *If you wish, continue straight on the railway bed for four or five minutes to a bridge over a small stream—a good place to picnic or spot birds and wildlife. Retrace your steps from the bridge to Point 7.*

8. After following the forest road for about ten minutes, you'll reach the small paved road at the hamlet of Labrede in the heart of an old farm. Turn left and walk a short distance to another paved road. Go left and follow this road back toward Villandraut. *Notice the communal bread oven on your left, a vestige of the time when locals made their own bread in shared ovens. Some are still in use.* Continue on the road as it passes Point 6.

9. At the next paved road, make a right toward the village center.

10. At the next road, turn left. Follow this tiny village road around as it curves to the right, back to your car.

▼

PLACES ALONG THE WALK

■ **Château de Villandraut.** *For information, contact the Association Adichats (see below). Open daily 9:30-12:30 and 3-7 Jun.-Sep.; Sat., Sun., and holidays 10-12:30 and 2-5 Oct.-May. Admission.*

■ **Association Adichats.** Those interested in getting involved in archaeological projects can select from various summer programs. *Maison Labat, Villandraut 33730, tel. 56-25-87-57.*

OTHER PLACES NEARBY

■ **Château de Roquetaillade.** This impressive castle was built in the early 14th century by a nephew of Pope Clement V. Centuries-old trees adorn its park. *Mazeres, Langon 33210, tel. 56-76-14-16. Open daily 10:30-7 Jul.-Aug.; daily 2-5 Easter-Nov. and 2-5 Sun., holidays. Admission. From Villandraut, take rte. D11 to rte. D932 north and watch for the turnoff to the left for the chateau. From Langon, take rte. D932 south 6 km. until the turnoff to the right.*

■ **Château de Budos.** Catch this 13th-century castle before the tourist authorities discover it and start charging admission. Only recently did locals remove a tangle of vines and undergrowth from the impressive walls. *From Villandraut, take rte. D110 toward Balizac, but make a quick right on rte. D114 to Budos. Near the center of Budos, go right following the sign to the ruins, on the village outskirts.*

■ **Château de Cazeneuve.** An interesting fortified 17th-century castle, it has only recently been opened to visitors. *Préchac, Villandraut 33730, tel. 56-25-48-16 and 56-01-14-59, fax 56-65-27-87. Open daily 10-7 Jun. 15-Sep. 15; Sat., Sun., and holidays 2-6:30 Easter-Oct. Admission. From Villandraut, take rte. D9a south to Préchac; make a right to enter village on rte. D11E, then a quick left on rte. D9.*

■ **Château de la Trave.** Only a few walls remain of this once redoubtable castle overlooking the Ciron river in a lovely rural spot. It is said that the legendary Black Prince of the Hundred Years War lived here for a while (*see* St-Macaire, Experience 17). Like the castle at Budos, this place can be visited at any time. *From Villandraut, take rte. D9a south to Préchac. From there, make a left on rte. D11E toward Uzeste. The ruins are on your right, just before the Ciron river.*

▼

■ **Sauternes.** The humid Ciron valley creates just the conditions necessary to produce this region's famed sweet white dessert wines, named after the tiny town. You'll see signs offering *dégustations,* or tastings, and there's a cooperative shop in the heart of the village.

DINING

■ **Domaine de Fompeyre** (moderate to inexpensive). The menu offers simple but flavorful meat, fish, and game garnished with fresh local produce and served in an inviting room with large windows and warm colors. On our visit, the inexpensive menu featured *pâtes fraîches à la crème de saumon fumé* (fresh pasta with a salmon cream sauce) and *entrecôte aux échalotes* (rib steak grilled with shallots). *Bazas 33430, tel. 56-25-98-00, fax 56-25-16-25. Closed Sun. evening Oct. 15-May 15. Take rte. D932e9 south of Bazas for about 2 km. toward Captieux; look for a sign indicating the turnoff for the hotel.*

■ **La Table du Sauternais** (moderate to inexpensive). Local wines and food products show up in all of this chef's offerings, among the most refined in the region. On the menu, you might find *escalope de truite de mer au Sauternes* (thinly cut sea trout served with Sauternes wine) or *entrecôte à la sauce bordelaise et ses garnitures de légumes* (rib steak with red wine sauce, garnished with fresh vegetables). *Preignac 33210, tel. 56-63-43-44. Open daily except Mon. From Villandraut, go north on rte. D8 11 km. to rte. D116. Turn left toward Pujols, and watch for signs. It's in the tiny hamlet of Boutoc.*

■ **Cirons-Loisirs** (inexpensive). Here you'll eat simple, hearty meals with locals in a very casual, friendly atmosphere. Good choices include *pâté de campagne* (restaurant-made pâté), *côte de mouton grillé* (grilled lamb chops), and *daube de canard à l'ancienne* (a local stew of duck, red wine, onions, and more). *Noaillan 33730, tel. 56-25-89-79. From Villandraut, take rte. D110 about 1 km. toward Balizac, turn right on rte. D114, and look for a sign for the restaurant.*

LODGING

■ **Domaine de Fompeyre** (moderate). This 35-room hotel outside Bazas mixes modern comforts with country charm. Set in a manicured

▼

garden and park, the contemporary hotel offers a pool, golf, and horse-back riding. The cheerful guest rooms have been decorated with a European charm that makes the place feel much older than it is. There's cable TV and a phone in every room. *Bazas 33430, tel. 56-25-98-00, fax 56-25-16-25. Open year-round. Take rte. D932e9 south of Bazas for about 2 km. toward Captieux; watch for signs pointing to the hotel.*

■ **Arbieu** (moderate). Three charming rooms and a suite are open to guests in this *chambres d'hôte,* part of a large country home built in 1850 on a huge private park outside of Bazas. Like the local nobility, you can sit by the private pool and admire the gardens and fields about you. You can even cook a simple meal in the poolside kitchen; other-wise, guests can request a moderately priced dinner. *Rte. D655, Bazas 33430, tel. 56-25-11-18, fax 56-25-90-52. Open Easter-Nov. 1; otherwise upon reservation. Closed for 15 days around Christmas. From Villandraut, take rte. D11 east to Bazas, then rte. D655 toward Casteljaloux. Watch for signs on the right just outside of Bazas.*

■ **La Bastide** (inexpensive). This *chambres d'hôte* offers two clean rooms, each with private bath and toilet. The clucking of chickens and the barking of dogs may greet your arrival, and the home's simple rustic decor and surroundings and the friendly elderly owners will charm those who want to taste the variety of rural life in France. *Rte. D8, Préchac 33730, tel. 56-65-21-17. From Villandraut, take rte. D8 south-west 8 km. The house is at a small intersection on your left.*

FOR MORE INFORMATION
Tourist Offices:
Office de Tourisme de Villandraut. *Pl. de la Mairie, Villandraut 33730, tel. 56-25-31-39, fax 56-25-89-33. Open Mon.-Wed. and Fri.-Sat. 2:30-6, Thu. 10-12:30.*

Maison de Tourisme de la Gironde. *21 cours de L'Intendance, Bordeaux 33000, tel. 56-52-61-40, fax 56-81-09-99. Open Mon.-Sat. 9-7. Closed major holidays.*

In conjunction with the regional government, Barry Byrne can assist you with canoe and bike rentals, hiking, nature walks, and guides. Contact *Barry Byrne, Conseil Géneral de la Gironde, Esplanade*

▼

Charles de Gaulle, Bordeaux 33000, tel. 56-99-33-33, ext. 3611 (during business hours); or La Barthe, Budos 33720, tel. 56-62-59-48 (Mon.-Fri. 6 p.m-8 p.m.).

For Serious Walkers:

The regional government has organized the construction of five long but easy walks (coded yellow for the longer walks and green for the local circuits). To obtain a map, contact the Maison de Tourisme de la Gironde. For the walking tour in this experience, use IGN map 1539E (east). There are also terrific long-distance bicycle trails.

Bastides of Bordeaux

EXPERIENCE 17: ST-MACAIRE

When you drive south out of the busy wine-growing region of Bordeaux along the right bank of the Garonne river, you enter a delightful region long neglected by French and foreign tourists alike. In the Middle Ages, the Garonne river saw plenty of

> **The Highlights:** A walled town, beautiful views of the Garonne river, an impressive Romanesque church, an idyllic canal walk.
>
> **Other Places Nearby:** The wine-growing region of Bordeaux, a castle where Toulouse-Lautrec spent his last days, the beautiful basilica where he was buried.

action, plied frequently by boats carrying wine and wheat in times of peace and warriors in times of war. St-Macaire was a rich city then. But the vagaries of commerce brought on centuries of decline, leaving St-Macaire an insignificant backwater. And therein lies its charm.

During the prosperous medieval era, the towns of this region took on the look they have today: Merchants built their homes side-by-side and erected outer ramparts to protect their wealth from jealous neighbors and marauders. These distinctive cities became known as *bastides,* and hundreds of them still exist in southwest France, south of Bordeaux, many in the region surrounding Agen, upriver from St-Macaire. The *bastide* of St-Macaire still looks much as it did then, unal-

▼

tered by so-called progress. On Walk 1, outlined below, you'll visit some of the **old gates** and **ramparts** that defended the city, as well as its beautiful arched Gothic **marketplace** and the impressive 13th-century **Eglise St-Sauveur**.

The history of this place is linked to wine, which the invading Romans probably introduced to the Gauls. At first, the Romans imported the wine they needed from Italy, but even before the time of Christ vineyards had spread throughout Mediterranean France. The Bordeaux region emerged as an important port for wine exporters serving the newly conquered lands of England. The vineyards in Gaul had taken on such importance by the 1st century A.D. that Italian producers pressured the Roman emperor to have half the vineyards in Gaul destroyed. But this did not impede the Gauls for long. They developed wooden barrels, far more suitable for the transport of wine than the porous amphora (ceramic jugs) used by the Romans, and the Garonne river was thronged with boat traffic carrying tons of wine produced throughout the region.

The fall of Rome and the invasion by barbarians certainly reduced the flow of wine. But when the Vikings developed a taste for it, that created a new market for Bordeaux vintners in Normandy, Flanders, and Scandinavian countries. During the Dark Ages, monks maintained whatever wine-growing activities survived and even improved wine-producing techniques. The man for whom St-Macaire is named—Macaire, born into a prosperous Greek family in Rome in the late 4th century—was a monk who eventually ended up in the Garonne valley, where he organized a group of monks not far from St-Macaire.

Legend has it that one St. Brandon came to St-Macaire each year from Ireland to partake in the wine harvest. As recounted by Robert Escarpit in *Les Contes de la St-Glinglin,* the saint one year brought with him a hapless monk named Galahan O'Galahan. When the saint and the monk landed at the **town dock,** which you pass on Walk 1, a young girl named Lurette asked Galahan his name. Unable to pronounce it, she called him Glinglin. Learning that he had a terrible memory, she taught him how to remember, and Glinglin returned happily to

▼

Ireland with his new powers. The next year, when he returned to St-Macaire with St. Brandon and learned of Lurette's early death, he lost his power of memory again.

After his death, Glinglin spent years trying to find his way to heaven's gate, having forgotten the route the monks had told him. When he finally got there, St. Peter asked him some basic questions about his life, including the date of his baptism. Glinglin could not recall it. "When can I enter Paradise?" Glinglin asked St. Peter. "The day of St. Glinglin," St. Peter told him, going back into Paradise and closing the door. To this day, the story goes, Glinglin sits on a cloud outside of heaven trying to remember the day of his baptism so that he can enter heaven. And that's why, Escarpit explains, when the French say "à la St-Glinglin," they mean "never."

During the Middle Ages, the French and English struggled for control of the Bordeaux region. Through a succession of marriages, much of the local aristocracy was connected to English kings, who kept them loyal by giving them relative autonomy. To defend Bordeaux from French encroachment, King Edward II sent his oldest son, Edward of Woodstock, named the Black Prince (perhaps because of his dark-colored armor). Sweeping through the countryside, he confirmed English rule, and between 1356 and 1367 he acted as a virtual monarch, earning tremendous respect from the nobles and the merchant class. But in 1369, some local nobles resisting a new tax called upon the French king, Charles V, for help. Declaring himself ruler of the entire region, Charles V demanded that the Black Prince come to Paris to pay homage. When the Black Prince refused, war broke out. Various sieges and several cycles of famine and plague crippled the town of St-Macaire, until the French finally forced the English out of the Gironde once and for all in 1453.

Relative peace prevailed for a couple of centuries, and St-Macaire profited from laws protecting the Bordeaux region from competition farther up the Garonne river valley. The religious wars of the 16th century brought havoc to the area, however, and St-Macaire suffered further sieges, from which it never recovered. It was not until recent years and the growing interest in France's patrimony that the town rebounded.

Walk 2 leads you along one of the great engineering boondoggles

▼

of French history—the **Canal Latéral de la Garonne,** a 200-km.-long (120-mile-long) canal that parallels the Garonne near St-Macaire. It was supposed to form a network of waterways connecting the Mediterranean Sea to the Atlantic Ocean. When the canal was conceived in the 1820s, many of the Garonne river towns argued that it would be cheaper simply to dredge and restore the Garonne. The advent of the railroad and steam-powered ships diminished the need for such a waterway, but the authorities proceeded with the project anyway. Just two months after the canal opened in 1856, a parallel rail link went into service.

GETTING THERE:

By car:

From Bordeaux, take *autoroute A61* south to the Langon exit. After the toll, follow the road into Langon, where you'll see signs for St-Macaire, just 4 km. east on *rte. N113*. In a short distance, go right at the turnoff for St.-Macaire onto *rte. D672e6*. When you reach St-Macaire, park in the lot in front of the town's main entrance, marked by a medieval tower.

Walk 1 Directions

TIME: 1 hour
LEVEL: Easy
DISTANCE: 1 1/2 miles
ACCESS: By car

This short walk takes you through the ancient *bastide* of St-Macaire, by the old marketplace and the Eglise St-Sauveur, down to the riverside where St. Brandon is said to have landed each year. You can pick up picnic provisions in the village of St-Macaire.

TO BEGIN

Walk through the opening in the 14th-century tower, the *Porte de Benauge,* onto the *rue Canton.*

1. At the *16th-century Maison de Pays* (Tourist Board), on your

▼

right, turn left onto the *rue Carnot, lined with old homes.*

2. Turn left onto the *pl. du Mercadiou to see the medieval market square. You might also stop by the Musée-Régional des P.T.T. d'Aquitaine (Regional Museum of the Postal Service of Aquitaine), housed in a 16th-century hotel.* Then retrace your steps and continue on the *rue Carnot.*

3. At the end of the road, make a right, then walk to the left of St. Sauveur Church, onto a terrace beside the church and above the Garonne river. Admire the view, then walk toward the church front.

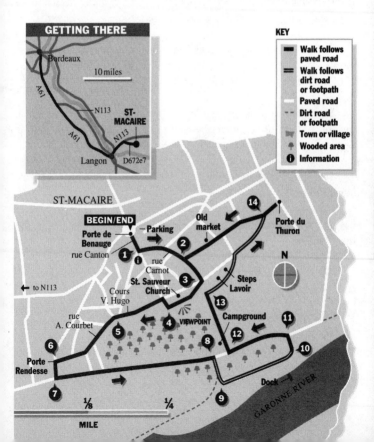

GETTING THERE

Bordeaux

10 miles

A61
N113
ST-MACAIRE
A61
N113
Langon
D672e7

KEY

▬ **Walk follows paved road**

＝ **Walk follows dirt road or footpath**

Paved road

-- **Dirt road or footpath**

Town or village

♣ **Wooded area**

ⓘ **Information**

ST-MACAIRE

BEGIN/END
← Parking

Old market

14

Porte du Thuron

Porte de Benauge
1
rue Canton

ⓘ

2

rue Carnot

St. Sauveur Church
3

Steps Lavoir

← to N113

Cours V. Hugo

13

N

rue A. Courbet

4 **VIEWPOINT**

Campground

11

5

8

12

6

10

Porte Rendesse

7

9

Dock

GARONNE RIVER

⅛   ¼

MILE

▼

4. When you get to the front of the church, *note the intricately carved 13th-century portal.* Then, with your back to the church entrance, go straight on the *Cours Victor Hugo* and walk gradually downhill.

5. At the *pl. Porte Neuve,* turn left down the *rue Amiral Courbet.*

6. Go through the old city gate and make a left. Walk about 25 feet.

7. Turn left, following the signs saying *"Remparts" (the town's old walls). Note the effect of frequent flooding on the buildings closest to the river and you'll understand why the town stands on the hill above.*

8. In front of a park, turn right on a dirt path under a wooden post, toward the riverbank. Tall poplar trees will be to your left, as you're outside the village now, on the river's flood plain.

9. At the riverbank, make a left and walk along the river on a path toward a stone dock. *Somewhere in this area, St. Brandon and St. Glinglin would have landed after their trip from Ireland.*

10. Turn left at the stone dock and follow the small road back toward town.

11. When you reach a paved road just a dozen yards from the river, turn left.

12. When you come to a little paved road heading back to the village, turn right. The park will be on your left as you proceed toward town.

13. In front of the new stone city gate, turn right and walk alongside the old ramparts. Follow the path between the cornfield and the ramparts to the old *lavoir* (communal washing area). Go down to the *lavoir* and then go up the stairs on its other side. Go right onto a dirt

▼

alley. As you head into the village, you'll pass *old homes with tiny gardens awash with color during much of the year.*

14. When you reach the paved road leading back to the town center, *make a right to see the 14th-century tower, the Porte du Thuron.* Then retrace your steps to Point 2 through the old market. When you reach *rue Carnot*, go right, back to the Maison de Pays and your car.

Walk 2 Directions

This stunning, simple stroll takes you alongside the Canal Latéral de la Garonne just at its junction with the Garonne. Admire the impressive locks and the countryside along this tranquil, tree-shaded waterway. Pick up provisions in Langon or St-Macaire and picnic anywhere. To get there from St-Macaire, drive on *rte. N113* to *rte. D226,* following signs to Castets-en-Dorthe. Cross the Garonne river and turn left immediately after the bridge on a small road leading to the locks of the canal. Park your car and cross a small footbridge leading over the locks. Just past the footbridge, make a right and follow the path leading along the canal bank. Ignore the trail that leads off into the woods to your left. Enjoy this beautiful setting.

When you reach the next set of locks, continue straight. In the next 1 km., you come to two bridges over the canal. At either bridge, cross the canal, then make another right onto the trail following the other side of the canal. It will lead you back to your car.

PLACES ALONG THE WALK

■ **St. Sauveur Church.** *Guided visits of the interior available afternoons in summer, Sun. afternoons or by appointment the rest of the year. For information, contact La Mairie (mayor's office), 8 allées des Tilleuls, St-Macaire 33490, tel. 56-63-03-64.*

■ **Musée-Régional des P.T.T. d'Aquitaine.** *Pl. du Mercadiou, St-Macaire 33490, tel. 56-63-08-81. Tours daily except Tue. 10-12 and 2-6:30 Apr. 1-Oct. 15; Sat. and Sun. 2-6:30 Oct. 15-Dec. 1. Closed Dec. 1-Apr. 1.*

▼

OTHER PLACES NEARBY

■ **La Réole.** This small but stunning town overlooking the Garonne features an abbey dating to the time of Charlemagne, many medieval homes, and a rare Romanesque town hall. *14 km. east of St-Macaire on rte. N113.*

■ **Château Malromé.** Here you can visit the 14th-century castle where the artist Toulouse-Lautrec lived for a short time before his death at the age of 37. Several small rooms with lovely views can now be rented in this quiet, beautiful spot. *St-André du Bois 33490, tel. 56-76-44-92, fax 56-76-46-18. Open Sun. and holidays 10-12 and 2-7 Easter-Nov. 1; daily Jun. 1-Sep. 15. The rest of the year, reserve in advance. Admission. About 6 km. north of St-Macaire by way of rte. D672.*

■ **Basilique de Verdelais.** Since medieval times, people have come here in pilgrimage to honor the Virgin Mary. Rebuilt in the 17th century, it houses statuary from much earlier times. In the cemetery, you'll find the grave of Toulouse-Lautrec. *Presbytère de Verdelais, Verdelais 33490, tel. 56-62-02-50, fax 56-62-05-74. Open daily 9-12 and 2-6. Located 4 km. north of St-Macaire by way of rte. D19E.*

■ **Monségur.** To explore this other stunning *bastide,* you can follow a short walking loop that takes you through the town and the river valley below. IGN map 1737O (west) covers the region; walking maps are available across from the town marketplace at the *Syndicat d'Initiative, Monségur 33580, tel. 56-61-60-12. From St-Macaire, take rte. N113 east to La Réole; then take rte. D668 northeast to Monségur.*

DINING

See also Experience 15, St-Symphorien, and Experience 16, Villandraut.

■ **Claude Darroze** (expensive to moderate). Critics dispute the food's quality, with some holding it in high esteem and others unimpressed; we had a sumptuous meal here that handled game and fish with equal aplomb. For an appetizer, you might find *salade de langoustine tiède aux petits artichauts* (warm prawn salad with tiny hearts of artichokes), or as an entrée, *fantaisie de boeuf et riz de veau au foie gras et aux champignons sauvages* (beef and sweetbreads cooked with

▼

pâté and wild mushrooms), or as a dessert, *feuilleté crème légère aux poires caramélisées* (a flaky pastry with light cream and caramelized pears). *95 Cours Géneral Leclerc, Langon 33210, tel. 56-63-00-48, fax 56-63-41-15. Closed Oct. 15-Nov. 5 and Jan. 5-25. Located 3 km. west of St-Macaire by way of rte. N113.*

LODGING

■ **Château de Valmont** (expensive). Nineteen elegant rooms in a winery recently converted into a hotel and located on the edge of a small town. *Circuit du Sauternais, Barsac 33720, tel. 56-27-28-24, fax 56-27-17-53. Open year-round. From St-Macaire, take rte. N113 following signs to Barsac. When you enter town, follow the signs to the hotel.*

■ **Château du Parc** (expensive). Stay in a completely renovated former wine chateau with a friendly English-speaking couple, themselves former winemakers. Beautifully furnished rooms, great views, and a tranquil setting make this a luxury experience for much less than you'd spend elsewhere in France. *Rte. D139, St-Ferme 33580, tel. 56-61-69-18, fax 56-61-69-23. No credit cards. Open year-round. From St-Macaire, take rte. N113 to La Réole, then take rte. D668 to Monségur. From there, take rte. D16 to St-Ferme, where you follow rte. D139 toward Castelmoron d'Albret. The* chambres d'hôte *appears on your right in 1 km.*

■ **Château de la Buche** (moderate). This charming, recently renovated *chambres d'hôte* is located on the edge of the *bastide* town of Monségur. The large, nicely furnished rooms in this 18th-century house have wonderful views of vineyards, hills, and castles. Breakfast is included, and an inexpensive dinner is available with a reservation. *10 ave. de la Porte des Tours, Monségur 33590, tel. 56-61-80-22, fax 56-61-82-04. Open year-round. From St-Macaire, take rte. N113 east to La Réole, then rte. D668 to Monségur. The hotel is at the edge of a park on the outskirts of town on the road to Duras.*

FOR MORE INFORMATION

Tourist Office:

Maison de Pays de St-Macaire. *8 rue Canton, St-Macaire 33490, tel. 56-63-32-14. Hours change frequently.*

Cave Dwellers of France

EXPERIENCE 18: NOIZAY

For most visitors, the Loire valley's massive chateaus illustrate mankind's fundamental desire to build up and out. To those in the know, the region also demonstrates mankind's desire to build in and down, for almost nowhere in the world will you find a better array of cave homes.

> **The Highlights:** Troglodyte homes; sweeping landscapes of farms, vineyards, and the Loire valley.
>
> **Other Places Nearby:** The wine-making village of Vouvray, the chateaus of Amboise and Blois.

The word *troglodyte* evokes images of cave people living in dark and dank places, but the Loire valley's troglodyte homes don't fit that image. Instead, they are cheerful, energy-efficient homes built into the steep southern-facing hillsides of the Loire and Cher valleys. These homes maintain a relatively constant temperature of between 48 and 57 degrees Fahrenheit and aren't likely to go up in smoke, and if you need another room, you just dig deeper or sideways.

Troglodyte homes are one of the surprises in this area, famed not only for chateaus but also for white wines. The walks outlined below take you through vineyards offering beautiful views of the peaceful valley. You'll pass by a tiny wine-making operation in an old troglodyte dwelling, where, if he's home, winemaker Guy Cosme will let you taste

▼

his inexpensive Vouvray wine, which has a following among locals. You can also taste and purchase good local wines at Domaine J. P. Pincendeau and Andre Delalou, other local winemakers along this walk who are open if you come during the day and if they're home.

Y ou'll also pass the home of Francis Poulenc, the 20th-century composer who lived here for many years before his death in 1963. (The house is now privately owned and closed to the public.) Rock singer Mick Jagger has a home near here (a secluded chateau on *rte. D1* just east of Pocé-sur-Cisse), and many locals you'll meet may turn out to be refugees from Paris and other big European cities who were looking for a cheerful retreat from urban life.

Cave dwellings and ancient rock refuges dot the French countryside; while some are naturally occurring caves, many others are manmade. Prehistoric cave dwellings were a matter of convenience—momentary stops in a nomadic lifestyle. In Neolithic times, humans began to make caves their long-term homes, driven underground by the climate, aggression, and lack of solid building materials. With the coming of the Iron Age, the movement flourished. Troglodytes were already present in the Loire valley when the Romans invaded Gaul—Julius Caesar mentions them in his writings.

During dangerous times in the Dark Ages and during the medieval era, people dug tunnels into hillsides to take refuge from invaders like the Vikings. One example of this is the fortress of La Roche-Guyon, built into a cliff near Giverny (*see* Experience 4). In the early Dark Ages, other caves were used by hermits to serve as primitive chapels; one such cave is the grotto at Mont Ste-Baume (*see* Experience 12). Caves also served religious purposes as funeral chambers or as a place to pay homage to subterranean deities.

During the Middle Ages, as the population grew, rock was mined extensively to build towns, churches, and castles, in mines that sometimes stretched for miles into the hillsides. The men who quarried the rock might, in exchange, use the carved-out space as a home for their family. The rock miner could save the cost of wood, carpenters, and so on, and at the same time the local nobleman got cheap rock for his

▼

own building needs. Thus it is no coincidence that cave dwellings coexisted with the great stone chateaus of this region, such as the nearby **Château d'Amboise,** which you can spot from a hillside on the walk.

A drive along the road named *rte. D58, rte. D1,* and *rte. D46* as it progresses the 30 km. between Onzain and Vouvray on the north side of the Loire lets you discover the range of troglodyte dwellings in the region. Some are barely modified caves, with just a door and maybe a small wall between the outside and the dwelling. Others have a full man-made facade (often quite elaborate), some with a house attached in front, others with a detached house in front. On the walking tour below, you'll also see a vertical troglodyte home built down into the ground. In this case, several rooms surround an open courtyard dug into the earth, permitting all rooms to get natural light.

To the east of Tours, troglodyte dwellings line the cliffside north of the Loire for miles. The famous wine-growing village of **Vouvray** (just west of Noizay) may once have been almost totally underground. In some cases, you'll find troglodyte homes three stories deep in this area.

Some of the newer-looking cave homes you'll see on the walk may occupy space lived in for hundreds or even thousands of years. There has been a gradual decline in this manner of living, perhaps accelerated by a stigma attached to it in France. Today, many of the troglodyte homes have been abandoned or converted for use as wine cellars or storage areas. But between Vouvray and Onzain you can see probably hundreds of still-inhabited dwellings, many of them unchanged for hundreds of years, their chimneys protruding from the rock above.

GETTING THERE
By car:

From Tours, take *rte. N152* east toward Amboise. About 5 km. before Amboise, exit left onto *rte. D78* toward Noizay. When you reach the village, turn right on *rte. D1* and go about 1 km. to a small road with signs pointing left to Beaumont and La Roche de Cestre. Go left until you reach an intersection in front of Les Jours Verts, a *chambres d'hôte* marked with a green *gîtes de France* sign, where you park.

From Amboise, take *rte. D5,* following signs for Nazelles-Negron.

▼

In the village, make a left onto *rte. D1* following signs to Vouvray. After about 2 km., turn right on a small paved road with signposts pointing to Beaumont and La Roche de Cestre. In about 1/4 km., you reach an intersection in front of one of the recommended *chambres d'hôte,* marked with a green *gîtes de France* sign.

Walk 1 Directions

TIME: 1 1/2 hours

LEVEL: Moderate

DISTANCE: 3 miles

ACCESS: By car

This walk is a loop that begins and ends near the village of Noizay, swinging out into the forests and vineyards of the surrounding countryside. Although you begin and end on paved roads, most of the walk is on dirt paths; you'll switch at one point from a trail with blue blazes to one with yellow blazes, but follow the walk directions carefully since the blazes are often difficult to find. Lovely places to picnic exist all along the vineyard portion of the walk, with some pretty good views available toward the end; pick up provisions in Amboise.

TO BEGIN

Walk up the paved road away from *rte. D1* for about five minutes, following the blue blazes on the *rue de Beaumont* toward the hamlet of Beaumont. *Notice the cave homes on your right.*

1. At the first intersection, a Y, take the road to the left, following the blue blazes. You'll see a sign for Cosme, *viticulteur.* The paved road soon ends, and you continue straight on a dirt road that leads you toward a forest (there will be a field to your left). For about 15 minutes, you walk through the Bois de l'Olive (Forest of Olive).

2. When you come out of the woods, the road ends at a T intersection at the edge of a vineyard. Go left. You'll walk through the vineyards for less than ten minutes to the next four-way intersection. Ignore a trail to the right along the way.

3. Turn right on a farm road that heads toward the woods lying off to your

▼

right. *You have now left the blue-blazed trail for a yellow-blazed trail, but the blazes are hard to find.* Walk for about five minutes.

4. Just before you reach the edge of the forest, make a right. There is a field on your right, vineyards to the left. The trail soon veers left, toward another small forest in the distance. Continue straight, ignoring trails that join in from the right and the left.

5. At a T intersection near some trees, turn right. Walk approximately 50 feet.

6. At the next intersection, turn left and follow the trail (blazed yellow, if you can find the marks) through vineyards

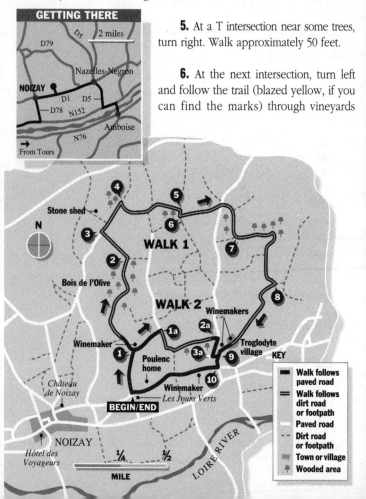

GETTING THERE

2 miles

D79
D5
D5
Nazelles-Negron
NOIZAY
D1 D5
D78
N152
Amboise
N76

→ From Tours

Stone shed
N
WALK 1
Bois de l'Olive
WALK 2
Winemakers
Winemaker
Troglodyte village
Poulenc home
Château de Noizay
Winemaker
Les Jours Verts
BEGIN/END
NOIZAY
Hôtel des Voyageurs
¼   ½
MILE
LOIRE RIVER

KEY

▬	Walk follows paved road
═	Walk follows dirt road or footpath
—	Paved road
- - -	Dirt road or footpath
🌳	Town or village
🌲	Wooded area

▼

offering extensive views of farmland and the Loire valley. After less than ten minutes, you'll cross a paved road. Continue following the trail for another ten minutes or so as it winds around to the right.

7. At a T intersection, turn left onto a dirt road (there are more vineyards on your right). Just a few minutes later, the road curves to the right away from some woods. *You soon reach the top of a hill, where the Loire valley opens up before you. In the distance, to your left, you can make out the Château d'Amboise, especially during winter.* Follow this trail downhill, ignoring an intersection along the way.

8. At another T, make a right downhill, with the Loire valley off to your left and more vineyards to your right. The dirt road veers left and then right toward a tiny village, where the road becomes paved. *Vauvelle is a typical village of troglodyte homes: Notice the chimneys sticking out of the hillside. There's an unusual vertical troglodyte home on your left as you enter the tiny hamlet. In just a few minutes, on your right, you reach the home of Guy Cosme, a local viticulturist. If he's in, visit his picturesque wine-making operation in an old troglodyte dwelling. The next house you pass contains the more modern operations of the Domaine J. P. Pincendeau, which sells good local wines.*

9. Just after the home of M. Pincendeau, make a left at a Y in the road and walk toward a stop sign.

10. At the stop sign, turn right on the *chemin Francis Poulenc*, which parallels *rte. D1.* You'll soon pass *another local winemaker, André Delalou,* on the left. Continue to pass occupied cave homes on your right. *Not far from the winery, on your right, you'll see a large ivy-covered wall with a big orange metal gate. Composer Francis Poulenc, who lived from 1899 to 1963, occupied this home for many years before his death. (The now-private home is marked by a hard-to-find plaque on the wall.)* Walk a few minutes more on the *chemin Francis Poulenc* and you'll be back at your car.

▼

Walk 2 Directions

TIME: 3/4 hour

LEVEL: Easy

DISTANCE: 1 1/2 miles

ACCESS: By car

This walk is basically a shortcut for Walk 1. The terrain is much the same, though you won't tramp through so many vineyards. Less of the route is blazed, and you'll miss the best views. You will also pass the private grounds of one of the many lesser chateaus that dot this region.

TO BEGIN

Park and begin in the same place as in Walk 1. When you reach the Y at Point 1, leave the blue-blazed trail and go right on a paved road for about five minutes.

1A. Just beyond a house on your right, turn right onto a farm road into the vineyards. In a few minutes, you follow the road as it curves left. Continue straight toward some woods. In less than five minutes, you reach the edge of the wooded grounds of a chateau.

2A. Turn right at a paved road.

3A. Turn left at the next intersection. At the next intersection (Point 9 on Walk 1), make a right. Make another right at Point 10 to return to your car.

OTHER PLACES NEARBY

■ **Château d'Amboise.** This clifftop castle looming above the Loire has lost many of its buildings over the years, but it remains an impressive structure. The spot has probably served as a fortress since Gallic-Roman times. You can visit the gardens, a terrace with a beautiful view of the Loire, a 15th-century chapel, and the king's apartments. *Amboise 37400, tel. 47-57-00-98, fax 47-57-52-23. Open daily 9-12 and 2-6:30 Apr. 3-Sep. 30; 9-6:30 Jul. 1-Aug. 31; 9-12 and 2-5 the rest of the year. Closed Christmas, New Year's. Admission. Located in center of Amboise.*

■ **Vouvray.** The town, known for its white wine, has a number of impres-

▼

sive troglodyte homes. *About 8 km. west of Noizay by way of rte. D1 and rte. D46.*

■ **Blois.** This historic town retains a medieval character and features one of the best-known castles in the region, the **Blois Château,** located in the center of town. *Blois 41000, tel. 54-78-06-62. Open daily 9-6 Mar. 15-Nov. 1; 9-12 and 2-5 Nov. 2-Mar. 14. Closed Christmas, New Year's. Admission. About 32 km. east of Noizay by way of rte. N152.*

DINING

■ **Domaine des Hauts de Loire** (expensive). No muddy shoes are welcome in this plush, elegant dining room perfect for a dressed-up romantic dinner. The chef has a creative bent, with such offerings as *fond d'artichaut et homard au coulis d'herbes aromatiques* (artichoke hearts with lobster and thick herb sauce), *salade de langoustines rôties et pomme de terre à l'huile vanillée* (salad of roasted prawns and potato with an oil spiced with vanilla), and *boeuf poché au vin de Montlouis* (beef poached in red wine). *Onzain 41150, tel. 54-20-83-41, fax 54-20-77-32. Closed Dec., Jan., and Feb. From the village of Onzain, take rte. D1, following signs to Mesland. You'll see the hotel on the right shortly after the road enters the countryside.*

■ **Château de Noizay** (expensive to moderate). In this lovely, upbeat setting in a beautifully maintained 16th-century chateau, you'll find such refined presentations of local fish, game, and duck as *cuisse de canard croustillante au verjus* (crispy duck thigh with a wine sauce) and *pintade à la graine de moutarde* (young game hen cooked with mustard seed). Neat dress is required. *Rte. D78, Noizay 37210, tel. 47-52-11-01, fax 47-52-04-64. Closed Nov. 15-Mar. 15. Less than 1 km. north of the village of Noizay on rte. D78.*

■ **Hôtel des Voyageurs** (inexpensive). Locals promise a graciously served, inexpensive meal with much less complicated menus than you'll find in the more expensive restaurants—and a pleasant, casual atmosphere. The least expensive menu on our visit featured *terrine de carpe à la crème citronnée* (terrine of carp with a lemon cream sauce) and *onglet à l'échalotte* (a fine cut of beef with shallots). *39 rue de la République, Noizay 37210, tel. 47-52-11-49. Open Fri.-Wed. Closed for ten days in March. On the main road of this village.*

■ **Ferme-Auberge Les Grillons** (inexpensive). Eat simple but tasty

▼

and fresh farm cooking with the locals on this small farm. There are about ten tables available for one dinner seating at 7:30. Attire is strictly casual, decor simple but cheerful. On our visit, during springtime, the menu featured *terrine de lapin aux noisettes* (rabbit terrine with hazelnuts), *feuilleté au jambon et Gruyère* (flakey pastry with ham and Gruyère), and *veau rôti aux oignons et à la tomate* (veal roasted in tomatoes and onions). *Limeray, Amboise 37530, tel. 47-30-11-76. Open for dinner daily, for lunch Sat.-Tue. Closed from three weeks before Christmas through first week of Jan. From Amboise, cross the river to rte. N152 and go east for about 2 km. to rte. D201; turn off for Limeray. You'll see signs on your right.*

LODGING

■ **Domaine des Hauts de Loire** (very expensive). This beautiful 33-room hotel in an early-19th-century hunting lodge has luxury, charm, elegance, and an enormous wooded park with extensive trails. But the bevy of expensive cars and elegantly dressed people—as well as its relatively large size—afford little escape if you already live in an opulent area. Nonetheless, lovers of fine hotels will not be disappointed with the tastefully furnished luxury rooms, the attractive views of forest and field from nearly every window, and the adjacent swimming pool and solarium. *Onzain 41150, tel. 54-20-83-41, fax 54-20-77-32. Closed Dec.-Jan. From village of Onzain, take rte. D1, following signs to Mesland. You'll see the hotel on the right shortly after the road enters the countryside.*

■ **Château de Noizay** (very expensive). You get the impressive setting of a 16th-century chateau on a hillside overlooking the Loire valley, along with beautifully furnished rooms, without quite the pomp and ceremony of the pricier Domaine des Hauts de Loire. Also a member of the Relais & Châteaux network, this hotel seems a bit more low key than some of its celebrated counterparts. The best rooms visited were No. 5, with a four-poster bed, and No. 1, a large and elegantly furnished corner room with (unfortunately) no view. Most of the 14 rooms provide views of the valley. There's TV and minibars in the rooms, plus a pool and tennis. *Rte. D78, Noizay 37210, tel. 47-52-11-01, fax 47-52-04-64. Closed Jan. 5-Mar. 15. Less than 1 km. north of the village of Noizay on rte. D78.*

■ **Hotel Château des Tertres** (expensive). For those who want

▼

the feel of staying in an old French home but don't have the money for luxury, there's plenty of charm, comfort, value, and, above all, peace and quiet in this lovely late-19th-century home. Of the 19 rooms, all have shower and bath, and 10 face the front with a view of the gardens and the Loire valley beyond. *Rte. de Monteaux, Onzain 41150, tel. 54-20-83-88, fax 54-20-89-21. Closed Nov. 11–Mar. 20. From Onzain, take rte. D58 following signs for Monteaux. Hotel signs clearly mark the entrance, on your right.*

■ **Château de Pray** (expensive). Good river views and large, elegant rooms are among the benefits of this hotel, a member of the Relais & Châteaux hotel group. Room 12 has a great view and a four-poster bed. The less expensive rooms lack views and are smaller but still well decorated. An annex behind the chateau has modern rooms that look onto the garden. Dinner is available in a beautiful dining room. *Amboise 37400, tel. 47-57-23-67, fax 47-57-32-50. Closed Jan. About 4 km. east of Amboise on rte. D51.*

■ **Le Clos des Vignes** (moderate). A very pleasant *chambres d'hôte* in a newly renovated old home, operated by an English-speaking couple in a tiny, quiet village. *Pocé-sur-Cisse 37530, tel. and fax 47-57-71-20. A moderately priced dinner is available with advance notice. Open year-round. No credit cards. Just north of Amboise and the village of Pocé-sur-Cisse on rte. D431.*

■ **Les Jours Verts** (moderate). If you would like to stay in the lovely country home of a friendly English-speaking couple, put away the hotel guides and savor this tiny *chambres d'hôte* located in the countryside and just at the start of the troglodyte walking tour. All three rooms are clean, with tasteful decor, and have private, modern bathrooms. The home itself dates to the 16th century but has been lovingly restored in a relaxed country motif. Since the price includes breakfast, it's really on the high end of inexpensive. *Mme. Bosma, Vallée de Beaumont, Noizay 37210, tel. 47-52-12-90. Open year-round. No credit cards. From Tours, follow the directions in Getting There, above. From Amboise, take rte. D5 following signs for Nazelles-Negron. In the village, make a left onto rte. D1 following signs to Vouvray. In about 2 km., turn right on a small paved road with signposts pointing to Beaumont and La Roche de Cestre. In*

▼

about 1/4 km., you reach an intersection in front of one of the recommended chambres d'hote, *marked with a green* gîtes de France *sign.*

■ **Le Petit Manoir** (moderate). Located less than 3 km. to the south of Amboise, this is slightly far afield of the troglodyte experience, but it has two charming rooms. The ivy-covered home stands out in a field with a tree-shaded garden in back and expansive views of the Loire valley and Amboise in the distance. *Mme. Party, rte. de Chenonceaux, Amboise 37400, tel. 47-30-59-50. Open year-round. No credit cards. In Amboise, make a left just west of the tourist office, following signs to Montrichard. Go straight at a light. At the next light, in less than 2 km., make a right on rte. D81 following a sign to the Novotel. You will see the entrance to the* chambres d'hôte *several kilometers up the hill on your left.*

FOR MORE INFORMATION
Tourist Office:

    Office de Tourisme. *Quai Géneral-de-Gaulle, Amboise 37400, tel. 47-57-09-28, fax 47-57-14-35. Open 9-12:30 and 3-6 Oct.-Jun. and Sep.-May; 9-8:30 Jul.-Aug. Along the Loire river near the chateau.*

For Serious Walkers:

The region has many blazed walking trails, including many day-trips. The walks are detailed in a series of French-language booklets on sale at the *Comité Touraine de la Randonnée, Office de Tourisme, Tours 37042, tel. 47-61-02-57. Open Mon., Wed., and Sat. 9-12 and 2-6.* For Noizay Walks 1 and 2, use IGN map 1922E (east).

Lonely Chateau

EXPERIENCE 19: GUE-PEAN

The tour buses come nowhere near Gué-Péan, a castle next to a forest in the Loire valley region. The only activity is in the meadow below, where birds swoop and sing and butterflies dance above the wild flowers. It's a scene that has changed little since 400 years ago when the fortress was built.

The region's most famous chateaus, like nearby **Chenonceaux,**

> **The Highlights:** Old farms, rural paths, fields of sunflowers, an isolated chateau surrounded by a forest and a meadow unchanged for centuries.
>
> **Other Places Nearby:** The famous chateau of Chenonceaux, the troglodyte homes of France (*see* Experience 18), the Roman ruins of Thésée (*see* Experience 20).

see throngs of people throughout the year, but dozens of lesser-known chateaus like Gué-Péan also dot the area. They were built by lesser nobles, who either aspired to greater things or simply wished to live near the action.

This walking itinerary takes you to Gué-Péan on old forest foot-paths that have surrounded the chateau for centuries. The several rooms and halls that are open to the public contain furniture from the time of Louis XV and Louis XVI, tapestries, and a library containing souvenirs and autographs of such notables as Victor Hugo, Napoleon, General Charles de Gaulle, François Mauriac (*see* Experience 15), Jean Cocteau, and many others. You can even stay overnight at the chateau (*see* Lodging, below).

▼

The official history of this lesser-known castle, written by a recent owner, exemplifies the rich past of myriad smaller chateaus off the tourist trails in the Loire valley. The story begins early in this millennium, when Foulques Nerra, Count of Anjou, built the castle along with several others to protect his domain from Norman invasions in the Loire and Cher valleys. Assaulted by the Normans and then the English during the Hundred Years War, it was finally taken by the English in 1346 and partially destroyed. You can still see remains of its moat and the original towers beside the current entrance to the inner courtyard. The most likely explanation for the name Gué-Péan relates to the castle's location above a pond (what is now the meadow below the chateau). A *gué*, or ford, near the site of the current footbridge allowed carts and horses to cross the pond. Peasants taking their grain to the property's mills had to pay a toll there—hence the name Gué-Payant ("paying ford"). Another hypothesis is that the name is based on Gué-Puant, or "foul-smelling ford," since the pond was shallow and possibly stagnant.

Over the centuries, the owners of Gué-Péan never had the will or the money to make this a great architectural monument on the scale of the most famous castles in the region. The English were expelled in 1429, but afterward, restoration was gradual and no serious work was done until the beginning of the 16th century.

Starting in the early 1500s, the chateau had a succession of owners with ties to royalty. Nicholas Alaman, the castle's first known seigneur (lord of the manor), held posts close to Kings Louis XII and François I. Alaman's son François also held several important but secondary posts—he was, however, influential enough to have his property elevated to the status of *chatellenie* (feudal estate), with full rights of justice over the local inhabitants. During this period, the chateau's current architectural style took shape, with an Italian influence perhaps related to the family's Italian ancestry.

With full feudal rights, the property had considerable value, and its ownership was sold or contested in court numerous times over the centuries. The heirs of François Alaman had to fight a lawsuit over rights to the property in 1565. Later in that century, the family had to take the

▼

property away from a hard-partying son.

In 1676, the property was purchased by the Count d'Aspremont, who earned the favors of Louis XIV through his military deeds. The Count and Countess further expanded and modernized the castle. After the Count died, the young widow fell in love with a 16-year-old page. When the young man resisted her advances, she imprisoned him in a tower, albeit in great luxury. He managed to escape and filed a complaint with the local lord, the Duke of St-Aignan. Under pressure from the Duke, the Countess quickly married a more respectable partner.

The last owners of the property before the French Revolution were the Amelot family. In 1776, in the Grand Salon, Antoine Jean Amelot assisted the Marquis de La Fayette and colleagues in writing a tract addressed to the French king favoring the liberation of America from England. Amelot spent much of his time away from Gué-Péan at the French court, but local residents rose to his defense during the Revolution when a band from Tours tried to attack the place. As the story goes, the Marquis surrendered in order to prevent bloodshed and was later beheaded in Paris. Sold as a national asset, the chateau was bought by the mayor of Tours.

After the fall of Napoleon, the property returned to the hands of the Amelot family, which later sold it. Maintained by its current owners as a quasi-private residence, the chateau does not have the spit and polish of a government museum, but that is part of its charm. In its halls and rooms and its surrounding forests and meadows echo memories of hundreds of people who lived here on the sidelines of history.

GETTING THERE
By car:

From Tours, take *rte. N76 east* to Montrichard, then go left over the Cher river, picking up *rte. D176* and following signs to Bourré. After passing through the village of Bourré, watch for signs pointing to Monthou-sur-Cher. Make a left following signs to Monthou-sur-Cher on *rte. D21* and follow it for about 2 km. into the village. Continue past the church and the café and bear left at the first intersection as you head out of the village. Cross a tiny stream and park on a little road just

▼

beyond, which veers off toward a house on the left. You'll see the sign indicating the outer limits of Monthou and a beautiful old stone farm.

Walk Directions

TIME: 1 1/4 to 2 hours
LEVEL: Easy to moderate
DISTANCE: 2 1/2 to 4 miles
ACCESS: By car

Walking from the village of Monthou-sur-Cher through fields and forest, you pass an old mill and an old farm, before reaching the chateau of Gué-Péan. Then make a loop to pick up the end of the trail back to your car. Dense forest and trails overgrown with vegetation make the full version of this itinerary a moderate walk, and the footbridge was in a sorry state of repair on our last visit. The chateau's owner says it will be fixed, but less ambitious walkers can turn this into an easy itinerary with a shortcut at Point 4. Yellow blazes mark most of the walk, but they're not always easy to find. Nearby Montrichard (7 1/2 km. west on *rte. D176*) offers picnic provisions.

TO BEGIN

Cross the paved road and head up a dirt road to the left of a rambling cluster of old stone farm buildings. The dirt road continues into the forest and dwindles to a dirt path.

1. The path veers left up a hill into the woods above a tiny stream, the Bavet, which lies below to your right. (Ignore a footpath that goes right to the stream.) In one stretch you will enter a particularly brushy area—*watch out for nettles.*

2. After about 15 minutes of walking through forest, you come out on the edge of farmland. Follow the trail as it swings to the right down a ravine; there will be fields above you to your left. *In summer, if you're in luck, the fields will be aflame with blossoming sunflowers.*

3. At the bottom of the ravine, you come upon an intersection near

▼

an old mill converted into a private home along the stream. Go left on a narrow trail for five to ten minutes as it weaves slightly from the forest into the fields and back again. *At times, it's clear that you're on the remains of a very old, once frequently used road.*

4. Just after going into the forest again, the trail hits a junction. The trail leading to your right goes down toward the Gué-Péan chateau. *To shorten the walk, you go right on this trail to the chateau, from where you retrace this route back to your car.*

For the full walk, continue on the trail that leads straight ahead, with fields to your left and the forest to your right. Soon you will pass the ruins of an ancient farm on your left, buried under brambles and vines. About five minutes beyond that, you cross another area that may be thickly overgrown. To bypass the overgrowth, bear to the left of the trail through the forest for a distance of 30 or so feet, and then bear right to get back on the trail.

5. Within 20 minutes of Point 4, you reach the edge of a field. Turn right on a broad path that goes across the small field, over a small bridge in ill repair (be careful), and back into the forest. Follow this trail through the woodlands for a few minutes.

6. Go right on a trail that veers diagonally off into the forest. Follow this straight for a few minutes.

7. When you come to a major intersection, go left and walk a short distance.

8. Turn right at the first intersection and go straight a few dozen yards until the chateau comes into view. *The Gué-Péan chateau stands alone in a large clearing surrounded by the ancient forest and sweeping meadows.* You can cross the grassy field along the left side of the chateau to enter. To your left, you'll see the stables. After visiting the chateau, proceed out the main gate and along the small paved access road for about five minutes.

▼

9. At an intersection by an abandoned house, take the tiny paved road that veers off to the right, and then quickly make an abrupt right across the field, *where you will get another stunning view of the chateau, much as it must have appeared 300 years ago.* Continue straight across a small wooden footbridge into the forest and up a hill back to Point 4, where you turn left. From here, retrace your steps to your car.

PLACES ALONG THE WALK

■ **Château de Gué-Péan.** *Monthou-sur-Cher 41400, tel. 54-71-43-01. Open daily 9-7. Admission. From Thésée, go west on rte. D176 about 2 km. to rte. D21. Go right into center of the village of Monthou-sur-Cher and follow the signs.*

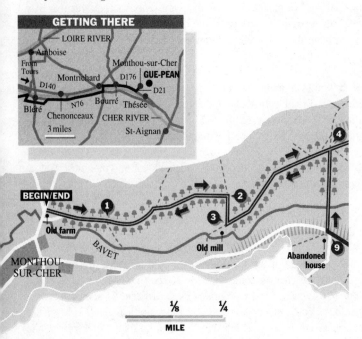

▼

OTHER PLACES NEARBY

■ **Montrichard.** A small, unspoiled town along the Cher river, Montrichard has attractive old houses and a castle. Access to the castle is in the center of town; the castle keep offers fine views of Montrichard and the Cher valley. *Castle tel.: 54-32-05-10. Open daily 9:30-11:30 and 2-6 Jun. 13-Aug. 31; weekends only 9:30-11:30 and 2-6 Apr. 4-Jun. 13 and Sep. Admission. Located 4 1/2 km. west of Thésée on rte. D176.*

■ **Chenonceaux Château.** Probably one of the most celebrated of the Loire river castles, this beautifully proportioned structure straddles the Cher river. The 16th-century chateau has an impressive collection of furnishings, tapestries, and paintings. *Chenonceaux 37150, tel. 47-23-90-07. Open daily 9-7 Mar. 16-Sep. 15; 9-6:30 Sep. 16-30; 9-6 Oct. 1-15;*

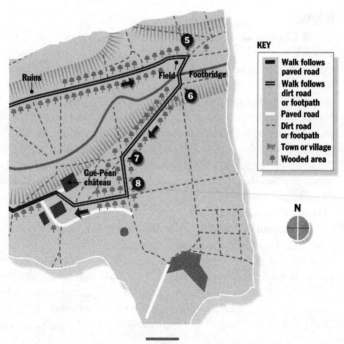

▼

9-5:30 Oct. 16-31; 9-5 Nov. 1-15; 9-4:30 Nov. 16-Jan. 31; 9-5 Feb. 1-15; 9-5:30 Feb. 16-29; 9-6 Mar. 1-15. Admission. About 18 km. west of Thésée on rte. D176.

■ **Les Maselles Roman ruins.** These remains were once either an administrative post or a warehouse, depending on which experts you believe (*see* Experience 20). *Rte. D176, Thésée 41140, tel. 54-71-40-20. Interior open during summer every day except. Wed. 10-12 and 3-6:30. Admission.*

■ **Musée de Thésée-la-Romaine.** Here you'll find Roman artifacts, most of them discovered in Thésée, along with representations of Roman homes and commercial sites. *La Mairie (town hall), just off rte. D176, Thésée-la-Romaine, tel. 54-71-40-20. Open daily except Tue. 10-12 and 2-6 Jun. 15-Sep. 15; weekends and holidays 2-5 Easter-Jun. 15 and Sep. 15-Oct. 15. Admission.*

DINING

■ **Château de la Ménaudière** (moderate). Views of a beautiful park accompany elegant country dining with gourmet meals based on fresh local ingredients. Among the appetizers, we chose the *mosaique de sandre et saumon au pistil de safran* (a carefully crafted plate of salmon and a local freshwater fish spiced with saffron) and the *goujonnette de volaille au basilic* (tiny morsels of fried chicken flavored with basil), and for the main course, *pintadeau braisé au gingembre* (pan-cooked game hen flavored with ginger). *Rte. D115, Chissay-en-Touraine 41401, tel. 54-32-02-44, fax 54-71-34-58. Open daily except Sun. evening and Mon. mid-Mar.-late Nov.; daily May-mid-Oct.; open major holidays. From Montrichard, take rte. D115 toward Amboise about 2 km., then turn right following signs to the hotel/restaurant.*

■ **Château de Chissay** (moderate). A charming dining room combines the old walls of this chateau with floor-to-ceiling windows offering a view of the medieval courtyard. On our visit, the menu featured *cuisse de lapin rôtie au miel* (rabbit thigh roasted with honey) and *pavé de saumon poêlé au velouté de champignons* (salmon with a white mushroom sauce). *Chissay-en-Touraine, Montrichard 41400, tel. 54-32-32-01, fax 54-32-43-80. Closed mid Nov.-early Mar. From Montrichard,*

▼

take rte. D176 west just 2 km. to Chissay, where you'll see a sign for the hotel/restaurant.

■ **Le Saint-Vincent** (inexpensive). Delicious offerings, many focused on local ingredients. Recommended dishes include *pot au feu de pigeonneau* (pigeon stewed in wine with *foie gras*) and *fricassé de coquilles St. Jacques,* scallops served in a cream sauce. *Oisly 41700, tel. 54-79-50-04. Open daily except Sun. eve. and Mon.*

■ **Les 2 Caves** (inexpensive). Homemade terrines along with grilled fish and meats are served in an old troglodyte home. *Bourré 41000, tel. 54-32-08-63. Open daily during summer. Otherwise, weekdays for lunch; weekends for lunch and dinner. About 3 km. east of Montrichard on Rte. D71.*

LODGING

Cost-conscious travelers can find less expensive accommodations near Noizay (*see* Experience 18), which is only a half-hour drive away.

■ **Château de la Ménaudière** (expensive). Built in the middle of the 16th century, this old home has been carefully restored into a top hotel and restaurant. The 25 guest rooms combine the modern with the traditional, though some are small (Rooms 8, 14, 17, 21, 23, and 24 are the biggest). You'll find absolute peace and beautiful countryside here. *Rte. D115, Chissay-en-Touraine 41401, tel. 54-32-02-44, fax 54-71-34-58. Closed mid-Nov.-mid-Mar. From Montrichard, take rte. D115 toward Amboise about 2 km., then turn right following signs to the hotel.*

■ **Château de Chissay** (expensive). This fortified castle transformed into a luxury hotel has seen such famous residents as Charles VII, Louis XI, and Charles de Gaulle. The 30 beautifully furnished rooms, most with river views, provide all the modern conveniences in a cheerful (yet medieval) atmosphere. *Chissay-en-Touraine, Montrichard 41400, tel. 54-32-32-01, fax 54-32-43-80. Closed mid-Jan.-early Mar. From Montrichard, take rte. D176 west just 2 km. to Chissay, where you'll see a sign for the hotel/restaurant.*

■ **Manoire de la Salle du Roc** (expensive). For a little less money, you can still get a charming combination of ancient and new at this intimate *chambres d'hôte.* Originally a 13th-century fortified castle, the

▼

home is set against a cliff above the road and the river, and it has been lovingly transformed into a country escape with beautiful gardens. There are four attractive guest rooms; all have private bath, television, and telephone. The owners have a private island on the Cher. This is a bed and breakfast, but the owners accept credit cards; they also speak some English. *69 rte. de Vierzon, Bourré 41400, tel. 54-32-73-54. About 4 km. east of Montrichard on rte. D176.*

■ **Château du Gué-Péan** (expensive). This *chambres d'hôte* was vandalized by people who managed the chateau for the owners, who have now reclaimed the property and vow to renovate. The setting and chateau have potential, but inquire about the state of renovations before booking. *Monthou-sur-Cher 41400, tel. 54-71-37-10, fax 54-71-35-77. From the church at Monthou-sur-Cher go north less than 1 km. on rte. D21 and bear right on a paved road, following signs to the chateau.*

FOR MORE INFORMATION
Tourist Office:

Montrichard Office de Tourisme. *1 rue du Pont, Montrichard 41400, tel. 54-32-05-10. Open daily 9-12 and 2-6:30.*

For Serious Walkers:

The area has a wide variety of walking trails, with information available from the *11 pl. du Château, Blois 41000, tel. 54-78-55-50.* For the walk at Gué-Péan, use IGN map 2022E (east). *See* also Experience 20, Thésée.

Lifestyles of the Gallic-Romans

EXPERIENCE 20: THESEE

Outside the village of Thésée-la-Romaine, in the hills where you walk on the tour outlined below, there have been farms since at least 100 years before Christ. On the road you follow coming toward the Roman ruins of **Les Maselles,** farmers probably walked 2,000 years ago on their way to town or market. This experience lets you

The Highlights: Sweeping farmland panoramas, vineyards, Roman ruins, a magnificent walk along the Cher river.

Other Places Nearby: The Chenonceaux Château, the little-known castle of Gué-Péan (*see* Experience 19), and the charming town of Montrichard.

feel the peaceful side of day-to-day life under the Romans and provides you with panoramic views unchanged since ancient times.

The ruins in Thésée are not of historic proportions—the spot is bypassed by most tourists visiting such Cher river valley chateaus as the famous **Château de Chenonceaux** or the castle in the charming small town of **Montrichard,** 9 km. west of Thésée. But this former stop along a major Roman road provides archaeologists with fascinating clues to the lives of ordinary Gallic-Roman inhabitants during the more than 400 years of Roman occupation that started around 100 B.C.

Known as Tasciaca in Roman times, the name Thésée may refer to a property owned by someone named Tasius. Though archaeologists

▼

have found some traces of occupation dating to Neolithic times (6,000-2,000 B.C.), this river valley town was probably founded by Romans. It appears in a Roman traveler's guide written in the 3rd or 4th century by a man named Peutinger and is shown on his map as a place to stay along the Bourges-Tours road.

While modern Thésée lies only on the right bank of the Cher, the ancient town apparently spanned the river—remnants of homes, shrines, wells, ovens, mills, docks, walls, and buildings have been found on both sides. The only still-visible ruins lie just west of the town, at Les Maselles, which you can visit on this walk. Three principal buildings surrounded by a wall lie about 250 yards off the present riverbank, along what is now *rte. D176.* Although no one is certain of the buildings' origins, archaeologists believe they served as either an administrative office complex or a warehouse.

While the major cities of Gaul were developed along the lines of Roman cities, with public forums, baths, theaters, and amphitheaters, Tasciaca was a small town that never benefitted from grandiose public works. Little is known about these more humble population centers, so a site such as this yields invaluable clues about life in Gallic-Roman times. Many of the artifacts unearthed here are on display at the **Musée de Thésée-la-Romaine** in the town hall in Thésée-la-Romaine.

Only the largest public buildings, like Les Maselles, were built of stone using Roman techniques. The richest homes had stone foundations, but their walls were built of crude brick or *torchis* (clay mixed with straw). Houses were decorated with paint and mosaics, but they were more Gallic than Roman—nearly square, with a single story and several rooms. Furniture was made of wood or wicker, with a square or rectangular dining table and three-legged stools. Locals used chests and wooden boxes to store household goods and unlocked them with metal keys. The rich had a Roman-style hot-air heating system; humbler folk relied on braziers of clay or metal or simply used the kitchen fireplace for warmth. Light came from clay or bronze lamps fueled by oil or grease or from candles of suet or wax.

Local meals consisted of round bread, cheese, a vegetable soup

▼

with bread cooked in water or milk, grilled fish in vinegar or cumin, chicken or stuffed milk-fed pigs, salted meat, and eggs from chickens, geese, or pigeons, which were served fried or soft- or hard-boiled. Spices and condiments included capers, pine nuts, anise, cumin, coriander, fennel, cilantro, basil, mint, thyme, pepper, and parsley. A fish sauce known as *garum* probably approximated the Indochinese sauce *Nuoc Mâm*. Most people ate on plates of clay, while the rich had silverware. Locals drank beers made of fermented barley or of wheat and honey; they also drank a wine spiced with honey, pepper, rose, and absinthe.

Many people in Tasciaca earned a living by making ceramics, which served as the basic material for most dining and storage utensils. Made of heated clay, ceramics were fragile and absorbed liquid, so they needed to be frequently replaced. It's believed that the ovens in Tasciaca manufactured brick used in construction, as well as large storage urns, everyday plates, and fine dinnerware. Boats probably played a big role in transporting these ceramics, for the ovens and storage facilities were located near riverside docks.

Roman gods mingled with those of the local Gallic peoples, including such deities as Epona, Sucellus, and Cernunnos, each with different attributes and powers. Although no traces of Roman temples have been found at Thésée, a *fanum* of Celtic origins is believed to have existed there. *Fanums* were tiny house-shaped shrines that faced east, with a room housing the statue of the revered god. It is believed that the *fanum* in Thésée honored a water god helpful in healing eyes (a tool used in ophthalmology was excavated).

When you come upon the ancient ruins in the Cher river valley while walking this rural landscape of farmlands and vineyards, you cannot help but feel a close connection with those ancient times. Perhaps life has not changed that much after all.

GETTING THERE

By car:

From Tours, take *rte. N76* east to Montrichard, where you make a left crossing the Cher river. From Montrichard, take *rte. D176* along the north bank of the river, following signs to Bourré. After passing through

▼

the village of Bourré, watch for a signpost indicating a turnoff for Monthou-sur-Cher (not far from the starting point for the walk to Gué-Péan—*see* Experience 19). Turn left on *rte. D21* and follow it to the village of Monthou, less than 2 km. Park in front of the church.

Walk Directions

TIME: 2 hours
LEVEL: Easy to moderate
DISTANCE: 3 1/2 miles
ACCESS: By car

This relatively long walk provides a pleasant morning or afternoon escape for vigorous walkers. You'll start in the village of Monthou-sur-Cher and walk through forests, fields, and vineyards to the Roman ruins, then follow a riverside trail along the Cher back to Monthou. If all you want is a beautiful short stroll, you can drive directly to the ruins at Les Maselles (on *rte. D176* in Thésée), and pick up this walk from Point 4, walking down to the Cher river, where you can enjoy idyllic views of this beautiful valley. Then retrace your steps from the river to your car at Les Maselles. Nearby Montrichard (7 1/2 km. west of Monthou on *rte. D176*) offers you the best selection of picnic provisions.

Gatepost

Concrete pole

8

LA VERRERIE

rte. de la Verrerie

7

6 Warehouse

Footbridge

N

KEY

| Walk follows paved road |
| Walk follows dirt road or footpath |
| Paved road |
| Dirt road or footpath |
| Town or village |
| Wooded area |

▼

TO BEGIN

From your parking space in front of the church, walk up to *rte. D21* (*rue du Château*) and turn left, toward a café. At the café, turn right and go uphill on the *rue de la Croix*. You're on a long-distance *GR* trail marked with white-and-red blazes that are sometimes difficult to spot. The *rue de la Croix* leads you

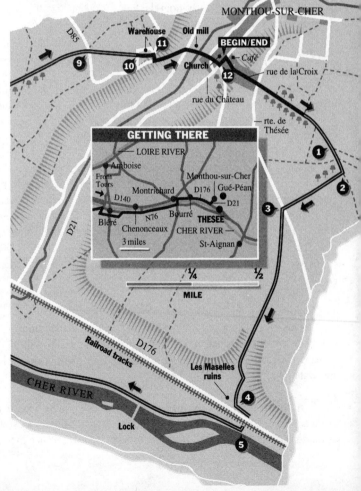

▼

along the edge of the village, across a small paved road (*rte. de Thésée*), and onto an unnamed dirt road leading toward the woods. You'll pass an old country house on the right called the Villa Riane. After about ten minutes, you emerge into vineyards, and then the trail runs next to a fence to your left, which you parallel for about five minutes.

1. About 15 minutes from the walk's starting point, you reach a Y in the farm road; bear right, away from the fence. Continue on this broad dirt path for a couple of minutes, ignoring the next trail to the right.

2. Turn right on the second farm road leading off to your right. You will see the white-and-red blazes of the *GR* trail on a fence post on your left. (You've missed this turn-off if you penetrate into woods.) Follow this farm road for about ten minutes, through a mix of woodlands, agricultural fields, and vineyards. You'll see the white-and-red blazes of the *GR* trail from time to time.

3. Cross the small paved *rte. de Thésée.* Continue straight on the farm road, bordered to your left by a small forest and to your right by more vineyards. *As you proceed, vast views of the finely manicured vineyards, farmlands, and forests of the Cher valley unfold. Before long, the walls of the Roman ruins appear ahead in the valley below, rising up over fields, looking much as they did to the approaching traveler 2,000 years ago.* Follow the trail directly down toward the ruins of Les Maselles and explore them.

4. From the ruins, turn left onto *rte. D176,* the main road running past Les Maselles. The white-and-red markings of the *GR* trail run alongside the road. After less than a five-minute walk on *rte. D176,* turn right, crossing the road and going through a tunnel under the railroad tracks and walking a short distance to the river.

5. At the bank of the river, make a right. You will now be on a trail marked with yellow blazes (the white-and-red-blazed *GR* trail goes off to the left). *This is one of the landscapes people come to France for—a*

▼

deep, narrow, slow-flowing waterway bordered by thick foliage of trees and wildflowers. Follow the riverside trail for about 45 minutes, *noticing the special little clearings and platforms fishermen have built for themselves, to fish from and take in the view. Along the way, you pass a lock to accommodate boat and barge traffic around a waterfall.* Eventually you'll cross a bridge over a tiny tributary of the Cher.

6. Just after the bridge, you come upon an intersection. Turn right, away from the river, and leave the yellow-blazed trail and head toward a warehouse and the railroad tracks. Cross the tracks and cross *rte. D176,* then make a left. You will follow the road for less than ten minutes, passing some troglodyte homes (elaborate cave homes described in Experience 18, Noizay).

7. Shortly after passing a right-hand turnoff for a dead-end street, make a right on the *rte. de la Verrerie.* Follow the direction indicated by the signposts to Les Arcis and La Verrerie. Stay on this paved road for less than 15 minutes, going through the outskirts of a village, where forest mingles with a mix of old and newer country homes. Keep your eyes out for an old country house on the left with a single ornate dormer window.

8. Just past this house, you will see a concrete telephone pole on the left marked with yellow and white-and-red blazes. Go right, following the white-and-red-blazed *GR* trail, which plunges into a forest on your right. (You have gone too far on the paved road if you reach the concrete gateposts and white gates of a house on the left.) In a few minutes, the trail brings you out into an open field. Follow the trail through vineyards, passing to the left of a copse of wood. The hamlet of Arcis, with its old houses, appears in the valley to your left as you go uphill on the grassy trail. Keep going straight on the trail for about ten minutes, through various intersections with other trails and dirt roads. The Cher valley appears to your right, shouldered by endless vineyards.

9. When you reach a paved road, *rte. D85,* cross it. Bear right onto a farm track heading toward the village of Monthou-sur-Cher, whose

▼

homes you can see in the valley before you. The grassy track proceeds down a shallow ravine to the left of some small power-line poles.

10. The footpath ends at a small paved road. There will be a small office and warehouse on your left. Walk straight through the parking lot of the office building toward a tiny country road.

11. Go right on the small road. Proceed downhill to the larger *rte. D85,* where you go left. Follow *rte. D85* straight back into Monthou-sur-Cher, announced by a signpost as you enter the village. You cross one small bridge and then another. *Admire a beautiful old wooden mill on your left at the entrance to the village.*

12. At a stop sign, turn left toward the small café. Your car is parked just before it, outside the church.

PLACES ALONG THE WALK
See Experience 19, Gué-Péan.

DINING & LODGING
See Experience 19, Gué-Péan, or Experience 18, Noizay.

FOR MORE INFORMATION
Tourist Office:
   Montrichard Office de Tourisme. *1 rue du Pont, Montrichard 41400, tel. 54-32-05-10. Open daily 9-12 and 2-6:30.*

For Serious Walkers:
   The area has a wide variety of walking trails; for information, contact the *Office de Tourisme, 11 pl. du Château, Blois 41000, tel. 54-78-55-50.* For the walk at Thésée, use IGN map 2022E (east) and 2023E (east). *See* also Experience 19, Gué-Péan.

Valley of the Lily

EXPERIENCE 21: ARTANNES

I n his acclaimed *Le Lys dans la Vallée* (*The Lily in the Valley*), the great 19th-century novelist Honoré de Balzac describes the route taken by the novel's main character, Félix de Vandeness, to a chateau in Touraine: "To go to the chateau of Frapesle, people on foot or on horseback shorten the

The Highlights: Walks in the footsteps of Balzac, extended vistas of rolling farmland, the Indre river valley, quiet country roads.

Other Places Nearby: Chateaus of Azay-le-Rideau and Villandry.

route by passing by the Landes de Charlemagne, untilled land situated at the top of the plateau that separates the valley of the Cher from that of the Indre, and from where leads a shortcut that one takes to Champy. These melancholy forests, flat and sandy, mark the path to Saché...."

This is the same path Balzac himself walked so often from the city of Tours, where he was born, to **Saché,** where an old family friend had a chateau. Balzac visited this chateau on many occasions, and he wrote or conceived some of his greatest works there. In this landscape, still almost identical to his description, you can discover the special places that were such a source of inspiration to this major French writer. And you won't have to wander far from the great tourist sites of the Loire

▼

valley, for Artannes is but a short escape from the city of Tours, the chateaus of **Azay-le-Rideau,** Ussé, and Langeais, and the old city of Chinon and its castle.

The valley Balzac calls the Lys actually is that of the Indre river, which flows for about 265 km. from Montluçon to the Loire river. Balzac's favorite section, referred to so often in his novels, stretches from the village of Artannes to Saché. To get there from Paris, Balzac would go to Tours by carriage (a 23-hour trip) and then, especially in his younger days, walk the last 12 or so miles through a mixture of forest trails and farm roads. At the village of Artannes, he wrote: "There is revealed a valley that begins at Montbazon, finishes at the Loire, and seems to bound under chateaus poised on its double hills: a magnificent emerald cup in the bottom of which the Indre slithers like a snake." Balzac's route to Saché follows part of the ancient Roman road connecting Caesarodunum (modern-day Tours) and Caino (now called Chinon). You can clearly see the remnants of the Roman road in the forests and fields here today. His route crossed the **Landes de Charlemagne,** where the Europeans defeated the Saracens in an important battle in October 732. A Saracen army led by Abd-er-Rhaman mounted a raid on Tours in hopes of capturing its rich religious treasures. Passing by the Pont-de-Ruan, the Saracens met a force coming from Tours. In this quiet forest, the local troops killed the Muslim chief, captured his booty, and returned to Tours without even pursuing the retreating Arabs. The site of this historic skirmish, which adventuresome walkers can visit, lies undisturbed by development.

Balzac, a master of realism, borrowed heavily from the people and places in his life to create his fictional worlds. The characters and places in his books often represented composites of real places and individuals, altered to suit his literary purposes. Local historian J. Maurice has carefully documented the places borrowed from the region in *Le Lys dans la Vallée.* In this novel, sort of a tribute to the place Balzac loved so much, he used the real name of Saché, but the Château de Clochegourde is really the **Château de Vonne** that you pass on the walk. The Château de Frapesle in the book is actually the Château de

▼

Valesnes (closed to the public) near Saché. Mme. de Mortsauf, one of the heroines of the book, probably was Mme. Le Breton de Vonne, who now lies in the cemetery in Saché.

The great writer's curious nomadic lifestyle—he lived in many places, often at the homes of friends—brought him here a dozen times or more to undertake a rigid regime of writing and contemplation. His letters reveal little affection for the owner of this chateau, M. de Marganne, yet he kept returning. Each time he visited, he fell into the following routine: He went to bed at ten and set his alarm clock to go off between two and three in the morning. He made his own coffee, ate several slices of bread with jam, and got back in bed to write with paper and a quill pen. He kept his shutters closed even during the day and would work like this until 5 p.m., stopping only to take a couple of quick catnaps or to make more coffee, of which he drank prodigious amounts. At 5 p.m., he would get dressed and descend to take part in the evening functions, which included dinner, games, and perhaps a walk in the park.

For all his success, Balzac went through periods of deep debt. During one such time, in 1830, he decided to make his way to Saché, where he knew he could stay at no cost. On a particularly hot day, he made the journey on foot from Tours to Saché by the path we've described. Exhausted and thirsty, he wandered from his route to the Manoir de l'Alouette, where he asked the owner, Mme. Martin, for something to drink. Apparently he did not pay her for the bowl of milk she gave him, supposedly telling her that he "didn't have any change."

Later, the historian Maurice tells us, he repaid her by referring to her in a book, *Le Médecin de Campagne* (*The Country Doctor*), in which a character gives a Mme. Martin several coins and adds an extra bonus for the orphans she takes care of. The real-life Mme. Martin probably never knew he had immortalized her, since she could not read.

Why did he so often return here to write? "At Saché, I am free and happy like a monk in his monastery. I go there to meditate some serious work. The sky is so pure, the oaks so beautiful, the calm so vast. There, I wrote *Louis Lambert,* dreamed up *Le Père Goriot,* and restored my courage for the horrible struggles of my material interests," wrote

▼

Balzac in a letter to a friend. Perhaps you too will find inspiration for some great project in this beautiful, unspoiled rural landscape.

GETTING THERE

By car:

From Tours, take *rte. D751* toward Ballan-Miré. About 2 km. beyond Ballan-Miré, turn left onto *rte. D8* toward Pont-de-Ruan.

Drive about 5 km. toward Pont-de-Ruan, then go left on *rte. D121*, following signs to Artannes-sur-Indre. In less than 1 km., you enter the village. Park in the square, the *pl. des Tilleuls*.

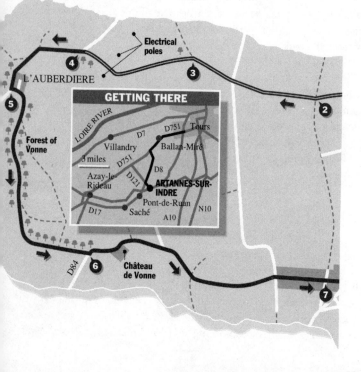

▼

Walk Directions

TIME: 1 1/2 to 2 1/2 hours
LEVEL: Easy
DISTANCE: 3 to 5 miles
ACCESS: By car

This route loops through sweeping landscapes in the Indre river valley, near the village of Artannes. You'll walk on paved and dirt roads through open farmland, hills, and rich forests. A shortcut described in Point 2 will shorten the walk considerably, but the terrain is easy enough that anyone with sufficient time can do the full route. Pick up picnic provisions in Artannes, and enjoy a lunch just about anywhere along the way. Yellow blazes mark the entire route,

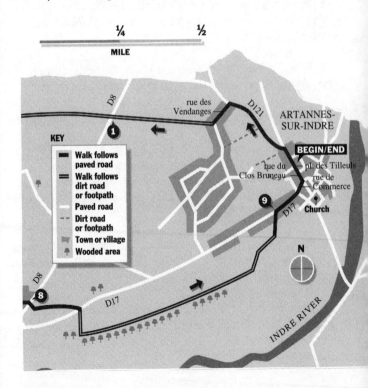

▼

but they won't always be easy to find in the open fields.

TO BEGIN

Walk back out of town on *rte. D121,* heading uphill. After about ten minutes, turn left on the *rue des Vendanges,* a small paved road heading into a new housing development. In about 100 feet the paved road goes left, but you continue straight, out into the open fields. Walk straight ahead for another ten minutes or so.

1. Cross *rte. D8* and continue straight on the well-marked trail for another 15 minutes or so. You will pass the ruins of an old stone shed.

2. When you reach a crossroads of blazed trails, continue straight. *Or, if you want a shortcut, turn left here onto a purple-blazed trail that will take you directly to Point 7.*

3. Soon you reach a Y intersection out in the fields, marked by a solitary old tree. Bear left, heading toward electrical poles in the distance.

4. When you come upon a small paved road, turn left and follow it downhill.

5. At the bottom of the hill you reach a three-way intersection of paved roads just before a tiny bridge in the hamlet of L'Auberdière. Go left. (Do not cross the bridge.) *This small paved road goes through the Bois de Vonne (Forest of Vonne).*

6. When you reach *rte. D84,* go left up the hill. *In just a moment, you'll pass on your right the Château de Vonne,* privately owned and closed to the public.

7. From the chateau, ten minutes or less of walking will bring you to a four-way intersection marked by a little sign pointing left to L'Alouette. Here, the mauve- and yellow-blazed routes intersect. Go straight.

▼

8. Cross *rte. D8* and continue straight. You'll soon reach *rte. D17*, where you make a sharp right onto a small trail running alongside houses and heading away from *rte. D17* and toward the Indre river. This trail abruptly veers left behind the houses and follows a small footpath for about 1/2 mile, then turns into the *rue de la Fontaine aux Mères*.

9. You rejoin *rte. D17* just outside the village of Artannes. Turn right onto *rte. D17*. As you enter the village, go straight onto the *rue de Commerce*. (*Rte. D17* veers sharply to the right.) Walk a short distance and then turn left on the *rue du Clos Bruneau*. It's another 100 or so feet from here to the *pl. des Tilleuls* and your car.

OTHER PLACES NEARBY

■ **Saché.** Visit the tiny room used by Balzac during his stays there. Manuscripts, portraits, original editions, and letters are on display. *Saché 37190, tel. 47-26-86-50. Open daily 9:30-12 and 2-5 Feb. 1-Mar. 14; 9:30-12 and 2-6 Mar. 15-Jun. 30; 9:30-6:30 Jul.-Aug.; 9-12 and 2-6 Sep.; 9:30-12 and 2-5 Oct. and Nov. Closed Dec. and Jan. Admission. From Artannes take rte. D17 6 km. west to Saché and follow signs to the chateau.*

■ **Azay-le-Rideau Château.** One of the most celebrated of the Renaissance-style chateaus in the region, Azay-le-Rideau has striking interiors, many of them authentically furnished, and a lovely tree-shaded setting along the Indre river. *Rue Nationale, Azay-le-Rideau 37910, tel. 47-45-42-04. Open daily 10-12:30 and 2-5 Oct.-Mar.; 9:30-6 Apr.-Jun.; 9-7 Jul.-Aug.; 9:30-6 Sep. Closed major holidays. Admission. From Artannes take rte. D17 8 km. west to Azay and follow signs to the chateau.*

■ **Villandry Château.** Magnificent re-creations of 16th-century French gardens occupy a beautiful setting near the Loire river. *Rte. D7, Villandry 37510, tel. 47-50-02-09. Gardens open daily 9-dusk; chateau open daily 9-6 Feb. 15-Nov. 15. Admission. From Artannes take rte. D121 about 10 km. north to Villandry and follow signs.*

DINING

■ **Auberge du XII Siecle** (expensive to moderate). With beautiful

▼

surroundings indoors and out, this restaurant serves updated traditional cuisine. Despite the elegant table settings, the atmosphere is casual, befitting an afternoon spent in the countryside. Specials on our visit included *aiguillettes de canard rosées en réduction de Chinon* (slices of duck flavored with a sauce of local white wine) and *filet de boeuf en casserole, ragoût de champignons sauvages* (a beef fillet cooked in a casserole with wild mushrooms). *Saché, Azay-le-Rideau 37190, tel. 47-26-88-77. Open daily Jul.-Aug.; daily except Wed. Mar.-Jun. and Sep.; daily except Tue. evening and Wed. Oct.-Jan. Closed Feb. On rte. D17, 6 km. east of Azay.*

■ **Le Grand Monarque** (expensive to moderate). In a lovely atmosphere, highly regarded cuisine is served by a chef who cooked for Valerie Giscard d'Estaing when he was president. On our visit, specials included *emincé de rillon tiède à la crème* (minced pork with a cream sauce), *brochette du Sandre au beurre d'herbe* (a local fish cooked on a skewer with herb butter), and *petit gâteau de semoule aux fruits de saisons* (a cake of semolina wheat and fresh fruit). *Pl. de la République, Azay-le-Rideau 37190, tel. 47-65-40-08, fax 47-45-46-25. Closed Dec. 15-Jan. 31. About 100 yards east of the intersection of the rue Nationale and the rue du Château.*

■ **L'Aigle d'Or** (moderate). In this intimate, comfortable village restaurant, the menu features such specialties as *salade de langoustines au foie gras* (a salade of prawns with a pâté of goose liver) and *filet de boeuf au Chinon*, a fillet of beef in white wine sauce. *10 ave. Adelaide-Riche, Azay-le-Rideau 37190, tel. 47-45-24-58, fax 47-45-90-18. Closed Sun. evening and Wed.; closed Tue. in fall and winter. About 200 yards west of the intersection of the rue Nationale and the rue du Château.*

■ **Le Fournil** (inexpensive). You get rustic atmosphere and good food popular with locals. On our visit, specials included *l'escalope de sandre rôtie, beurre blanc au vinaigre de framboises* (a perchlike freshwater fish that is grilled and served in a butter sauce flavored with raspberry vinegar) and *le suprême de volaille à la crème de morilles,* breasts of chicken served in a wild mushroom cream sauce. *22 rue du Val de Loire (Rte. D39); Azay-le-Rideau 37190, tel. 47-45-43-06. Closed Sun. eve. Located in the town of Azay.*

▼

LODGING

■ **La Rémonière** (very expensive). A beautiful small chateau with six rooms located adjacent to the main chateau at Azay-Le-Rideau. The Charles VII room has a four-poster bed and a beautiful fireplace. There's a large pool alongside some Gallo-Roman ruins. *Cheille 37190, Azay-le-Rideau, tel. 47-45-24-48. On rte. D17 just outside of the town of Azay-le-Rideau.*

■ **Château Le Gerfaut** (expensive). A stately country home built in 1910 (it looks much older) on beautiful grounds at the edge of a forest, this *chambres d'hôte* provides near-luxury living at reasonable prices. All six rooms have private bath and charming decor. You can play tennis and rent bicycles. English is spoken. *Azay-le-Rideau 37190, tel. 47-45-40-16, fax 47-45-20-15. Closed Nov.-Mar. From rte. D751 at the edge of Azay-le-Rideau, make a left on rte. D39 in the direction of Villandry and then the first right, following signs to the chateau.*

■ **Le Clos Philippa** (moderate). This old home in the center of Villandry has four rooms, two of which face a garden. The Green Room is the biggest; the Beige faces the garden. All the rooms are clean and pleasantly decorated, but rooms facing the road may get street noise. *10 rue Pineau, Azay-le-Rideau 37190, tel. 47-45-26-49.*

■ **Chez Mme. Balitran** (moderate). This modern house in an old country village provides two charming rooms, and the feeling of living in a French home. One room has its own entrance and a solarium that serves as the living room. The other, which once served as an artist's studio, provides guests with lots of space. *La Sablonnière, Saché 37190, tel. 47-26-86-96. From Saché, go north on a little road over the Indre river, with a sign pointing to La Sablonnière. Turn left on rte. D84. The house is on your right in the heart of the tiny hamlet.*

■ **La Gallaisière** (inexpensive). The single room in this farmhouse is rustic but comfortable. An inexpensive meal is served for those who reserve in advance, and horseback riding is available. *La Gallaisière, Artannes 37260, tel. 47-65-70-36. No credit cards. Leave Artannes on rte. D121, cross rte. D8, go about 1 km., and turn left at a small road sign pointing to Auberdière and Les Erables. Go a short distance to some stables and turn right on a small paved road; follow it to the right,*

▼

behind the farm, where the house is located.

FOR MORE INFORMATION
Tourist Office:

Office de Tourisme de Tours. *Blvd. Heurteloup, Tours 37042, tel. 47-05-58-08, fax 47-61-14-22. Open Mon.-Sat. 9-12:30 and 1:30-6 Oct.-Apr.; Mon.-Sat. 8:30-6:30 and Sun. 10-12:30 and 3-6 May and Sep.; daily 8:30-7 Jun.-Aug.*

For Serious Walkers:

The region has an incomparable number of blazed walking trails, including many day-trips for experienced walkers. There's a series of booklets for sale at the *Comité Touraine de la Randonnée*, adjacent to the Tours tourism office. Unfortunately, almost all of the information is in French, but even those unable to read French can use the maps in conjunction with IGN maps to create realistic itineraries. For more information, contact the walking organization *c/o Office de Tourisme, Tours 37042, tel. 47-70-37-35, fax 47-61-14-22. Open Mon., Wed., and Sat. 9-12:30 and 2-6. Closed holidays. (The walking group has hours different from those of the tourist office.)* For the Artannes walk, use IGN map 1823E (east).

The Longest Day

EXPERIENCE 22: OMAHA BEACH

When you come to Omaha Beach, don't park at the American Military Cemetery like everybody else does. Instead, drive over to Les Moulins and park near the beach. Look uphill toward the wooded plateau on which the cemetery rests, or down to the

> **The Highlights:** An awesome World War II battlefield, quiet beaches, rugged coastline, the American Military Cemetery.
>
> **Other Places Nearby:** The treasures of Bayeux, an exquisite Romanesque monastery, incomparable countryside.

peaceful sandy beach. Then try to imagine what happened here on one bloody morning, June 6, 1944, when heroic American soldiers stormed this beach under horrendous enemy fire.

Omaha Beach was the code name for one of the beachheads of the D day invasion, in which Allied forces landed on Normandy beaches and moved inland to attack the German line of defense. From a military standpoint, D day was a tremendous success, with fewer losses in men and equipment than envisioned by military planners. But that was little consolation to the men who came ashore on Omaha Beach; they suffered the greatest concentration of losses of any of the forces that landed in France that day. The American Military Cemetery bears silent witness to their sacrifice, with the staggering sight of nearly 10,000 white crosses arrayed in perfect rows.

Omaha Beach, nearly four miles long, forms the only break in the cliffs lining this part of the Normandy coast. Military planners had little

▼

choice but to select this as one of the assault points, since it is among the few gaps through which tanks, armored carriers, and trucks could reach the interior. The assault especially targeted four tiny valleys formed by streams coming off the plateau. Through here, the Allies would build roads on which to unload the enormous quantity of supplies needed for the invasion of France.

Unfortunately, the Germans knew the strategic importance of the position and had significantly fortified it, stationing the crack 352nd German infantry division near this sector just before the battle. Allied intelligence failed to detect their presence; General Omar Bradley learned of it too late to warn the troops.

The Allied plan was clear. Troops would be directed against the four strategic valleys up and down the beach in sectors given code names such as Fox Green, Fox Red, Easy Red, and Easy Green. The first wave of demolition experts was to land at 6:30 a.m., just one hour before low tide. Their job was to clear a path through the spikes, mines, and other obstacles placed by the Germans on land and underwater. Within half an hour, the next wave of troops would arrive, followed by another wave every ten minutes until 9:30.

The Americans knew most of the difficulties. Big guns in fortified bunkers, machine-gun nests, and mortar and artillery positions lined the hills above the beach, especially the four valleys following the streambeds up to the plateau. To reduce these German defenses, the Allies launched an enormous naval and air bombardment in the early morning hours of June 6. The deafening roar of explosions and the bright lights of fires probably boosted Allied troop morale, but it did not have the desired effect on the Germans. Fog and smoke hindered the efforts of Allied target spotters, who had difficulty directing the bombardment. Rocket launchers, brought up close to shore in the half hour before the landing, created a heartening roar but had little apparent effect.

As the first wave of men approached, the area was eerily devoid of enemy fire, which must have further encouraged the soldiers. They didn't know that German troops were under orders to hold their fire until American forces began to land. The enemy fire, when it came, was

▼

devastating. Landing forces confronted a cross-fire of heavy cannons, artillery, mortars, and automatic weapons, with hardly any cover. Those demolition experts who got to shore alive or unhurt lost much of their equipment. Many soldiers drowned even before reaching shore. Those who did survive found meager cover behind German antitank devices. Many lay prostrate in the shallow waters of the incoming tide, moving forward with only their heads out of the water. Pinned down on a narrow strip of beach under heavy fire and blinded by thick smoke and fog, the attackers could not use their flamethrowers, rocket launchers, or automatic rifles.

This narrow strip of beach was covered with soldiers, many of them dead or wounded, and wave after wave of incoming men poured in over them, facing the same disastrous situation. Some of the worst losses occurred in the Easy Red sector, near where you begin the walk described below. By 10:30 a.m.—four hours after the first wave—3,000 dead or wounded lay on this narrow beach, one man for every six feet of beach.

Allied naval forces bore down on enemy positions, inching as close to shore as possible in the incoming tide. Gradually, a few groups of men made their way across the beach, through the mine fields, to the base of the sandy wooded cliffs facing the sea. The first Americans broke through to the plateau near the present-day American cemetery at around 8 a.m. and walked through the woods where the cemetery now stands to knock out German positions overlooking the Easy Red sector.

After five hours of carnage, the situation began to improve. By about 11:30, Bradley got the first reports of movement into the interior. By 1:30 p.m., troops pinned down in Easy Red, Easy Green, and Fox Red sectors began to advance. One colonel led his men across the beach through a mine field shouting the now-famous order: "Two kinds of people are staying on this beach, the dead and those who are going to die—now let's get the hell out of here." By the end of the day, American forces had knocked out most of the German defenses in the sector and had formed a firm bridgehead at Omaha Beach, with men and equipment already beginning the move into the interior.

On the described walk, you climb through the same little valley

▼

that some of the first Americans passed through as they made their way up onto the plateau. On either side of the hill lay hidden a fearsome array of defensive positions designed to halt the Allied advance. Once the Americans had taken this valley, the 5th Engineer Special Brigade, whose monument you will pass on your walk, went to work preparing the route for the huge convoys of equipment.

To the west of this theater of operations, another daring assault took place at **La Pointe du Hoc,** where a tremendous German gun emplacement was located. The huge naval barrage that preceded the American assault scattered the German troops defending the position, but the Germans returned to their posts just in time to greet the Americans landing on the beach. A group of 225 Rangers had been given the daunting job of climbing the 100-foot rock cliffs with ropes. The Germans strafed them with bullets and lobbed hand grenades as the Rangers attempted to climb the cliffs. With the help of close naval support, the Americans made it to the top and overtook the fortifications in a fierce battle, only to find the guns moved elsewhere.

For the next day, the Rangers were effectively pinned down, facing counterattack after counterattack. Naval support helped, but they could expect no new supplies for a while from the troops struggling to survive on Omaha Beach. The Rangers resorted to using the weapons they had captured from the enemy, only to be fired on by fellow Americans who mistook them for Germans by the sound of their guns. By the time they were freed by other troops, only 90 of the original 225 men were in condition to continue fighting.

Most tourists approach La Pointe du Hoc by way of a well-marked country road off *rte. D514,* but you can approach this spot from a different direction, along an easy and well-marked clifftop walk that takes about an hour to get to the monument and back. If you're up to more of a challenge, you can even approximate the Rangers' courageous climb up the cliff, on a path only locals know about. Drive to the hamlet of Levèvre (for directions, *see* Other Places Nearby, below) and, facing the ocean, turn left on the white-and-red-blazed coastal walk (signs call it "Sentier du Littoral"), which passes through a bird sanctuary, past battle-churned landscape, to the area of the monument. About 125 steps from

▼

your starting point, you may notice a gap in the thick brush bordering the cliff. This leads to a very steep cliffside trail descending to the sea, where you can get a close-hand look at the obstacles the Rangers had to overcome in their assault on La Pointe du Hoc. Do not stray too far from the ladder, however, unless you know the hours of high tide; unwary people have been stranded against the cliffs and even drowned in the swift tides.

In this region of Normandy, the charming town of **Bayeux** and the beautiful **Abbaye de Cerisy-la-Forêt** also attract visitors. Often bypassed by tourists, the mostly modern cities of St-Lô, Caen, and Coutances were once beautiful cities with numerous charming streets. In an effort to block German retreat, Allied air forces unleashed deadly bombardments on these major French cities, hoping to render their major road and rail intersections impassible. Whether or not the strategy succeeded is subject to dispute, but no one argues the fact that the area was devastated. For the duration of the Normandy operations, from June 6 through August 1, some 12,000 French civilians were killed in this theater of operations and many more were wounded. Hardly a family in the region was spared the loss of a loved one or a dwelling. Allied liberators generally received a warm welcome from locals, but resentment smoldered under the surface. There were some reports—perhaps spread by Germans—of isolated sniper attacks against Allied soldiers by French civilians. A generation of Normans silently asked themselves whether it was necessary to kill so many civilians, and most locals still will not talk with Americans about this sad chapter in the otherwise-magnificent story of the Normandy invasion.

GETTING THERE

By car:

From Rouen, take *autoroute A13* west to Caen, then *rte. N13* to Bayeux, from which you continue on *rte. N13* 15 km. west to a right-hand exit for *rte. D517,* Formigny and Omaha Beach. Continue on *rte. D517* toward the beach and the hamlet of Les Moulins. When you get to the beach and the war monument to the American 1st Division, turn right and go 1 km. to the end of the road, where you'll find a parking area for a monument to the 2nd Division.

▼

Walk Directions

TIME: 1 to 1 1/2 hours
LEVEL: Easy
DISTANCE: 2 to 2 1/2 miles
ACCESS: By car

This walk includes a mixture of paved country roads, forest footpaths, farm tracks, and sandy beach as you head to the cemetery, past some war monuments, and back along the beach. You will encounter a few muddy spots in wet weather. You can trim the route slightly with the shortcut described in Point 3, though you'll miss the most stunning view of Omaha Beach. Your best bet for picnic provisions is to buy them in Port-en-Bessin or Grandcamp-Maisy, though a few shops sell food in the small villages of Vierville-sur-Mer, St-Laurent, and Colleville-sur-Mer. You'll find picnic spots on the beach and near the war memorial to the 5th Engineer Special Brigade.

BEGIN/END
OMAHA BEACH
Parking
Monument

American Military Cemetery

VIEWPOINT
VIEWPOINT
Monuments

① ③
②
⑦
⑥
⑧
Parking

④ ⑤

N

GETTING THERE

Les Moulins
OMAHA BEACH
American Cemetery
D517
D6
D29
N13
D96
Bayeux

4 miles

KEY

▬▬ Walk follows paved road
═══ Walk follows dirt road or footpath
—— Paved road
- - - Dirt road or footpath
🌲 Town or village
🌲 Wooded area

⅛ ¼

MILE

▼

TO BEGIN

Walk uphill away from the beach along the only paved road heading up the valley.

1. When the paved road veers abruptly to the right, continue straight on a dirt road. You should now see the white-and-red blazes of a long-distance *GR* trail, which you will follow all the way to Point 7. Continue straight for a few minutes.

2. At a three-way intersection, go left, following the white-and-red blazes down a hill. You will cross a stream and enter a damp area with a tangle of trails. Follow the blazed trail uphill, ignoring trails that go off to your left.

3. Toward the top of the hill, you will reach another intersection. Continue straight.

4. When you reach large water tanks, go left on a dirt road toward the access road to the cemetery.

5. The dirt road ends at the paved access road, in front of the gate marking the cemetery entrance. *To visit the cemetery, go left at Point 5 and walk about 300 yards to the cemetery. From there, you can retrace your steps to Point 5 or proceed to the viewpoint overlooking the beach, from where you can descend on a well-marked path through the dunes to the sea, where you go left and return to your car.* If you choose not to visit the cemetery, cross the road and proceed on dirt through a narrow strip of trees onto another paved road. Turn left toward the monument to the 5th Engineer Special Brigade, still following the white-and-red blazes.

6. You reach the parking lot for the war memorial in less than ten minutes. Here, go right and proceed through the parking lot toward some war memorials and the sea.

7. Cross a paved road, walk to the right about 30 feet, and then go

▼

left on a paved footpath to the war memorials. You have now left the *GR* trail. Descending straight toward a blockhouse and the monument to the 5th Engineer Special Brigade. *From this fortified hillside, the Germans held back the American assault until nightfall on June 6. The spot now provides one of the most impressive views of Omaha Beach.* Facing the monument, turn right down a grassy track toward a beach-side parking area and a cluster of buildings.

8. In a very short distance, go left, downhill toward the beach and a dirt road. When you reach it, go left and walk toward the beach. There, go left for the 20-minute walk back along the beach to your car. *Here, you walk where Americans took the heaviest losses on the day of the invasion. Above this beach, at about the location of the American cemetery, a detachment of the 1st Division was able to get a foothold as early as 8 a.m. By noon, it had almost reached the entrance to Colleville, where it would remain blocked until the evening.*

PLACES ALONG THE WALK

■ **American Military Cemetery.** *Colleville-sur-Mer 14710, tel. 31-22-40-62. Open 9-6 Mar. 16-Oct. 14.; 9-5 Oct. 15-Mar. 15. Off rte. D514 between St-Laurent-sur-Mer and Colleville-sur-Mer.*

■ **Monument to the 5th Engineer Special Brigade.** *About 100 yards from the cemetery, near Point 7 on the walk.*

OTHER PLACES NEARBY

■ **Abbaye de Cerisy-la-Forêt.** One of the finest examples of Romanesque architecture in Normandy, the existing abbey was built in the 11th century on a site occupied by a monastery perhaps as early as the 6th century. Visits are accompanied by concerts of Gregorian chants and other music. *Cerisy-la-Forêt 50680, tel. 33-56-10-01. Guided visits daily 10:30-12:30 and 2:30-6:30 Easter-Nov. 15. From Bayeux, take rte. D5 west 14 km. to Le Molay-Littry. Pass through the village and make a left on rte. D160 following signs to Cerisy, 6 km.*

■ **Bayeux.** This attractive Normandy town with old homes and a cathedral spared destruction during the war is home to the famed tapes-

▼

tries and a well-preserved Gothic cathedral (*see* Tapisserie de la Reine Mathilde, below). *From Omaha Beach, take rte. D514 to Port-en-Bessin and then rte. D6 to Bayeux, a total distance of 19 km.*

■ **Tapisserie de la Reine Mathilde (Museum for the Tapestry of Queen Matilda).** World-renowned, this magnificently restored tapestry celebrates the deeds of William the Conqueror. Its highly detailed depictions of life in the 11th century yield a first-hand look at the way these medieval people lived. *Rue de Nesmond, Bayeux 14400, tel. 31-92-05-48, fax 31-92-06-41. Open 9-7 Apr. 30-Sep. 17 and Easter weekend; 9:30-12:30 and 2-6 Oct. 16-Mar. 15; otherwise 9-12:30 and 2-6:30. Admission.*

■ **Cathédral Notre-Dame.** Thankfully spared the effects of Allied bombing, this striking edifice is a mix of Norman and Gothic architecture and contains art from the 11th to the 19th centuries. *Near the corner of the rue des Chanoines and the rue Leforestier, Bayeux.*

■ **La Pointe du Hoc.** An outdoor monument open year-round, it commemorates the bravery of the Rangers who held this position on D day. Areas where mines might lie are fenced off, but you can still see the huge craters and wrecked bunkers of the battle. *4 km. east of Grandcamp-Maisy off rte. D514. To reach the starting point of the coastal walk, take rte. D514 to Vierville-sur-Mer, and from the intersection with rte. D517, go straight 4 1/2 km. to the hamlet of Levèvre; turn right onto a paved road next to a farm hangar and go 1 km. to a cul-de-sac.*

■ **Musée Omaha.** This private museum displays memorabilia of the German occupation and D day. *St-Laurent-sur-Mer, tel. 31-21-97-44, fax 31-92-72-08. Open daily 9:30-1:30 and 2:30-6:30 Mar.-Nov. 15; daily 9:30-7:30 Jul.-Aug. On rte. D514 in St-Laurent-sur-Mer, just 4 km. west of turnoff for American Cemetery.*

DINING

■ **Restaurant La Marée** (moderate). Lovely views of the fishing port accompany a menu featuring fresh fish. Specialties include *huîtres chaudes gratinées* (warmed oysters with melted butter) and *poisson grillé à la cheminée* (grilled fresh fish of the day). *On the port in Grandcamp-Maisy 14450, tel. 31-22-60-55, fax 31-92-66-72. From*

▼

Bayeux, take rte. N13 west toward Isigny-sur-Mer. Just before Isigny, exit right onto rte. D514 following signs to Grandcamp.

■ **La Belle Marinière** (inexpensive). Although there are no views here, you'll find a pleasant dining room and simple, carefully prepared offerings of seafood and meats such as *terrine de saumon et toasts chauds* (salmon terrine with toast), *huîtres farcies* (oysters with butter and shallots), and *raie au beurre et aux câpres* (skate with butter and capers). *9 rue du Petit Maisy, Grandcamp-Maisy 14450, tel. 31-22-61-23. Open daily Jul.-Sep. Closed Tue. evening and Wed. Oct.-Jun. and three weeks around Christmas. From Bayeux, take rte. N13 about 30 km. west toward Isigny-sur-Mer. Just before Isigny, exit right onto rte. D514 following signs to Grandcamp. It's one block from the port.*

■ **Le Duguesclin** (inexpensive). Enjoy ocean views from this comfortable, informal, lively dining room. Straightforward seafood and meat offerings include *coquilles St-Jacques, pavé de morue fraiche à l'oseille* (cod steak with sorrel), and *côtes d'agneau grillé* (grilled lamb chops). *4 quai Crompon, Grandcamp-Maisy, tel. 31-22-64-22. Closed Jan. 15-Feb. 5. From Bayeux, take rte. N13 about 30 km. west toward Isigny-sur-Mer. Just before Isigny, exit right onto rte. D514 following signs to Grandcamp. The restaurant is just off the port in front of the beach.*

■ **Hotel de France** (inexpensive). This spot is obviously popular with locals. On our visit, specials included *sole au cidre* (a fillet of sole flavored with local cider) and *huîtres chaudes farcies cinq sauces* (oysters served hot in a sauce of five spices). *13 rue E. Demagny, Isigny-sur-Mer 14230, tel. 31-22-00-33, fax 31-22-79-19. Open daily Easter-Oct. 31. Closed Fri. evening and Sat. Nov.-Mar.; Dec. 15-Jan. 15. Located 31 km. west of Bayeux.*

■ **Ferme-Auberge La Piquenotière** (inexpensive). A particularly attractive dining room is in this working Norman farm in the heart of the countryside. Specialties are meats, poultry, and foie gras. *St-Martin-de-Blagny, Trévières 14710, tel. 31-21-35-54. Reservations required. Take rte. D5 14 km. east of Isigny-sur-Mer to Bernesq; then go 2 km. south on rte. D145.*

LODGING

■ **La Chenevière** (very expensive). One of the only luxury hotels

▼

in the region, La Chenevière is a converted 19th-century home in a quiet park. *Rte. D6, Port-en-Bessin, tel. 31-21-47-96, fax 31-21-47-98. Closed Dec.-mid-Mar. 1 1/2 km. south of Port-en-Bessin.*

■ **Le Château de Colombières** (very expensive). A beautifully maintained 14th-century chateau with beautiful rooms, gardens, and a perfectly intact moat. You can't go wrong in the Tower Suite, but all of the rooms have style and comfort, and the count and countess who own the home offer an especially warm welcome to Americans. *Colombières 14710, tel. 31-22-51-65, fax 31-92-24-92. Closed between Christmas and New Year's and for one week in Jul. Located about 8 km. east of Isigny-sur-Mer off rte. D5.*

■ **Ferme Fortifiée de L'Hermerel** (moderate). Four charming rooms are available on this 17th-century farm with a recently renovated 15th-century chapel. The top-floor room has the most space and charm, but the others have better views. *Géfosse-Fontenay 14230, tel. 31-22-64-12. Closed between Christmas and New Year's and for one week in Jul. Located 6 km. northeast of Isigny-sur-Mer on rte. D199A.*

■ **Manoir de la Rivière** (moderate). A beautiful old working farm offers four lovingly appointed rooms. Most of the antiques have been handed down through the family. The Blue Room is huge, and there's a cozy appartment in an old tower near the main house. *Géfosse-Fontenay 14230, tel. 31-22-64-45, fax 31-22-01-18. Located 6 km. northeast of Isigny-sur-Mer on rte. D199A.*

■ **Château Vouilly** (inexpensive). Here's a wonderful opportunity to relive history—stay at this medieval farm used by the press corps during the first weeks after D day. Big rooms, beautiful farmland views, and extremely friendly owners round out the experience. *Rte. D113, Vouilly, Isigny-sur-Mer 14230, tel. 31-22-08-59, fax 31-22-90-58. Open Mar.-Nov.*

■ **Ferme-Auberge de la Rivière** (inexpensive). Pleasantly furnished rooms and views over Norman marshlands accent this old farm. The Jaune (yellow) and Rose (pink) rooms give you the most space, but all are attractive and have fine views. Inexpensive dinners are available. *Rte. D124, St-Germain du Pert 14230, tel. 31-22-72-92. Closed Nov.-Mar. Reservations required. Located 8 km. west of Isigny-sur-Mer.*

▼

■ **Ferme de L'Abbaye** (inexpensive). Once a nunnery, now a private home, it offers three rooms as well as a house for up to four people. Attractive furnishings and friendly hosts make this a good value. Dinner is available upon request. *Ecrammeville, Trévières 14710, tel. 31-22-52-32. Located 10 km. east of Isigny-sur-Mer on rte. D124.*

FOR MORE INFORMATION
Tourist Office:

Office de Tourisme. *Pont St-Jean, Bayeux 14403, tel. 31-92-16-26, fax 31-92-01-79. Open weekdays and Sat. 9-12:30 and 2-6:30; Sun. 10-12:30 and 3-6:30 in summer only.*

For Serious Walkers:

This part of France has woefully few walking trails. Those following the walk above might wish to purchase IGN map 1411S (south).

The Peaceful Side of Mont-St-Michel

EXPERIENCE 23: CAROLLES

F ew places in France attract more tourists than **Mont-St-Michel,** and for good reason: Its unique setting in a huge tidal bay, its almost unparalleled mixture of medieval architecture, and its long colorful history make this a must for many tourists. But as a result, it's unlikely you'll visit the place in peace.

The Highlights: A spectacular view of the legendary island, a dramatic coastal walk through moors and forests where Romans and medieval monks once roamed.

Other Places Nearby: Mont-St-Michel, incomparable Norman landscapes, ancient abbeys, beaches, the bustling port town of Granville.

So when you've taken in the principal sights and have had enough of the crowds, a drive of less than half an hour will bring you to a spectacular vantage point from which to view Mont-St-Michel across the bay. You'll be able to savor it in the quiet of the countryside, far from the crowds—and then, if the weather's right, enjoy a visit to the busy beaches in nearby Jullouville and Carolles.

The Bay of Mont-St-Michel forms a large tidal inlet separating

▼

Normandy and Brittany. The mouth of the bay stretches between the Norman city of **Granville** to the north and Point Grouin to the south-west, near the Breton port of St-Malo. Mont-St-Michel rises up on an islet off the south coast of the bay. This experience takes you up along the north coast into the famous *bocage* of Normandy, a magnificent pastoral landscape crisscrossed with elaborately pruned hedgerows of ancient trees and bushes.

O nce you leave the main roads, you enter a world of small green pastures and farmland surrounded by fences of flowers, bushes, and trees, their sides often pruned into a sort of living wall. The *bocage* emerged in medieval times as a way to preserve a little woodland—needed for firewood, mushrooms, and edible forest plants—while expanding fields to grow wheat or other crops. In the 19th century, tilled fields gradually gave way to pastureland for cattle, but the *bocage* was left standing.

Walking or driving through this Normandy countryside, one would hardly guess that forestland covers only about four percent of the region. Walls of trees and hedgerows line the old roads, creating the impression that you're in a deep forest when actually you're surrounded by open fields. The *bocage* creates a natural shelter from the winds and rains that frequently sweep through this temperate, verdant region near the Atlantic coast.

To many, the *bocage* is a distinctive element of France's patrimony; to farmers, hard-pressed to compete in the global economy, it simply gets in the way. The tiny parcels of land surrounded by the living fences are too small for modern agricultural techniques, especially for growing corn, which is increasingly important in this region. Farmers lose too much time negotiating the tiny fields with their tractors. This has led to *remembrement,* or regrouping of farmlands, through which farmers create larger, more productive parcels. With *remembrement,* precious *bocage* is often destroyed, infuriating environmentalists and nature lovers. As with most issues, there are no easy solutions.

Set in the heart of *bocage* country, the **Abbaye de la Lucerne** can be reached on foot from Carolles by serious walkers. It's a 15-mile

▼

round-trip through mostly flat, lush countryside (*see* For Serious Walkers, below). The remote, tranquil setting makes it easy to imagine yourself in any era you wish, without the distractions of modern life.

The walking tour outlined below takes you through other characteristic local landscapes as well—seaside moors and forested valleys, just as striking as the *bocage* and just as evocative of the past. This small region between the coastal road and the sea has been spared development and features a fine network of walking trails. On the Pointe de Champeaux, which juts out into the Bay of Mont-St-Michel just south of Carolles, rocky windswept clifftops form a narrow strip of moorland overlooking the sea. The thin soil supports little growth, but it is speckled with wildflowers a good part of the year. Through the seaside highlands, the tiny Lude river has carved a deep valley to the sea, filled with a humid, junglelike forest.

Where the river trickles through a cleft in the cliffs into the sea, there's a rocky shelf called the **Port du Lude** that's often submerged during high tide. It's far too dangerous for normal boat traffic, but it's so remote that over the centuries it probably has seen a fair share of illicit landings. You'll also pass **La Cabane Vauban (Vauban Cabin),** a 17th-century stone shelter for coastal sentries searching for smugglers. It was named for the French engineer Sébastien Vauban, known for significantly improving French defenses in the 17th century (*see* Experience 7, Vézelay). From here, you get a dramatic view of Mont-St-Michel rising up from the sea far in the distance.

About 300 feet beyond La Cabane Vauban lie impossible-to-find vestiges of a **medieval monastery.** Some believe it to be the lost Abbaye de Maudane, where saints Pair and Victor were said to have lived during early medieval times. Some believe that the place has had religious significance since the 6th century, perhaps as a sanctuary for lepers. You'll also walk past traces of a **Roman fort,** in the form of long dirt walls in the forest and undergrowth.

If you don't have time to explore the region but still want an impressive view of Mont-St-Michel, drive to Genêts, 9 km. west of Avranches on *rte. D911.* Park on the left just before the village church, in a lot alongside a stream pouring into a tidal inlet. Walk across the

▼

tiny bridge to the eastern side of the stream, then go to your right, toward the sea. You'll see Mont-St-Michel looming in the distance. The trail quickly veers to the left, paralleling the tidal areas. You can walk for miles, enjoying the views and the rural solitude. With IGN map 1215E (east), you can easily create shorter or longer loops.

GETTING THERE

By car:

From Mont-St-Michel, take *rte. D275* (which becomes *rte. D43*) to *rte. N175* to Avranches. Exit for *rte. D911* toward Jullouville. After 17 km., just before the entrance to the village of Carolles, turn left on a small paved road following signs to La Cabane Vauban. Drive to the end of the road and park.

Walk Directions

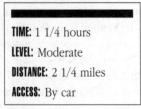

TIME: 1 1/4 hours
LEVEL: Moderate
DISTANCE: 2 1/4 miles
ACCESS: By car

This is only one of many loops in the open lands around La Cabane Vauban. You can shorten this walk by going just to La Cabane Vauban (Point 1, below) and back, or you can extend the walk with the help of maps available at the Carolles tourist office. Most of the walk is along a marked coastal trail, with several ups and downs but only one difficult descent, which you can avoid by taking the shortcut described in Point 1. You'll find numerous secluded spots above the seaside cliffs for a picnic; buy provisions in Carolles.

TO BEGIN

Walk about 100 steps toward the sea.

1. When you reach a wooden signpost providing information (in French) on the *GR* "Sentier du Littoral" (Coastal Walk), make a right toward La Cabane Vauban, marked by a sign. *Along this portion of the*

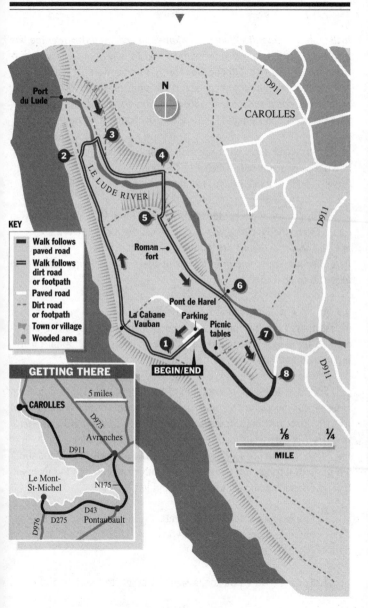

KEY

- **Walk follows paved road**
- **Walk follows dirt road or footpath**
- Paved road
- Dirt road or footpath
- Town or village
- Wooded area

N

Port du Lude

CAROLLES

D911

D911

LE LUDE RIVER

Roman fort

Pont de Harel

La Cabane Vauban

Parking

Picnic tables

BEGIN/END

D911

⅛ ¼

MILE

GETTING THERE

CAROLLES

5 miles

D973

Avranches

D911

Le Mont-St-Michel

N175

D976   D275   D43   Pontaubault

▼

walk, take in magnificent views of Mont-St-Michel presiding over the bay in the distance. At La Cabane Vauban, coastal sentries took shelter during patrols. From La Cabane Vauban, continue walking on the trail along the towering clifftop for about 15 minutes. *In the brush to your right was located an ancient abbey, possibly the Abbaye de Maudane.* Pass by a wooden sign and follow the arrow to Port du Lude.

2. You will soon reach another signposted intersection. Go right down a very steep hill, which can be muddy and slippery when wet. Cross a small concrete bridge over the Lude river.

3. In just a few more steps, you reach a three-way intersection. Go right. *To see the Port du Lude and walk on the rocky, rugged shore, go left and walk for about five minutes. Be careful walking on the beach here. The tide can come in quickly and sweep unsuspecting walkers out to sea. Retrace your steps to Point 3.*

4. After walking a few minutes from Point 3, you reach another intersection. Take the trail to the right, which crosses a bridge and is marked by a sign pointing to La Cabane Vauban. Head uphill on this broad trail, ignoring a trail part way up the hill to your left.

5. At a T intersection at the top of the hill, go left. *You will notice a ridge of dirt paralleling the trail on your right; this is part of the Roman fortification. Just a short distance later, beyond the field thick with underbrush, tiny trails lead into the dense forest and along the edge of one of the ancient dirt walls of the fort.* Follow the trail straight for about ten minutes through the forest and gradually downhill into the river valley. Ignore trails going off to the right and left.

6. On the valley floor, a trail enters from the left at the Pont de Harel. Continue straight on the trail you're on, heading uphill and to the right of pastureland.

7. At the top of an incline, a signpost points to the right and uphill

▼

to La Cabane Vauban. Continue straight for a few minutes. *You can go right here to shorten the walk.*

8. When you reach the paved access road, turn right and follow the road for less than ten minutes, uphill to your car.

OTHER PLACES NEARBY

■ **Abbaye du Mont-St-Michel.** No visit to this part of Normandy would be complete without a stop at the famous abbey island and religious shrine. Tourists jam a main street filled with souvenir shops, but the visit to the striking hilltop church and abbey offers unique views of architecture spanning the Carolingian, Romanesque, and Gothic periods. *Manche 50116, tel. 33-60-14-14. One-hour guided tours May 15-Sep. 15 9:30-6; Sep. 16-May 14 9:30-11:45 and 1:45-4:15. Closed Christmas, New Year's, May 1, and Nov. 11. Admission. From Carolles, take rte. D911 to Avranches, then N175 toward Pontorson. At Pontaubault (7 km. south of Avranches), exit onto rte. D43 west to Mont-St-Michel. When this road reaches rte. D976, go right for 2 km.*

■ **Abbaye de la Lucerne.** The setting as much as the ruins themselves make this a delightful stop. Some of the main structures date from the 12th century, and the entire complex sits within a peaceful wooded valley untouched by time. *La Lucerne d'Outre-Mer 50320, tel. 33-48-83-56. Open daily 9-12 and 2-6:30 Easter-Oct.; Sat., Sun., and school holidays 9-12 and 2-6:30 the rest of the year. Admission. From Carolles, take rte. D61 east 8 km. to Sartilly; then take rte. D35. Make a quick left on rte. D335 and go 4 km. to the abbey.*

■ **Granville.** This bustling seaside vacation site and fishing center has an interesting historic center and ramparts offering attractive coastal views. *12 km. north of Carolles on rte. D911.*

■ **Abbaye de Hambye.** These imposing ruins in the Sienne river valley were once an abbey founded in the 12th century. The architecture spans the 13th, 14th, and 15th centuries. *Hambye 50650, tel. 33-61-76-92. Open daily except Tue. 10-12 and 2-6. Closed Dec. 15-Jan. 31. Admission. From Carolles, take rte. D61 8 km. to Sartilly, then rte. 35 about 8 km. to La Haye-Pesnel. Go north 17 km. on rte. D7 to Gavray*

▼

and follow signs east on rte. D9 to an intersection with rte. D198, which you follow 7 km. to the abbey.

DINING

For the largest selection of restaurants, go to the nearby towns of Granville or Avranches.

■ **Le Jardin de L'Abbaye** (moderate to inexpensive). One of the best values of any restaurant we visited, Le Jardin de l'Abbaye is located deep in the heart of Norman countryside. The menu featured such creative yet accessible combinations as *cuisse de lapereau à l'estragon* (thigh of rabbit with tarragon), *fricassée de sole au beurre d'agrumes* (sole with citrus-flavored butter), and *faux-filet aux poivres façon bordelaise* (sirloin steak with bordelaise sauce). The decor is elegant and appealing, with dark-stained wooden beams and posts. *La Croix Barrée, St-Pierre-Langers 50530, tel. 33-48-49-08, fax 33-48-18-50. Open daily except Mon. Jul.-Aug.; daily except Sun. evening and Mon. the rest of the year. Closed late Sep.-Oct. 15 and first three weeks of Feb. From Carolles, take rte. D68 8 km. to Sartilly. Go left on rte. D973 about 4 km. to rte. D143, where you go right and proceed for under 1 km.*

■ **Le Courtil de la Lucerne** (inexpensive). A group of farmers present simple but wholesome food in a renovated rectory. On our visit, specials included *flan de pommes aux gésiers* (a custard of potato and gizzard) and *pintade du Courtil (roasted young Guinea hen). Le Bourg, La Lucerne d'Outremer 50320, tel. 33-61-22-02, fax 33-61-22-15. In summer, open daily except Sun. eve. Otherwise, closed Sun. eve., Mon. lunch, and Wed. 13 km. east of Carolles by way of rte. 61 and rte. D35.*

LODGING

Although the nearby beach resorts of Carolles and Jullouville attract crowds in summer, most of those visitors rent houses or apartments, so there are few hotels in the area.

■ **Le Manoir de Brion** (expensive). We couldn't see the bedrooms on our visit, but this ancient home, its earliest portions built in the 11th century, makes for an incredible *chambres d'hôte*. You

▼

can sleep where French kings stayed on their visits to Mont-St-Michel. *Off Rte. D911, Dragey 50530, tel. 33-70-86-45. Closed Nov.-Feb. Located 3 km. southwest of Carolles on rte. D911.*

■ **Villa Le Nid** (moderate). Clean, bright rooms in a modern home overlooking Mont-St-Michel. A seaside terrace with a barbecue is available to guests. *7 blvd. Stanislas, St-Jean-Le-Thomas 50530, tel. 33-68-10-37. Located 2 km. southwest of Carolles off rte. D911.*

■ **Les Cèdres** (inexpensive). A *chambres d'hôte* unlike any other we experienced in France, Les Cèdres offers a little bit of New York's SoHo in Normandy. Funky contemporary decor contrasts with the traditional lines of this 18th-century priory built just before the French Revolution. All rooms have clean, well-equipped private baths. The owners (who speak a little English) will help you take part in weekly guided tours that cross the bay at low tide to Mont-St-Michel. *Rue de l'Ortillon, Genêts 50530, tel. 33-70-86-45. Located 7 km. southeast of Carolles on rte. D911, just before the church of Genêts.*

FOR MORE INFORMATION
Tourist Office:
Syndicat d'Initiative de Carolles. *Carolles 50740, tel. 33-61-92-88. Open Mon.-Fri. 10-12:30 and 3-6:30, Apr. 15-Jun. 15 weekends, and daily Jun. 15-Sep. 15. During the off-season, contact the Mairie de Carolles, tel. 33-61-86-75.*

For Serious Walkers:
The tourist board in Carolles has extensive walking maps of the region, with many trails well marked with colored blazes. IGN map 1215E (east) covers this itinerary. Local bookshops and *Au Vieux Campeur* (*see* How to Use This Guide) sell French-language guidebooks of short walks in Normandy.

Castle in the Moors

EXPERIENCE 24: CAP FREHEL

Just a short distance away from the crowded tourist town of St-Malo and within easy access of Mont-St-Michel, Cap Fréhel lets you discover the essence of Brittany without a lengthy trip into the hinterlands.

The cape's most famous site, **Fort de la Latte,** attracts crowds of French and Europeans in summer, and nearby **Sables-d'Or-les-Pins** has been a popular seaside resort since 1924, when a

> **The Highlights:** Dramatic coastal scenery of dunes, moorlands, and cliffs; an ancient seaside castle; a lighthouse with spectacular views; a Celtic standing stone.
>
> **Other Places Nearby:** The busy seaside resort of St-Cast-le-Guildo, seaside walks, ruined pre-Roman fortifications, sandy beaches with coastline views.

tramway from Lamballe and St-Brieux was established. But these two walking tours let you discover this wild terrain on your own, undisturbed by tourists. You'll see this stunning landscape of cliffs, hidden coves, and windswept moors much as its inhabitants did hundreds, if not thousands, of years ago. You'll come upon the fort alone, seeing it rise above the foaming sea at the foot of a steep hill, and you'll pass a menhir, an ancient stone vestige of prehistoric life called **Le Doigt de Gargantua** (Gargantua's Finger).

From numerous prehistoric artifacts found in the region, it appears

▼

that people have lived here since at least 6,000 years before Christ. Archaeologists have found signs of man-made rock galleries, burial mounds, and stone and bronze hatchets and knives from prehistoric times. The first Romans probably came sometime around the time of Christ.

By A.D. 465, Bretons chased from English islands by the Saxons began to settle here. They named several villages with the designation "Plou," after a local leader; from this came the present-day names of **Pléhérel** and **Plévenon,** two villages that remain today on the sparsely populated cape. In the year 513, a Breton king named Riwal established a small domain in the region. One of his descendants defeated the Frankish king Charles the Bald in 846 and gained independence for his people, which lasted until the 10th century and the arrival of the marauding Vikings. Local nobility built the striking Fort de la Latte in the 13th century.

Cap Fréhel sat on the sidelines for the majority of France's most historic struggles but saw a little action during the Revolution, when locals rose up against the Republic. Many more residents died as soldiers in Napoleon's conquests. During World War II, the Germans occupied the entire cape. They installed an aircraft listening post, machine gun nests, and **pillboxes,** one of which you'll see the vestiges of on Walk 2.

What you'll probably remember most about Cap Fréhel is the unique seaside scenery. There are two sorts of moorlands here—those to the west, consisting of low, windswept shrubs and grasses; and those to the north and east, which are greener, with pockets of pine trees. On the sheltered eastern side of the cape you'll find humid conditions supporting small forests.

Bird-watchers will delight in the seaside bird sanctuary, **La Réserve Ornithologique du Cap Fréhel,** located on the northern tip of the cape and traversed on Walk 2. It supports large populations of birds who nest in the rugged cliffs. Attentive watchers will see the nearly all black shag cormorants, the white kittiwake sea gulls, the white-and-gray petrels, the black-and-white web-footed *torda* penguins, and the funny-beaked puffins; in tidal areas you might also glimpse the oyster-eating magpie, with its long orange beak perfect for digging up shellfish.

▼

GETTING THERE

By car:

From St-Malo, take *rte. D168* west through Ptoubalay, then *rte. D786* to Ste-Aide, about 1 km. before the small town of Fréhel. In Ste-Aide go right on *rte. D16* to Le Gros Moulin. There, you bear right on *rte. D16a,* which you follow all the way to the parking area for the Fort de la Latte.

Walk 1 Directions

TIME: 1 1/4 hours round-trip
LEVEL: Easy
DISTANCE: 2 miles
ACCESS: By car

Muddy footpaths in wet weather and a few short but steep pitches are the only obstacles on this walk through the countryside and along the cliffs to Fort de la Latte. Those who want only to see the fort and menhir can follow the signs and the tourists through the front gate for a ten-minute walk down the hill and take in the stunning cliffside panorama.

TO BEGIN

With your back to the entrance to the fort, walk back up the paved road the way you came, for about five minutes.

1. When you come to a paved road on the right, turn right, following the road through a few old farms.

2. Just about 100 yards before the small paved road ends at a stop sign, turn right onto a well-used farm track heading out into the fields.

3. The farm track soon hits an intersection with a well-worn footpath that cuts straight to the sea. Bear left on the farm track that runs along the right side of a field. *To shorten your walk, head straight down toward the sea from Point 3, picking up the itinerary a little east of Point 5. (You'll encounter a few short pitches that are slippery when wet.)*

4. You quickly reach a paved road, where you go right a few steps and then turn right onto another trail that leads into the forest.

5. Soon you come to the cliffs above the sea, where you encounter the coastal *GR* trail.

CAP FREHEL

Stone tower

Lighthouse

Bird sanctuary

Parking

Pointe du Jas

Pillbox ruins

WALK 2

Moors of Fréhel

Le Relais de Fréhel

Le Fanal Hôtel

D16

D34a

D16a

QUERIVET

LA MOTTE

PLEVENON

Port St-Geran

GETTING THERE

CAP FREHEL

D16a
St-Cast
St-Malo

D16

Ploubalay

D786

D768

D768

Plancoët

3 miles

WALK 1

Fort de la Latte

BEGIN/END

Menhir Parking

BAIE DE LA FRESNAYE

KEY

KEY

	Walk follows paved road
	Walk follows dirt road or footpath
	Paved road
	Dirt road or footpath
	Town or village
	Wooded area

¼   ½

MILE

▼

Turn right and follow the well-used footpath above the cliffs, *watching for the impressive Fort de la Latte to come into view. Several steep paths lead down to secluded beaches, some well-used by locals and fishermen.*

6. When you reach the fort (up to half an hour of walking away), you can stop for a visit or make a right on the broad trail leading back uphill to the parking lot. *Three-quarters of the way uphill, near the trail, you'll see Gargantua's Finger, a menhir, or standing stone.*

Walk 2 Directions

TIME: 4 hours
LEVEL: Difficult
DISTANCE: 8 miles
ACCESS: By car

Experienced walkers will find this a relatively easy experience, but novices will consider it a challenge, even though the route presents relatively few ups and downs. You'll take in much more of the seaside, farms, moors, and forests on this unspoiled cape.

TO BEGIN

Take the path from the parking area in Walk 1 downhill to the fort. Just before you reach the Fort de la Latte, turn left at Point 6 in Walk 1 onto a footpath blazed with the white-and-red blazes of a *GR* long-distance trail. Follow the clifftop trail through the moors and occasional woods; it will take you about one hour to reach Cap Fréhel and its lighthouse. As you approach, you'll see the concrete shape of a seasonal tourist restaurant near the cliff. Follow the trail to the right along the clifftops toward a small stone tower at the very tip of the cape.

1A. After admiring the view from the tip of the cape, walk away from the cape toward the lighthouse.

2A. Just after you've passed the lighthouse, follow the blazed trail all the way to the right of the parking lot and then to the right of a low stone wall. From the parking lot, a tangle of dirt paths head into the

▼

moors; follow the trail nearest the cliff for about ten minutes toward ruins of some pillboxes and a stone cabin.

3A. Shortly after the ruins, the trail bears sharply to the right, out onto the Pointe du Jas, following the edge of the cliffs above the sea. After another 20 minutes, it comes near a paved road, *rte. D34a*. As you parallel the road, you'll notice houses far off to your left on the other side of open fields. Look for a well-used farm track on your left that will take you over the moors toward the houses.

4A. After paralleling the road for about ten minutes, go left on any of the small trails cutting across to *rte. D34a* to pick up the farm track heading across the fields away from the sea. Cross *rte. D34a* and follow the dirt farm road across *La Lande de Fréhel* (Moors of Fréhel) for less than 15 minutes, heading straight across the fields toward the houses. You will pass through a small clump of trees.

5A. You'll reach *rte. D16* at a small picnic area. Go left, following *rte. D16* past Le Fanal Hôtel.

6A. Just a few minutes past the hotel, bear right on a country road marked by a road sign to Le Relais de Fréhel.

7A. When you reach Le Relais de Fréhel, turn right into the driveway. Make an immediate right on a small farm road heading toward a wooden gate. Follow the dirt road to the left past the gate and continue on it for less than ten minutes through woods and fields.

8A. When you reach a paved road in a tiny hamlet, turn left and follow that road for just a few minutes.

9A. Turn right onto the first paved road you come to. Follow it for another ten minutes to the tiny hamlet of Quérivet. Follow the road straight through Quérivet and continue straight on the small paved road to La Motte, another ten minutes or so.

▼

10A. When you reach a paved road at La Motte, make a left.

11A. Go right at the next intersection onto *rte. D16a*. Follow it for about five minutes.

12A. About 100 yards out of the village, look for a dirt road that goes to your left. It used to be a white-and-red-blazed *GR* trail, but it has been relocated, so what blazes you do see will be faint. Follow the path; when it turns abruptly left in a few minutes, stay on it.

13A. In a few more minutes, you will reach some houses. When you get to a paved road, go right. Follow the road downhill to the left until you reach another paved road. Go right, heading down the hill toward the bay and *Port St-Géran*.

14A. You will reach *Port St-Géran, a secluded little harbor for fishing and pleasure boats, and a small paved road. Stone Age people built stone walls in the bay to trap fish in pools of water when the high tide receded*. Go left on the white-and-red-blazed *GR* trail heading uphill onto a dirt trail. The well-blazed *GR* trail cuts across the wooded hillside below vacation homes and above the bay until it plunges into a wooded valley and crosses a little footbridge. Follow the blazes for about half an hour, past a footbridge and all the way back to the Fort de la Latte (Point 6 in Walk 1). Turn left at Point 6 to return to your car.

PLACES ALONG THE WALK

■ **Fort de la Latte.** *Plévenon, Fréhel 22240, tel. 96-41-40-31. Open daily 10-12:30 and 2:30-6:30 Easter-Sep. 30; Sun. afternoons Oct. 1-Easter. Admission. Follow directions in Getting There, above.*

■ **Cap Fréhel.** It has a lighthouse and a spectacular view of the sea and the rugged coast. *From Fréhel, take rte. D34 to Pléhérel Plage, then go right on rte. D34 following the signs to the cape.*

OTHER PLACES NEARBY

■ **Cap Erquy.** Another stunning cape offering seaside walks, these

▼

near the remains of pre-Roman fortifications. *From Fréhel, take rte. D786 west 10 1/2 km., following signs to Erquy.*

■ **Plages Pléhérel and Sables-d'Or-les-Pins.** Two sandy beaches lined with dunes and views of the coastline and offshore islands provide refreshment on those rare hot days in Brittany. *The Pléhérel beach lies east of the town, off rte. D34a.*

DINING

■ **La Voile d'Or** (moderate to inexpensive). An elegant dining experience overlooking a tidal inlet, it offers some ambitious renditions of such local seafoods as *langoustines royales grillées au paprika doux* (langoustines grilled with sweet paprika) and *lotte rôtie à la coriandre et confiture d'oignons* (monkfish roasted with coriander and onion jam). *Sables-d'Or, Fréhel 22240, tel. 96-41-42-49, fax 96-41-55-45. Open daily except Mon. Easter-Oct.; daily except Mon. and lunch on Tue. Nov. 15-Mar. 15. Southwest of Cap Fréhel on rte. D34.*

■ **Le Biniou** (moderate to inexpensive). This popular beachside spot has a polished but convivial dining atmosphere and views disturbed only by a parking lot. Offerings may include *filet de rouget à l'huile d'olive fruitée* (fillet of red mullet with fruit-scented olive oil on a bed of vegetables) and *pigeonneau farci aux trois champignons* (pigeon stuffed with mushrooms and a restaurant-made pâté). *Plage de Pen-Guen, St-Cast 22380, tel. 96-41-94-53. Open daily except Tue. Mar.-Nov.; daily Easter-Oct. Go east of the village of Fréhel on rte. D786 to rte. D19. Make a left, following signs to Plage de Pen-Guen.*

■ **Le Relais de Fréhel** (inexpensive). Dine on an old farm and enjoy such basic favorites as *moules marinières* (mussels marinara), *truite aux amandes* (trout with almonds), and *escalope de volaille à la crème* (escalope of chicken in cream sauce). *Fréhel 22240, tel. 96-41-43-02. Open daily Mar. 15-Nov. 5. Adjacent to Point 7A.*

LODGING

■ **Domaine du Val** (expensive). You've probably never stayed at a resort like this: beautiful old rooms in a chateau on huge grounds with two pools, a hot tub, exercize room, squash and tennis courts, excellent hiking trails, a secluded beach, and, of course, a restaurant.

▼

You can rent a home or apartment. *Planquenoual 22400, tel. 96-32-75-40; fax 96-32-71-50. Open all year. Located about 10 km. southwest of Fréhel off rte. D786. Get directions when you book.*

■ **Château du Val d'Arguenon** (expensive). You'll have no trouble capturing the mood of the past in this well-preserved 16th-century home. Rooms are large, with tall ceilings and antique furnishings and decor. The large, comfortable Châteaubriand Room is named for the famous Romantic author, who may have stayed there. *Notre Dame du Guildo, St-Cast 22380, tel. 96-41-07-03, fax 96-41-02-67. Open year-round. No credit cards. From Fréhel, take rte. D786 east through the village of Notre Dame du Guildo. Go left on a tiny paved road, following signs to the home. It appears shortly on your right.*

■ **Le Fanal Hôtel** (moderate). This is a curiously out-of-place wooden home on the moors of Cap Fréhel, along Walk 2. Rooms are modern, with country graces; many have pretty views of the moors and the ocean. Upper-level rooms—like 6, 7, 8, and 9—are particularly big and cheerful. In summer, book well in advance. *Rte. du Cap Fréhel, Plévenon, Fréhel 22240, tel. 96-41-43-19. Open Apr. 1-Sep. 30. From Fréhel, take rte. D786 1/2 km. east. Go left on a small road with a sign pointing to Plévenon. When you reach the village and rte. D16, go left and through the village following signs to Cap Fréhel and the hotel.*

■ **Le Relais de Fréhel** (moderate). A complete contrast to Le Fanal, this is for those who want the feel of an old farm. The rooms are small and most have baths. Room 4 is the best. *Rte. du Cap Fréhel, Plévenon, Fréhel 22240, tel. 96-41-43-02. Just beyond Le Fanal on the right.*

FOR MORE INFORMATION
Tourist Office:
Syndicat d'Initiative Pays de Fréhel. *Sables-d'Or-les-Pins, Fréhel 22240, tel. 96-41-51-97 (summer) or 96-41-40-12 (off-season). Located across from the casino on rte. D34 in Sables-d'Or-les-Pins.*

For Serious Walkers:
IGN map 1015S (south) covers the entire region of Cap Fréhel and Erquy.

Where Time Stands Still

EXPERIENCE 25: CHATEAU DE LA HUNAUDAYE

Nothing momentous happened at the Château de la Hunaudaye. It has no particular place in history, and it is bypassed by many tourists. Yet for the careful observer, a visit provides as much enrichment as a trip to Versailles or the Eiffel Tower. On the walking tour outlined below, you enter a world that gives you a great sense of what this region looked like during medieval times.

The Highlights: The ruins of a beautiful castle, peaceful Breton villages, and a farm museum.

Other Places Nearby: A lovely abbey in an ancient forest, the lonely grave of an American patriot.

Many things contribute to a sense of mystery in Brittany. The local mix of religion and superstition is manifested in a crucifix at nearly every intersection and strange calvaries in some churchyards. Local legends tell of the romantic lovers Tristan and Isolde; of the town of Is, engulfed by the sea; and of the 12 Washerwomen of Death, who prepare our bodies before Death takes our souls away. Then there are the ancient standing stones and tumuli that dot the region, relics of an early people about whom we know very little. Scientists believe that most of the megaliths in Brittany predate construction of the Pyramids or

▼

Stonehenge by 2,000 years or more. The largest structures are the alignments of huge standing stones, such as those at Carnac, almost on the scale of Stonehenge. Tumuli, such as the one at Garvinis (an island off the coast), are ancient burial mounds. Dolmens are rock tables formed by placing one huge slab over supporting stones; covered with soil and rock and now eroded away, they were probably burial chambers. Menhirs, which are plentiful in this region, are standing stones, often ten or more feet high, some weighing hundreds of tons (*see* Experience 24, Cap Fréhel). They might have been religious icons or perhaps fertility symbols, or they might simply have represented boundary lines between domains or peoples. Some stand by themselves, others in great numbers, although experts assume that the solitary stones might simply be lone survivors of larger groups.

Che Celts came from what are today the British Isles, and apparently settled near the Château de la Hunaudaye—probably on a site just north of the town of Langouhèdre, at a crossroads linking ancient regional capitals. When the Roman invaders came, they built their own roads, probably over the ancient ones. The Château de la Hunaudaye was built near one of these roads just to its north.

The walk begins in front of the chateau, which does attract tourist buses in high season. But the trail takes the walker over the ancient fortifications to the back of the castle and into the fields, where you will find a landscape that cannot have changed too much since the heyday of the castle's existence from the 12th to the 17th century, when it provided defense for a vast manor of farms held by the Tournemine family, which gained this land in return for its exploits in the wars with England. The picturesque structure has been reconstructed several times since the 12th century, but its towers, fully intact moat, and beautiful setting in a forested valley will enchant those who come to France to taste the past.

Not far from the castle, in the forest known also as Hunaudaye, lies the lonely grave of a Frenchman who, like the Marquis de la Fayette, played an important role in the American Revolution. Charles Armand Tuffin, Marquis de la Rouërie, served for several years under General

▼

George Washington, who became his good friend. He returned to France after the American Revolution. During the French Revolution, appalled at the imprisonment of the king, he became a leader in the *chouannerie,* which rose up in western France in opposition to the Republic. When the Marquis was killed in an accident, his friends secretly buried him near the **Château de Guyomarais.** A traitor revealed the location to the authorities, however, who unearthed the corpse, beheaded it, and reburied it. Locals have formed an organization honoring the Marquis, whose grave you can visit in its lovely spot behind the private chateau.

GETTING THERE

By car:

Exit Plancoët west in the direction of St-Brieuc on *rte. D768.* In just a short distance, bear left at a Y, continuing on *rte. D768.* In about 1 km., go left on *rte. D28* toward Pleven, about 6 km. Make a left about 1 km. west of the village on *rte. D28E.* In a little over 1 km., you arrive at a three-way intersection, where you go right. The Château de la Hunaudaye will appear through the woods on your right. Drive a short distance and park in the lot across from the castle.

Walk Directions

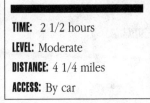

TIME: 2 1/2 hours
LEVEL: Moderate
DISTANCE: 4 1/4 miles
ACCESS: By car

This very special walk takes you into a wonderful rural landscape that includes fields, forests, old farms and villages. Almost the entire route is blazed yellow and red, except for a short segment along a paved road that will pose no navigational problems. If its open, the Ferme d'Antan provides insights into agricultural practices of the 19th century.

TO BEGIN

Facing the castle, walk on the path to its left along the moat. There's a farm on your left. You should see yellow-and-red blazes.

▼

1. Behind the castle, admire the view, then proceed straight on the blazed trail that goes toward a field.

2. In a short distance, the trail comes out on a paved road. Go left and follow the paved road and the blazes.

3. At a three-way intersection of small paved roads, continue

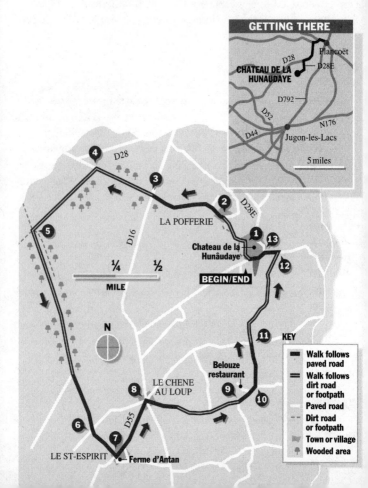

▼

straight on the broad dirt road that heads into the forest. This path can be muddy during wet weather.

4. Just before you reach a paved road, go left on a dirt path, still following the blazes. There will be a field on your right.

5. In about 15 minutes, you will reach a four-way intersection of broad dirt paths. Go left, following the blazes into a forest of holly trees. Ignore an overgrown old trail that parallels the main one to its left The trail traverses a deeply wooded area before it becomes paved and begins traversing farmland.

6. Shortly after passing a picnic table, you arrive at a four-way intersection of paved country roads. Continue straight toward a farm. You should still see the yellow-and-red blazes, among others.

7. After walking a short distance, you arrive at another four-way intersection in the tiny village of Le St-Esprit. Go left on the paved *rte. D55* toward the hamlet of Le Chêne au Loup, still following the blazes. *To visit the farm museum (Ferme d'Antan, otherwise known as St-Esprit-des-Bois) go straight at Point 7 and walk about five yards to another country road, where you go left and walk about 25 feet to the old farm's entrance. Retrace your steps to the intersection at Point 7, and go right.*

8. In the village of Le Chêne au Loup, you come to a crucifix and a six-way intersection of country roads. Walk onto the second road to the right—a small paved road that goes to the right of an electric pole and to the left of a small parking lot. A small sign points to the Clos Chantoux, and you should still be able to find the blazes. The country road quickly becomes dirt and bears left. You go straight onto a foot-path that descends into a ravine below farm fields. You will come to a well-used farm road; continue straight down into the ravine. You will pass yet another farm track; continue straight down in the ravine, walking beneath a large fallen tree. You'll arrive at a concrete fence and a concrete house. Follow the path leading down to the paved road.

▼

9. Go left on the paved road. In about 100 feet, you'll see another paved road on your left. Go left to visit the Bélouze restaurant. Otherwise, continue straight.

10. In just a short distance, you reach a Y intersection. Go left. Note that you are no longer following the blazed itinerary. The road leads through farmland.

11. At the next intersection, continue straight on a well-used dirt farm road. You are once again on a blazed itinerary. Follow this through farmland, watching on your left for the castle, which will appear through the forest as you proceed downhill.

12. When you get to a paved road, go left and walk a short distance toward the castle.

13. At a three-way intersection, continue straight to the parking lot and your car.

PLACES ALONG THE WALK

■ **Château de la Hunaudaye.** Although the interior is open part of the year, the setting is the real attraction. The area around the castle and the walk is open to the public all year. *Plédéliac 22270, tel. 96-34-82-10. Open daily 10-12 and 2:30-6 Jul.-Aug. Open 2:30-6 Apr., May, Sep. Admission.*

■ **Ferme d'Antan.** Visit an old farm restored to depict agricultural life in the 19th century. *Le St-Esprit 22270, tel. 96-34-14-67. Admission.*

OTHER PLACES NEARBY

■ **Armand de La Rouërie's grave.** Behind a private chateau is the tranquil resting place of this 18th-century Frenchman who fought in both the American and the French revolutions. *From Plancoët, take rte. D28 west through Pléven toward Lamballe. About 6 km. west of Pléven, in the hamlet of St-Aubin, go right on rte. D68. Go about 1 km., cross railroad tracks, and make the next right at an intersection of country*

▼

roads. *Go a short distance; a sign on your right indicates a right turn t[*
the grave (tombeau). Go right, downhill past the chateau, and park by
the river. A footpath follows the stream for about 100 yards, then cuts
abruptly left through a copse of wood to the tranquil site.

■ **Dinan.** Picturesque streets, striking views on the Rance estuary,
and abundant shops make this town a good place to stop for provisions
and a stroll before entering the isolated hinterlands of Brittany. *17 km.*
southwest of Plancoët by way of rte. D794. Just after passing over a four-
lane highway (13 km. south of Plancoët), make a left following signs into
the center of town.

DINING

■ **Jean-Pierre Crouzil** (expensive to moderate). One of the more
celebrated restaurants in the region features carefully presented creations
of local seafood, meats, and poultry. You might find *buîtres du belon*
chaudes et glacées au sabayon de Vouvray à la carotte (warm oysters
with a zabaglione of Vouvray wine and carrot), *trois oeufs en brouillade*
aux boucbées de homard du Fréhel (three eggs cooked with morsels of
local lobster), or *volaille bien élevée, sautée à l'estragon et aux oignons*
confits (chicken sautéed in tarragon and served with pickled onion). *Les*
Quais, Plancoët 22130, tel. 96-84-10-24, fax 96-84-01-93. Closed Sun.
eve. and Mon., except Jul.-Aug.; closed Nov. 2-16 and Jan. Located 17 km.
northwest of Dinan by way of rte. D794, just across from the Plancoët
train station.

■ **Manoir du Vaumadeuc** (moderate). Elegant country dining in
this 15th-century house is priced well below what you'll find in cities
for comparable quality and service. On the menu when we visited were
escalope de saumon a l'oseille (small salmon steak with sorrel), *emincé*
d'agneau au miel (slivers of lamb with honey), and *tarte feuilleté aux*
abricots (a tart of danish pastry and apricots). *Pléven, Plancoët 22130,*
tel. 96-84-46-17, fax 96-84-40-16. Closed Jan. 5-Mar. 15. Located 10
km. southwest of Plancoët on rte. D28.

■ **Manoir des Portes** (moderate). Locals recommend this old farm
converted into a hotel/restaurant for good, basic offerings like *terrine de*
lièvre maison (homemade terrine of rabbit), *medaillon de saumon au*

▼

lanc (small morsels of salmon in butter sauce), and *demi-*
neau rôti aux trompettes de la mort (half a young pigeon roasted
n mushrooms). *La Pôterie, Lamballe 22400, tel. 96-31-13-62, fax 96-*
31-20-53. Closed Mon. lunch May-Sep. 20; Sun. eve. and Mon. Sep. 20-
late Jan. and Mar.-Apr.; late Jan.-Mar. 1. Located 22 km. west of
Plancoët by way of rte. D28.

■ **Bélouze** (moderate). Here's a restaurant you could never find
back home. The owners take their home-grown farm products and turn
out dishes popular in medieval times, such as *hypocras* (an aperitif of
wine, spices, and flowers), *limonia à la porée blanche* (chicken with
lemon and almonds), and *pastes* (a platter of terrines served on a bed of
lettuce). An ancient farm setting and costumed waiters complete the
experience. *Plédéliac 22270, tel. 96-34-14-55. Open daily mid-Jun.-late*
Sep.; by reservation only the rest of the year. From Plancoët, take rte. D28
through Pléven and watch for signs.

■ **Ferme Auberge Le Grand Trait** (inexpensive). Just about
everything comes from the farm, the owner assures us. The basic but
wholesome offerings in this farmhouse setting may include *assiette de*
crudités et terrine de lapin (raw shredded vegetables with terrine of rabbit), *tourte au jambon et aux poireaux* (ham-and-leek pie), and *lapin*
au cidre et aux pommes (rabbit cooked with cider and apples). *Rte. de*
Dinard, Plancoët 22130, tel. 96-84-01-23. Open daily except Sun. eve.
Easter-Oct.; by reservation only the rest of the year. Just north of Plancoët
off rte. D768. Follow signs for the farm and make a right onto a country
road. Go a short distance uphill and to the left.

LODGING

■ **Manoir du Vaumadeuc** (very expensive to expensive). This magnificent 15th-century manor house, maintained with sophisticated warmth and
charm, is located in the heart of the countryside. Rooms 4, 5, and 6 are especially large and beautiful. Having owned the house for more than 300 years,
the host family will proudly and most graciously share with you its history,
detailed in a four-page guide available in English. *Pléven, Plancoët 22130, tel.*
96-84-46-17, fax 96-84-40-16. Closed Jan. 5-Mar. 15. Located 10 km. south-
west of Plancoët on rte. D28.

▼

■ **Manoir des Portes** (expensive). Ask for a room in the old wing of this 17th-century dwelling. All rooms are clean, with modern conveniences, but the new wing lacks charm. We particularly liked rooms 22, 24, 25, 36, and 37 for their combination of space and country decor. *La Pôterie, Lamballe 22400, tel. 96-31-13-62, fax 96-31-20-53. Closed late Jan.-Mar. 1. Located 22 km. west of Plancoët by way of rte. D28.*

■ **La Villerobert** (moderate). Conveniently located between Plénée and Cap Fréhel (*see* Experience 24), this 17th-century manor house has two beautiful rooms offering an excellent value, since breakfast is included in the price. *Rte. D19, St-Lormel, Plancoët 22130, tel. 96-84-12-88. Open Easter-late Oct. Located 5 km. north of Plancoët on rte. D19.*

■ **La Pastourelle** (inexpensive). There are five comfortable, country-furnished rooms in this semi-working farmhouse, four with private bath or shower. Breakfast is included, and an inexpensive dinner is available with reservations during the summer. *St-Lormel, Plancoët 22130, tel. 96-84-03-77. Open Easter-Oct. Located 2 km. north of Plancoët off rte. D19.*

FOR MORE INFORMATION
Tourist Offices:

Office de Tourisme de Dinan. *6 rue de l'Horloge, Dinan 22100, tel. 96-39-75-40, fax 96-39-01-64. Open daily 8:30-7 Jul.-Aug; daily except Sun. 8:30-12:30 and 2-6 the rest of the year. Closed major holidays.*

For Serious Walkers:

A large number of blazed circuits dot this part of France—some are poorly maintained. Local bookstores sell walking guides to the region, all in French. IGN map 1017O (west) covers the area of this walk.

's Travel Publications

t bookstores everywhere, or call 1–800–533–6478, 24 hours a day.

Guides

s.

Alaska
Arizona
Boston
California
Cape Cod, Martha's Vineyard, Nantucket
The Carolinas & the Georgia Coast
Chicago
Colorado

Florida
Hawaii
Las Vegas, Reno, Tahoe
Los Angeles
Maine, Vermont, New Hampshire
Maui
Miami & the Keys
New England

New Orleans
New York City
Pacific North Coast
Philadelphia & the Pennsylvania Dutch Country
The Rockies
San Diego
San Francisco

Santa Fe, Taos, Albuquerque
Seattle & Vancouver
The South
U.S. & British Virgin Islands
USA
Virginia & Maryland
Waikiki
Washington, D.C.

Foreign

Australia & New Zealand
Austria
The Bahamas
Barbados
Bermuda
Brazil
Budapest
Canada
Cancún, Cozumel, Yucatán Peninsula
Caribbean
China
Costa Rica, Belize, Guatemala
Cuba
The Czech Republic & Slovakia

Eastern Europe
Egypt
Europe
Florence, Tuscany & Umbria
France
Germany
Great Britain
Greece
Hong Kong
India
Ireland
Israel
Italy
Japan
Kenya & Tanzania
Korea

London
Madrid & Barcelona
Mexico
Montréal & Québec City
Morocco
Moscow, St. Petersburg, Kiev
The Netherlands, Belgium & Luxembourg
New Zealand
Norway
Nova Scotia, New Brunswick, Prince Edward Island
Paris
Portugal

Provence & the Riviera
Scandinavia
Scotland
Singapore
South Africa
South America
South Pacific
Southeast Asia
Spain
Sweden
Switzerland
Thailand
Tokyo
Toronto
Turkey
Vienna & the Danube

Fodor's Special-Interest Guides

Branson
Caribbean Ports of Call
The Complete Guide to America's National Parks
Condé Nast Traveler Caribbean Resort and Cruise Ship Finder
Cruises and Ports of Call

Fodor's London Companion
France by Train
Halliday's New England Food Explorer
Healthy Escapes
Italy by Train
Kodak Guide to Shooting Great Travel Pictures

Shadow Traffic's New York Shortcuts and Traffic Tips
Sunday in New York
Sunday in San Francisco
Walt Disney World, Universal Studios and Orlando
Walt Disney World for Adults

Where Should We Take the Kids? California
Where Should We Take the Kids? Family Adventures
Where Should We Take the Kids? Northeast